Kaplan Publishing are constantly finding new ways to make a difference to your studies and our exciting online resources really do offer [illegible] ng different to students looking f[illegible]

This book comes with free MyKa[illegible] hat you can study anytime, anywhere[illegible] resource is **not sold separately and is include[illegible] price of the book.**

Having purchased this book, you have access to the following online study materials:

CONTENT	AAT	
	Text	Kit
iPaper version of the book	✓	✓
Progress tests with instant answers	✓	
Mock assessments online	✓	✓
Material updates	✓	✓

How to access your online resources

Kaplan Financial students will already have a MyKaplan account and these extra resources will be available to you online. You do not need to register again, as this process was completed when you enrolled. If you are having problems accessing online materials, please ask your course administrator.

If you are already a registered MyKaplan user go to www.MyKaplan.co.uk and log in. Select the 'add a book' feature and enter the ISBN number of this book and the unique pass key at the bottom of this card. Then click 'finished' or 'add another book'. You may add as many books as you have purchased from this screen.

If you purchased through Kaplan Flexible Learning or via the Kaplan Publishing website you will automatically receive an e-mail invitation to MyKaplan. Please register your details using this email to gain access to your content. If you do not receive the e-mail or book content, please contact Kaplan Flexible Learning.

If you are a new user register at www.MyKaplan.co.uk and click on the link contained in the email we sent you to activate your account. Then select the 'add a book' feature, enter the ISBN number of this book and the unique pass key at the bottom of this card. Then click 'finished' or 'add another book'.

Your Code and Information

This code can only be used once for the registration of one book online. This registration and your online content will expire when the final sittings for the examinations covered by this book have taken place. Please allow one hour from the time you submit your book details for us to process your request.

Please scratch the film to access your MyKaplan code.

WUhW-MeN8-7QAP-FWu2

Please be aware that this code is case-sensitive and you will need to include the dashes within the passcode, but not when entering the ISBN. For further technical support, please visit www.MyKaplan.co.uk

KAPLAN PUBLISHING

CASH MANAGEMENT

Qualifications and Credit Framework

AQ2013 Level 4 Diploma in Accounting

British Library Cataloguing-in-Publication Data

A catalogue record for this book is available from the British Library.

Published by
Kaplan Publishing UK
Unit 2, The Business Centre
Molly Millars Lane
Wokingham
Berkshire
RG41 2QZ

ISBN: 978-1-78415-403-5

Printed and bound in Great Britain.

We are grateful to the Association of Accounting Technicians for permission to reproduce past assessment materials and example tasks based on the new syllabus. The solutions to past answers and similar activities in the style of the new syllabus have been prepared by Kaplan Publishing.

CONTENTS

INTRODUCTION

HOW TO USE THESE MATERIALS

These Kaplan Publishing learning materials have been carefully designed to make your learning experience as easy as possible and to give you the best chance of success in your AAT assessments.

They contain a number of features to help you in the study process.

The sections on the Unit Guide, the Assessment and Study Skills should be read before you commence your studies.

They are designed to familiarise you with the nature and content of the assessment and to give you tips on how best to approach your studies.

STUDY TEXT

This Study Text has been specially prepared for the revised AAT qualification introduced in September 2013.

It is written in a practical and interactive style:

- key terms and concepts are clearly defined
- all topics are illustrated with practical examples with clearly worked solutions based on sample tasks provided by the AAT in the new examining style
- frequent activities throughout the chapters ensure that what you have learnt is regularly reinforced
- 'pitfalls' and 'examination tips' help you avoid commonly made mistakes and help you focus on what is required to perform well in your examination
- practice workbook activities can be completed at the end of each chapter.

WORKBOOK

The workbook comprises:

Practice activities at the end of each chapter with solutions at the end of this text, to reinforce the work covered in each chapter.

The questions are divided into their relevant chapters and students may either attempt these questions as they work through the textbook, or leave some or all of these until they have completed the textbook as a final revision of what they have studied

ICONS

The study chapters include the following icons throughout.

They are designed to assist you in your studies by identifying key definitions and the points at which you can test yourself on the knowledge gained.

Definition

These sections explain important areas of knowledge which must be understood and reproduced in an assessment.

Example

The illustrative examples can be used to help develop an understanding of topics before attempting the activity exercises.

Activity

These are exercises which give the opportunity to assess your understanding of all the assessment areas.

Quality and accuracy are of the utmost importance to us so if you spot an error in any of our products, please send an email to mykaplanreporting@kaplan.com with full details.

Our Quality Co-ordinator will work with our technical team to verify the error and take action to ensure it is corrected in future editions.

UNIT GUIDE

Cash management covers both knowledge and skills

Principles of Cash Management (Knowledge)
2 credits
Cash Management (Skills)
3 credits

Purpose of the units

Organisations that fail to manage their liquid resources appropriately expose themselves to a higher risk of failure than organisations that effectively manage their liquid resources. This unit is designed to equip accounting technicians not only with an understanding of the theoretical principles of good cash management but also with associated practical skill.

These skills include being able to extract relevant data from a range of sources to forecast income and expenditure and to use these forecasts, together with information on expected payment patterns, to undertake the preparation and revision of cash budgets. It is important that students can also analyse a range of information on borrowing and investing options and make appropriate recommendations to management which adhere to organisational policy.

Learning objectives

On completion of this unit the learner will be able to:

- Use statistical techniques and financial information to prepare forecasts of information
- Prepare cash budgets
- Use cash budgets to monitor cash flow within the organisation
- Manage cash balances effectively
- Raise finance in accordance with organisational requirements
- Invest surplus funds observing organisational policies

Learning outcomes and Assessment criteria

The unit consists of six learning outcomes which are further broken down into Assessment criteria. These are set out in the following table with Learning outcomes in bold type and Assessment criteria listed underneath each Learning outcome. A K indicates a knowledge criteria and an S indicates a skill criteria. Reference is also made to the relevant chapter within the text.

To perform this unit effectively you will need to know and understand the following:

		Chapter
1	**Use statistical techniques and financial information to prepare forecasts of income and expenditure**	
1.1K	Explain how recording and accounting practice may vary in different parts of an organisation	1
1.2S	Prepare forecasts of income and expenditure using these statistical techniques: • moving averages • allowance for inflation • regression analysis	2
1.3K	Describe the relationship between cash flow and accounting for income and expenditure	1
1.4S	Ensure forecasts of future cash payments and receipts agree with known income and expenditure trends	2
2	**Prepare cash budgets**	
2.1K	Identify the characteristics of the main types of cash receipts and payments	1
2.2S	Estimate cash flows over the accounting period, and anticipate any exceptional receipts or payments	3, 4
2.3K	Explain the effect of lagged receipts and payments upon an organisation's cash management	3
2.4S	Prepare cash budgets in accordance with the organisation's preferred format and clearly indicate net cash requirements	4
2.5S	Undertake sensitivity analysis on elements with the cash budget and quantify the effects of possible	4

		Chapter
	changes in assumptions	
3	**Use cash budgets to monitor cash flow within the organisation**	
3.1S	Monitor cash receipts and payments against budgeted cash flow	5
3.2S	Identify significant deviations from the cash budget and take corrective action within organisational policies	5
4	**Manage cash balances effectively**	
4.1K	Explain how government monetary policies affect an organisation's treasury functions	6
4.2K	Identify the principles of liquidity management	6
4.3K	Describe how an organisation's principles of cash management will be determined by their specific financial regulations, guidelines and security procedures	6
4.4K	Identify statutory and other regulations relating to the management of cash balances in different types of organisations	6
4.5S	Take account of trends in the economic and financial environment in managing cash balances	7
4.6S	Observe the organisation's financial regulations and security procedures	7
4.7S	Manage cash, overdrafts and loans in order to maintain an adequate level of liquidity in line with cash forecasts	7
5	**Raise finance in accordance with organisational requirements**	
5.1K	Explain how an organisation can raise finance and the basic terms and conditions associated with each of these types of financing	7
5.2S	Anticipate cash requirements and arrange overdrafts and loans on the most favourable terms available	7

		Chapter
6	**Invest surplus funds observing organisational policies**	
6.1S	Assess different types of investment and the risks, terms and conditions associated with them	8
6.2S	Analyse ways to manage risk when investing, to minimise potential losses to the organisation	8
6.3S	Invest surplus funds according to organisational policy and with defined authorisation limits	8

Delivery guidance

This section provides detailed delivery guidance covering assessable topics and the depth and breadth to which these topics should be taught and learnt. The examples given of possible assessment tasks for each topic area are to provide guidance on the sort of tasks that students may be required to undertake but should not be considered as an exhaustive list. Task types include multiple choice, drag and drop, linked boxes, pick lists gap fill, and written tasks where students have an opportunity to provide evidence of their knowledge. Clear instructions are provided for each task and students should ensure that they follow these carefully.

The term cash in this unit is used to include bank accounts as well as coins and notes and cash payments include cheque payments, BACS, direct debits and standing orders.

The effective management of cash is not something that can be undertaken in isolation or without an awareness of the general financial environment in which organisations operate. Therefore it is important that students have a basic awareness of how the banking sector is structured, the relationship between different financial institutions and understand that legal relationships exist between lenders and borrowers.

Students should also be introduced to the sort of financial terminology which they could encounter in the workplace such as fixed and floating charges, brokers, term loans, maturity date, loan principal, annual percentage rates and money markets. These and other financial terms may be used in assessment tasks however students will only be expected to display knowledge or understanding of terms that are specifically noted in the delivery guidance and standards as assessable. The use of other terms will simply be to add reality to a task and the ability to undertake the task in a competent manner will not depend upon any detailed knowledge of such terminology.

Assessment tasks may relate to a range of different organisations including sole traders, partnerships and limited companies. Students will not be expected to have any prior knowledge of the structure or accounting regulations of these organisations as they will simply be used as a background setting to enable assessment. Receipts and payments that might be organisation specific – for example, corporation tax, dividends received, dividends paid – could be used in tasks but students will simply be required to treat these cash flows in accordance with the instructions in the assessment data. However students will be expected to understand the format of a statement of profit or loss (income statement) and a statement of financial position and accounting adjustments such as accruals, prepayments, depreciation and irrecoverable debts.

Cash receipts and payments and their relationship with profit (LO1, LO2)

Assessment criteria:

1.1K Explain how recording and accounting practice may vary in different parts of an organisation

1.3K Describe the relationship between cash flow accounting and accounting for income and expenditure

2.1K Identify the characteristics of the main types of cash receipts and payments

Although this unit is primarily concerned with cash flows for an organisation students need to understand how cash flow accounting relates to accounting profits and losses. Transactions may be recorded in different ways in different parts of an organisation and therefore accounting technicians may be required to use a range of different sources of information to determine appropriate forecasts of income and expenditure. This could include financial statements (statement of profit or loss (income statement) and statement of financial position), management reports, production information and budgets).

Financial statements are prepared using accounting adjustments such as accruals, prepayments, provisions and depreciation and therefore does not show the cash flow of an organisation. Knowledge of how figures from financial accounting statements can be adjusted to reverse the effect of accounting adjustments and thereby find the cash transactions to be included in a cash budget is essential.

Cash receipts and payments can be categorised in a number of ways according to their main characteristics. It is important to recognise the impact that each of these different types of receipts and payments has on the cash flow of an organisation and their differing patterns of cash flow. A cash budget needs to recognise different types of receipts and payments.

Statements of cash flows prepared under FRS1 and IAS7 format are not assessable in this Unit.

Assessment tasks may include:

- Identifying the characteristics of different types of cash receipts and cash payments and explaining their impact on cash flow (including regular, exceptional, capital, drawings, disbursements).
- Explaining how recording and accounting practices may vary in different parts of the organisation resulting in a variety of sources of information being available for determining likely patterns of cash flow.
- Deriving cash receipts and cash payments for a period from a range of given information whilst adjusting for accruals, prepayments and provisions. Information may be supplied in the form of financial statements, management reports, production information, budgets, ledger accounts and narrative, and may include information for more than one period.
- Explaining and demonstrating the impact of non-cash items e.g. depreciation on the cash flow of an organisation.
- Calculating the proceeds from or payments for non-current asset transactions. This may include using cost and accumulated depreciation or carrying amount, calculating or using a depreciation charge, dealing with disposals, splitting out additions paid for by cash with those made under finance leases.
- Using forecast information to reconcile operating profit with changes in cash including changes in equity, loans and tax.
- Using information provided in financial statements and narrative to determine the net change in cash position from the operating profit and reconcile the actual cash position to the forecast cash position.
- Creating an income statement from various financial records including extracts from summary bank statements and the trial balance. This will derive the income statement from the cash movements and the opening and closing balances.

Forecasting income and expenditure (LO1)

Assessment criteria:

1.2S Prepare forecasts of income and expenditure using these statistical techniques: moving averages; allowance for inflation; regression analysis (least squares regression analysis will not be tested).

1.4S Ensure forecasts of future cash payments and receipts agree with known income and expenditure trends

Known income and expenditure trends must be considered and incorporated into estimates of future cash receipts and payments that are to be included in a cash budget. Students will be required to use a range of statistical techniques to forecast income and expenditure, and use these forecasts to determine future cash payments and receipts.

Assessment tasks may include:

- Using moving averages to identify the basic trend of income or expenditure. Calculations may be based on odd or even points so students must understand and be able to calculate centred averages.
- Calculating seasonal variations (both additive and multiplicative).
- Using the trend and the seasonal variations to forecast income or expenditure.
- Forecasting future income and expenditure making allowances for inflation using percentage increases and index numbers. Calculating price and index numbers from a range of information given and calculation of the price at the start of the index. Compounding is assessable here as well as calculating percentage increases and decreases over time. The creation of an index from historical figures is also assessable.
- Using regression analysis to forecast income and expenditure. Students will not be assessed on the derivation of the regression equation using the least squares formula but they will need to know the generic equation y = a + bx where y is the sales forecast and x is the time period (a and b will be constants).
- Forecasting sales and purchases using mark up and margin.
- Using forecast income and expenditure to forecast future cash receipts and payments.

Patterns of cash flows (LO2)

Assessment criteria:

2.2S Estimate cash flows over the accounting period and anticipate any exceptional receipts or payments

2.3K Explain the effects of lagged receipts and payments upon an organisation's cash management

The preparation of a cash budget relies on identifying the expected payment patterns for receipts and payments accounting for differences in timings arising from selling or purchasing goods and services on credit terms and on cash terms and deposits made in advance.

- Using information obtained from a range of sources within an organisation to determine the likely pattern of different types of cash receipts and cash payments for inclusion in a cash budget. Given the potential impact of exceptional receipts and payments on the cash position of an organisation, these types of cash flows should be anticipated to ensure that they are included in the cash budget in the correct period so that their likely effect can be assessed.
- Mark up and/or margin could be assessed in this task to determine either sales prices or purchase prices and this could well lead into calculating the expected cash receipts and/or cash payments.
- Calculating the likely value of cash receipts for a number of periods using a range of information including the split of cash and credit sales, the expected pattern of receipts, expected sales volume and selling prices and opening receivables, and irrecoverable debts. Closing receivables, closing irrecoverable debts and discounts offered values or percentages may also have to be calculated.
- Calculating the likely value of cash payments for a number of periods using a range of information including the split of cash and credit purchases, different classes of expenditure such as materials, labour, overheads, capital purchases made by instalments and opening payables. Closing payables and discounts taken may also have to be calculated.
- Explaining the effect of lagging on the cash flow of a new business and an existing business.

Preparing cash budgets (LO2)

Assessment criteria:

2.2S Estimate cash flows over the accounting period and anticipate any exceptional receipts or payments

2.4S Prepare cash budgets in accordance with the organisation's preferred format and clearly indicate net cash requirements

2.5S Undertake sensitivity analysis on elements within the cash budget and quantify the effects of possible changes in assumptions

Cash budgets provide decision makers with an effective tool for cash management therefore students who are able to accurately prepare a cash budget from a variety of information will be equipped with a valuable practical skill.

The preparation of a cash budget will necessarily require students to use a range of information presented in a variety of ways depending upon the nature of the organisation and its activities. At this level students will be expected to be able to extract information from data that is presented in different ways.

Cash budgets do not have a statutory format and organisations may choose to present information in different ways. The assessment will use the following format:

- Analysis of sources of receipts leading to total receipts for the period
- Analysis of the sources of payments leading to total payments for the period
- Net cash flow for the period
- Opening cash balance
- Closing cash balance

Cash budgets are prepared using assumptions about the nature of cash flows. It is important to understand that net cash requirements will be affected by changes in those assumptions and that revised cash budgets will need to be prepared. Students must be able to quantify effects by value or by percentage.

Assessment tasks may include:

- Calculating sales receipts for inclusion in a cash budget after accounting for early settlement discounts, sales price fluctuations, irrecoverable debts and the effect of lagging.
- Calculating purchase payments for inclusion in a cash budget after accounting for early settlement discounts, purchase price fluctuations and the effect of lagging.

- Calculating other receipts and other payments for inclusion in the cash budget from a variety of information incorporating given payment patterns.
- Calculating VAT payments or refunds based on information provided for sales and purchases. All VAT will be standard rated only; there will be no inclusion of any complexities such as differing VAT rates, cash accounting for VAT or the Flat Rate Scheme.
- Calculating the sterling value of a receipt or payment when the amount in a foreign currency is known. An appropriate exchange rate will be given.
- Preparing a cash budget for at least two periods for a new or an existing organisation, clearly indicating the net cash position at the end of each period. Cash budget figures should be rounded to whole £'s following normal rounding conventions.
- Calculating and incorporating bank interest received and bank interest paid into a cash budget, as well as loan principal payments, bank loan interest and overdraft interest.
- Incorporating receipts and payments into a cash budget.
- Quantifying the effects of changes in volume, price and timing.
- Quantifying the effects of suppliers enforcing payments in line with contractual terms where payment terms have slipped or deviated.
- Quantifying whether discounts for early settlement should be accepted or offered.
- Quantifying the effect of special offers for purchasing early or using substitute materials or labour.
- Preparing revised cash budgets to account for changes in original assumptions.
- Explain or quantify the impact on cash flow of decisions to increase or decrease inventory levels.

Monitoring cash flows (LO3)

Assessment criteria:

3.1S Monitor cash receipts and payments against budgeted cash flow

3.2S Identify significant deviations from the cash budget and take corrective action within organisational policies

In addition to being a tool for predicting cash shortfalls and cash surpluses, a cash budget can be used to monitor and control cash inflows and outflows. Cash management is not simply about being able to prepare a cash budget it also involves being able to analyse significant deviations from budget offering explanations and suggesting possible courses of action to prevent recurrence.

Assessment tasks may include:

- Identifying significant deviations between actual and budgeted cash flows in line with organisational policy.
- Analysing the causes of significant deviations from budget accounting for information supplied.
- Suggesting corrective action for significant deviations having regard to the impact of such actions on the cash position of the organisation and on organisational policies. Ensure that possible courses of action are matched with the nature and cause of the variances.
- Identifying and explaining which variance(s) have had the greatest impact on the budgeted results.
- Discussing the inherent problems of forecasting figures and the strengths and weaknesses of cash budgets as a tool for monitoring and controlling cash flows.

Liquidity management (LO4)

Assessment criteria

4.1K Explain how government monetary policies affect an organisations treasury functions

4.2K Identify the principles of liquidity management

4.3K Describe how an organisation's principles of cash management will be determined by their specific financial regulations, guidelines and security procedures

4.4K Identify statutory and other regulations relating to the management of cash balances in different types of organisations

Adequate liquidity is the key factor in contributing to the success or failure of trading organisations. Students need to understand that cash is part of the working capital of the business and that the time taken to convert inventory, trade receivables and trade payables into cash affects the liquidity position of the organisation. Liquidity management involves monitoring cash flows through the working capital cycle, understanding that different types of cash flows have different timing patterns, using cash budgets to forecast and monitor the organisation's liquidity position, arranging finance to cover expected cash shortfalls and investing cash surpluses to achieve maximum returns. In short, to ensure that an organisation has access to sufficient funds to meet their liabilities as and when they fall due. In addition management should be able to recognise the indicators of possible future liquidity problems which include overtrading.

Students should also understand the role of the government in setting monetary policies to control the supply of money.

Assessment tasks may include:

- Explaining the purpose and elements of liquidity management.
- Explaining the working capital cycle/cash operating cycle and its relationship to liquidity management. Students will be expected to calculate the cash operating cycle from information given. When calculating trade payable days it is usual to use the cost of sales figure, however this is a rough approximation of the total purchases on credit. However if there are figures given for total purchases on credit or cost of sales and total purchases for cash then students should use the total purchases on credit when calculating trade payable days.
- Calculating liquidity ratios and using them to calculate the length of the cash operating cycle.
- Recognising generally accepted signs of overtrading (rapidly increasing sales linked to rapidly increasing trade receivables often with customers taking longer to pay and increases in irrecoverable debts, and also inventory increases in anticipation of future sales increases. These increases put added strain on the cash flow of the business as cash is tied up in inventory and receivables. The large increase in inventory and receivables is often funded by an increase in trade payables and increased use of a bank overdraft which will add to future cash flow issues when overdraft interest is paid); suggesting actions to reduce the risk of overtrading; explaining the impact of overtrading on liquidity management.
- Demonstrating an awareness of statutory and other organisational regulations and guidelines that relate to the management of cash balances. Students must be aware that some organisations are governed by mandatory regulations that need to be adhered to e.g. limited companies through the Companies Act are required to maintain proper accounting records and that directors have a fiduciary duty of care, and public sector organisations follow guidelines issued by HM Treasury.
- Explaining the 'treasury function'.
- Explaining how the government's monetary policy in controlling the supply of money in the economy, and the effect of this on the rate of inflation, economic activity (GDP growth and attempting to avoid recession) and interest rates, impacts an organisations treasury function. This includes an understanding of the principles of quantitative easing and explaining the role of the Bank of England in influencing interest rates.

Raising finance (LO4, 5)

Assessment criteria:

4.5S Take account of trends in the economic and financial environment in managing cash balances

4.6S Observe the organisation's financial regulations and security procedures

4.7S Manage cash, overdrafts and loans in order to maintain an adequate level of liquidity in line with cash forecasts

5.1K Explain how an organisation can raise finance and the basic terms and conditions associated with each of these types of financing

5.2S Anticipate cash requirements and arrange overdrafts and loans on the most favourable terms available

A cash budget is one method that an organisation can use to anticipate future cash shortages based on their forecast activities. A cash budget provides a periodic forecast of net cash positions that will enable management to select and arrange suitable financing options to cover any cash shortages.

Organisations can raise finance from a range of sources including bank loans and overdrafts, operating and finance leases, sale and leaseback, HP agreements, loan stock, bonds, equity and preference shares, factoring and invoice discounting. Students need to understand that all financing options have differing terms and conditions attached to them and that there are a number of factors that need to be considered before recommending a suitable form of finance. Different organisations may have established regulations, policies and guidelines governing the sources of, and terms under which, finance can be raised. An important point to recognise is that those charged with liquidity management owe a duty of care to the owners of the organisation either as a fiduciary or under an employment contract.

Assessment tasks may include:

- Explaining the main features, terms and conditions associated with bank overdrafts and loans, leases (including risks and rewards of ownership), equity and debt funding and bonds including availability, interest rates (fixed, variable and capped), fees, time period, repayment structure, security (mortgage, personal guarantee, fixed and floating charges), default, advantages and disadvantages.

- Students may be tested on their knowledge of finance leases and operating leases and the difference in the accounting treatment in the financial statements and how the leases will affect the gearing. The gearing ratio used in any assessment will be:

$$\frac{\text{Total debt (short term + long term)}}{\text{Total debt + equity}} \times 100$$

- Making justified recommendations of ways to finance given cash requirements. Recommendations should consider the possibility of combining different types of financing options to maintain an adequate level of liquidity at the lowest possible cost or the most favourable impact on cash flow having regard to the organisation's own guidelines and regulations.
- Calculating the costs associated with different forms of borrowing, including different types of interest. Flat rate interest is when the interest rate is calculated based on the loan principal. It is applied to the whole of the loan every year and does not take into account any repayments. For this reason the flat rate of interest can seem to be the lower option but in reality can be quite expensive. Calculating the simple interest on a loan or investment. The simple interest rate can be calculated by taking the total interest as a percentage of the original principal. Calculating interest charged from the loan term and repayments.
- Explaining the purpose and mechanics of annual percentage rate (APR) and how it is calculated on the amount of loan principal outstanding so that the interest charge reduces each time a repayment is made by the borrower. This means that the actual interest charged each month reduces in line with the reduction in the principal. Calculation of APR is not assessable.
- Explaining the importance of adhering to statutory regulations such as the Companies Act and public sector regulations as well as organisational policies when raising finance.
- Selecting the most appropriate borrowing having regard to the economic and financial environment.
- Explaining and calculating the impact of borrowing on gearing/credit rating and the concept of loan to value.

Managing surplus funds (LO4, 6)

Assessment criteria:

4.5S Take account of trends in the economic and financial environment in managing cash balances

6.1S Assess different types of investment and the risks, terms and conditions associated with them

6.2S Analyse ways to manage risk when investing, to minimise potential losses to the organisation

6.3S Invest surplus funds according to organisational policy and within defined authorisation limits

As well as being able to select suitable finance for dealing with cash shortages organisations need to utilise cash surpluses in the most appropriate manner to ensure that they receive acceptable return for acceptable risk. This may include repaying loans early or taking advantage of early settlement discounts which would offer a greater saving to the business than various investment opportunities Different organisations have different regulations and guidelines governing investment and students must take these into account when making recommendations. Investment options may include: property, land, shares (equity and preference, listed and private), bonds, gilts, money market accounts, treasury bills, deposit accounts, notice accounts, Certificates of Deposit (CD's), and gold or other commodities.

Assessment tasks may include:

- Explaining the main features, terms and conditions associated with different types of investments including availability, interest rates (fixed, variable and capped), fees/transaction charges, time period, liquidity, risk, advantages and disadvantages.

- Understand that when investing surplus funds the risk, reward and liquidity of the investment needs to be taken into account. In addition to this the portfolio effect will need to be considered where the diversification of investment into a number of options provides a balance of risk reward and liquidity and could create a better return than putting all their eggs into one basket.

- Understanding that different organisations will have their own financial regulations, guidelines and security procedures that must be observed when considering possible courses of action and making recommendations. Describing how these regulations, guidelines and procedures affect the organisations principles of cash management and the typical contents of an organisational policy.

- Identifying ways that an organisation could manage risk and exposure when investing surplus funds to try and ensure that potential losses are minimised and explaining the terms risk averse and risk seeking.
- Analysing the risk and return of different investment options.
- Assimilating a range of information and analysing the suitability of different investment options and making recommendations for investing surplus funds having regard to the organisation's policies and procedures, internal regulations, attitude towards risk, return, termination costs, realisation/maturity, authorisation limits and the economic and financial environment.
- Calculating the return on investments incorporating early cash-in penalties and bonus interest rates, dividend yield, yields on gilts. Identifying sums to be invested to achieve a specific return.

THE ASSESSMENT

The format of the assessment

The assessment will be divided into ten standalone tasks which cover all of the learning outcomes and assessment criteria. Three of the tasks will require free text responses and will be human marked. The remaining seven tasks will be computer marked.

Task	Learning outcome	Assessment criteria	Maximum marks	Title for topics within task range
1	1, 2	1.1K 1.3K 2.1K	12	Cash receipts and payments and their relationship with profit
2	1	1.2S 1.4S	14	Forecasting income and expenditure
3	2	2.2S 2.3K	14	Patterns of cash flow
4	2	2.2S 2.4S	16	Preparing a cash budget
5	2	2.5S	16	Sensitivity analysis
6	3	3.1S 3.2S	12	Monitoring cash flows
7	4	4.1K 4.2K 4.3K 4.4K	12	Liquidity management

Task	Learning outcome	Assessment criteria	Maximum marks	Title for topics within task range
8	4, 5, 6	4.5S 5.2S 6.1S	12	Saving and borrowing – terms, conditions and calculations
9	4, 5	4.5S 4.6S 4.7S 5.1K 5.2S	16	Raising finance
10	6	6.1S 6.2S 6.3S	12	Investing surplus funds

Time allowed

The time allowed for this assessment is **2 hours 30 minutes.**

STUDY SKILLS

Preparing to study

Devise a study plan

Determine which times of the week you will study.

Split these times into sessions of at least one hour for study of new material. Any shorter periods could be used for revision or practice.

Put the times you plan to study onto a study plan for the weeks from now until the assessment and set yourself targets for each period of study – in your sessions make sure you cover the whole course, activities and the associated questions in the workbook at the back of the manual.

If you are studying more than one unit at a time, try to vary your subjects as this can help to keep you interested and see subjects as part of wider knowledge.

When working through your course, compare your progress with your plan and, if necessary, re-plan your work (perhaps including extra sessions) or, if you are ahead, do some extra revision/practice questions.

Effective studying

Active reading

You are not expected to learn the text by rote, rather, you must understand what you are reading and be able to use it to pass the assessment and develop good practice.

A good technique is to use SQ3Rs – Survey, Question, Read, Recall, Review:

1 **Survey the chapter**

Look at the headings and read the introduction, knowledge, skills and content, so as to get an overview of what the chapter deals with.

2 **Question**

Whilst undertaking the survey ask yourself the questions you hope the chapter will answer for you.

3 Read

Read through the chapter thoroughly working through the activities and, at the end, making sure that you can meet the learning objectives highlighted on the first page.

4 Recall

At the end of each section and at the end of the chapter, try to recall the main ideas of the section/chapter without referring to the text. This is best done after short break of a couple of minutes after the reading stage.

5 Review

Check that your recall notes are correct.

You may also find it helpful to re-read the chapter to try and see the topic(s) it deals with as a whole.

Note taking

Taking notes is a useful way of learning, but do not simply copy out the text.

The notes must:

- be in your own words
- be concise
- cover the key points
- well organised
- be modified as you study further chapters in this text or in related ones.

Trying to summarise a chapter without referring to the text can be a useful way of determining which areas you know and which you don't.

Three ways of taking notes

1 Summarise the key points of a chapter

2 Make linear notes

A list of headings, subdivided with sub-headings listing the key points.

If you use linear notes, you can use different colours to highlight key points and keep topic areas together.

Use plenty of space to make your notes easy to use.

3 Try a diagrammatic form

The most common of which is a mind map.

To make a mind map, put the main heading in the centre of the paper and put a circle around it.

Draw lines radiating from this to the main sub-headings which again have circles around them.

Continue the process from the sub-headings to sub-sub-headings.

Highlighting and underlining

You may find it useful to underline or highlight key points in your study text – but do be selective.

You may also wish to make notes in the margins.

Revision phase

Kaplan has produced material specifically designed for your final examination preparation for this unit.

These include pocket revision notes and a bank of revision questions specifically in the style of the new syllabus.

Further guidance on how to approach the final stage of your studies is given in these materials.

Further reading

In addition to this text, you should also read the 'Student section' of the 'Accounting Technician' magazine every month to keep abreast of any guidance from the examiners.

3. Try a diagrammatic form – the most common of which is a mind-map.

The most common of which is a mind-map. To [illegible]

To make a mind-map, put the main heading in the centre of the paper and put a circle around it.

Draw lines radiating from this to the main sub-headings which again have circles around them.

Continue the process from the sub-headings to sub-sub-headings.

Highlighting and underlining

You may find it useful to underline or highlight key points in your study text – but do be selective.

You may also wish to make notes in the margins.

[illegible]

Kaplan has produced [illegible] material [illegible] examination preparation [illegible].

These include [illegible] questions [illegible] specifically in the style [illegible].

Further guidance on how to approach the final [illegible] your studies [illegible] covered in these materials.

[illegible]

In addition to [illegible] of the Accounting Technician [illegible] any guidance from the [illegible].

TERMINOLOGY FOR CSHM

There are different terms used to mean the same thing – you will need to be aware of both sets of terminology.

UK GAAP	**IAS**
Final accounts	Financial statements
Trading and profit and loss account	Statement of profit or loss or Income Statement
Turnover or Sales	Revenue or Sales revenue
Balance sheet	Statement of financial position
Fixed assets	Non-current assets
Net book value	Carrying amount
Tangible assets	Property, plant and equipment
Stock	Inventory
Trade debtors	Trade receivables
Trade creditors	Trade payables
Long term liabilities	Non-current liabilities
Capital	Equity
Profit and loss balance	Retained earnings
Net profit	Profit for the year

1 Cash and profit

Introduction

This chapter demonstrates how important cash is to a business. It looks at how cash differs from profit.

ASSESSMENT CRITERIA

Explain how recording and accounting practice may vary in different parts of an organisation (1.1K)

Describe the relationship between cash flow accounting and accounting for income and expenditure (1.3K)

Identify the characteristics of the main types of cash receipts and payments (2.1K)

CONTENTS

1 Types of cash flow

1.1 The importance of cash flow

The term **cash** in this unit is used to describe bank account balances as well as coins and notes; and cash payments include cheque payments, BACS, direct debits and standing orders.

Any business will wish to make a profit. This means that, over a period of time, revenue needs to exceed costs. However, even if the business is making a profit, it must also have **cash funds** available to pay suppliers, employees and other expenses.

1.2 Types of cash flow

There are different types of cash flow that a business is likely to have:

- Regular receipts and payments such as sales, purchases and expenses.
- Receipts and payments of a long-term nature, known as capital receipts and payments, such as the raising of share capital or the purchase of non-current assets.
- Payments made to the owners of a business either in the form of drawings for a sole trader or partnership or dividends for a company.
- Other costs such as the payment of taxes to the government.
- Unusual or exceptional receipts or payments, for example, cash received from the sale of a non-current asset.

A business will have different types of receipts and payments. The typical types of cash flows that you will come across are described below.

1.3 Cash inflows

- **Regular revenue receipts** for a business will be cash sales and cash from customers that have purchased goods on credit.
- **Capital receipts** will include cash raised by issuing shares or raising a loan.
- Other types of capital cash inflow such as the proceeds from the sale of non-current assets or the receipt of government grants. These are likely to be **irregular cash inflows**.

1.4 Cash outflows

- **Regular revenue payments** will include payments for cash purchases, cash paid to payables, wage payments, payment of bills, and cash payments of expenses.
- **Capital payments** could include the repayment of loans or the purchase of non-current assets. When new non-current assets are purchased this may be for a large sum on just one date or it may take the form of regular payments if, for example, the asset is acquired under a lease or hire purchase agreement.
- Businesses will also be likely to make payments or disbursements in the form of corporation tax, VAT and PAYE. These may be regular such as the monthly PAYE payments or one-off payments each year such as the annual payment of corporation tax.
- Payments will also be made to providers of finance such as dividends to shareholders and interest payments to banks and other providers of finance. The timing of these payments will vary but, for example, companies usually pay any dividend twice a year, a small interim dividend during the year and a larger final dividend after the year end.
- Finally, in a sole trader's business or a partnership, there may be either regular or irregular payments made to the owner or partners in the form of drawings.

1.5 Exceptional cash flows

The cash flows described above are the normal, everyday types of cash flows that most businesses will have. However in some cases there will also be exceptional cash flows which are **not part of normal business** operations.

- Exceptional cash outflows might include payment of legal damages or redundancy costs.
- Exceptional cash inflows might include items such as receipts from an insurance company for damaged inventory.

Activity 1

Cash receipts and payments take many different forms but they can be broadly categorised into regular, capital, exceptional and drawings.

Complete the table by selecting the correct description from the list of options below to match the type of cash receipt or cash payment (not all options need to be used).

Type of receipt or payment	Description
Capital receipts	
Capital payment	
Regular revenue receipt	
Exceptional payment	
Exceptional receipt	
Regular revenue payment	
Annual disbursement	
Drawings	

Options:

A Payment of electricity bill

B Receipt from an insurance claim

C Proceeds from the disposal of non-current assets

D Payments made to the owners of the business

E Lease new machinery

F Pay corporation tax for the year

G Payment of a redundancy package

H Customer paying their debt

Activity 2

Payments that relate to the purchase of non-current assets would be classified as:

A Capital payments

B Regular revenue receipts

C Drawings

D Exceptional receipts

Activity 3

Income received from an insurance claim for lost inventory would be classified as:

A Capital payments

B Regular revenue receipts

C Drawings

D Exceptional receipts

2 Cash flow versus profit

2.1 Cash flow and profit

Cash is not the same as profit. It is entirely possible for a profitable business to run short of cash.

- Profit is a figure on the Statement of Profit or Loss
- Cash is a current asset on the Statement of Financial Position

A typical Statement of Profit or Loss is shown below:

	£000
Revenue	X
Cost of sales	(X)
Gross profit	X
Distribution costs	(X)
Administrative expense	(X)
Operating profit	X
Finance costs	(X)
Profit before tax	X
Tax	(X)
Profit for the period	X

A typical Statement of Financial Position is shown below:

	£000
Non-current assets	
Property, plant and equipment	X
Other intangible assets	X
Goodwill	X
	X
Current assets	
Inventories	X
Trade and other receivables	X
Cash and cash equivalents	X
	X
Total assets	**X**

Equity and liabilities	
Equity	
Share capital	X
Share premium account	X
Revaluation reserve	X
Retained earnings	X
Total equity	X
Non-current liabilities	
Bank loans	X
Long-term provisions	X
	X
Current liabilities	
Trade and other payables	X
Tax liabilities	X
Bank overdrafts and loans	X
	X
Total liabilities	**X**
Total equity and liabilities	**X**

2.2 The difference between cash and profit

There are a variety of reasons why the profit of a business will not equate directly to cash:

- **Revenue** is recognised in the Statement of Profit or Loss when it is earned but this is not necessarily when the cash is received. A business may make credit sales thus creating receivables.
- **Costs** are recognised in the Statement of Profit or Loss when incurred but this is not necessarily when the cash is paid. A business may have credit with suppliers creating payables.
- **Accruals** are an expense that has been incurred during the period but has not been paid by the period end, so will reduce profit but will not have impacted on cash flow.

> **Definition**
>
> FRS 18 *Accounting Policies* defines the accruals concept as follows.
>
> 'The accruals basis of accounting requires the non-cash effects of transactions and other events to be reflected, as far as is possible, in the financial statements for the accounting period in which they occur and not, for example, in the period in which any cash involved is received or paid.'

- **Prepayments** are payments made during the period for an expense that relates to a period after the period end. This will impact the current period's cash flow as cash is being spent on an expense that will be accounted for in a future period's Statement of Profit or Loss.
- **Depreciation** is charged to the Statement of Profit or Loss, reducing profit, but it does not have any effect on cash. It is a non-cash expense.
- **Provisions for doubtful debts** are charged as expenses but they are not cash flows and will not reduce the cash balance of the business.
- **Purchases of non-current assets** are often large cash outflows of a business but the only amount that is charged to the Statement of Profit or Loss is the annual depreciation charge and not the entire cost of the non-current asset.
- **Sale of non-current assets** will result in an inflow of cash to the business but the figure appearing in the Statement of Profit or Loss is not the sales proceeds but any profit or loss made on the sale.
- **Financing transactions,** such as issuing additional share capital and taking out or repaying a loan, will result in large cash flows in or out of the business with no effect on the profit figure.

There are a number of different techniques that can be used to calculate the cash flows or changes in cash position.

3 Calculating cash flows

3.1 Introduction

To be able to produce cash budgets it is necessary to calculate the actual cash a business spends and receives during a time period. Figures from the Statement of Profit or Loss and Statement of Financial Position will be used for these calculations.

Note: Some of the concepts in this chapter are assumed knowledge. Please refer to Chapter 9 Assumed knowledge for more information.

3.2 Calculating cash flows

The adjustments include:

- Calculating the **actual cash received from receivables** – using the opening and closing receivables balance and the sales revenue for the period
- Calculating the **actual cash paid to payables** – using the opening and closing payables balance and the purchases for the period
- Calculating the **actual cash paid for various expenses** – using accruals and/or prepayments to adjust the expense for the period.

3.3 Cash receipts from receivables

Example

Opening receivables are £10,000 and closing receivables are £14,000. Revenue for the period has been £12,000. Assuming that all the sales were on credit. How much cash has been received from receivables in the period?

Solution

To calculate the cash received in relation to sales it is possible to use the trade receivables control account:

Trade receivables

Opening balance	10,000	*Cash received*	*8,000*
Sales	12,000	Closing balance	14,000
	22,000		22,000

Instead of using a T account:

cash received = sales plus opening balance less closing balance

= 12,000 + 10,000 – 14,000

= 8,000

3.4 Cash payments to payables

Example

Opening payables are £2,500 and closing payables are £3,250. Purchases for the period have been £2,250. Assuming that all the purchases were on credit. How much cash has been paid to payables in the period?

Solution

To calculate the cash paid in relation to purchases it is possible to use the trade payables control account:

Trade payables

Cash paid	*1,500*	Opening balance	2,500
Closing balance	3,250	Purchases	2,250
	4,750		4,750

Instead of using a T account:

cash paid = purchases plus opening balance less closing balance

= 2,250 + 2,500 – 3,250

= 2,250

= 1,500

3.5 Accruals

Example

Electricity has an opening accrual of £100 and a closing accrual of £50 relating to it. There is an amount of £200 recorded in the Statement of Profit or Loss for electricity.

Solution

To calculate the cash paid in relation to electricity complete the electricity account:

Electricity

Cash paid	*250*	Opening accrual	100
Closing accrual	50	Statement of Profit or Loss	200
	300		300

3.6 Prepayments

Example

Rent has an opening prepayment of £300 and a closing prepayment of £200 relating to it. There is an amount of £750 recorded in the Statement of Profit or Loss for rent.

Solution

To calculate the cash paid in relation to rent complete the rent account:

Rent

Opening prepayment	300	Statement of Profit or Loss	750
Cash paid	*650*	Closing prepayment	200
	950		950

3.7 Non-current assets

A business may buy or sell a non-current asset and the cash paid or received for this will be classed as a cash outflow or inflow.

It may be necessary to calculate this cash flow with reference to the Statement of Profit or Loss and the Statement of Financial Position.

Example

New fixtures and fittings were purchased in a part exchange deal. The trade in price for the old fittings was £1,200 and the new fitting had a list price of £3,000. What was the cash outflow for this purchase?

Solution

£3,000 – £1,200 = £1,800 cash outflow.

Example

During the year a printing press was sold that had originally cost £35,000. When the press was sold the asset had a carrying amount of £23,000. The loss on disposal was £5,000. What was the cash inflow from this sale?

Solution

Disposal

Printing press cost	35,000	Accumulated depreciation*	12,000
		Loss on disposal	5,000
		Cash received	*18,000*
	35,000		35,000

* calculated by subtracting the carrying amount (£23,000) from the cost (£35,000).

Alternative working:

If the carrying amount of the assets is £23,000 and a loss on disposal of £5,000 was made, then the cash received must have been £5,000 less than the carrying amount. Therefore cash received = £18,000

Example

The business decided to sell off one of its spare premises. The building had been depreciated at 5% on cost for the 5 years of ownership. The original purchase price was £50,000. There was a gain on disposal of £12,000. What was the cash received from this sale?

Solution

Disposal

Building cost	50,000	Accumulated depreciation*	12,500
Gain on disposal	12,000	*Cash received*	*49,500*
	62,000		62,000

* calculated by taking 5% of the original cost and multiplying it by the 5 years the building was owed for (50,000 × 5%) × 5.

In some cases you may need to work out the cash paid for additions or received from a sale by looking at figures for total assets not individual ones as per the previous examples. In such cases make sure you include the depreciation charge for the period.

Example

The carrying amount of non-current assets at the start of the period is forecast to be £30,000 and the carrying amount at the end of the period is forecast to be £37,000. Depreciation for the period will be £10,000. The company will pay for any additions immediately by cash. Calculate the cash to be paid for any additions.

Solution

Carrying amount of NCA

Opening balance	30,000	Depreciation charge	10,000
Cash paid for additions	*17,000*	Closing balance	37,000
	47,000		47,000

Non-current assets can be acquired by outright purchase (e.g. through raising a bank loan and paying cash) or via **finance leases**. A finance lease is a lease whereby the risks and rewards of ownership are transferred to the business using the non-current asset – for example the lessee has to maintain and repair the asset.

While the legal form is that the asset is still owned by the leasing company (the lessor) the commercial substance is that it is effectively the same as buying it. The accounting treatment reflects this:

- The finance leased non-current asset is recorded in the Statement of Financial Position and treated as a normal non-current asset.
- Lease and interest payments relating to the finance leased non-current asset are recorded in the Statement of Profit or Loss (note: you do not need to know the details of the accounting entries here).

Example

The carrying amount of non-current assets at the start of the month is forecast to be £300,000 and the carrying amount at the end of the month is forecast to be £370,000. Depreciation for the month was £30,000.

During the month the business will take out a new finance lease to acquire a new machine that would otherwise cost £40,000. The finance lease is payable at 5% per month.

The company will pay for any other additions immediately by cash. Calculate the cash to be paid for any additions in the month.

Solution

Carrying amount of NCA

Opening balance	300,000	Depreciation charge	30,000
Additions	*100,000*	Closing balance	370,000
	400,000		400,000

The total additions are £100,000 of which £40,000 is the finance lease. The cash paid for additions is therefore £60,000

Note: The cash paid for the finance lease will amount to £2,000 per month (£40,000 × 5%).

3.8 Other considerations

Non-cash items

Depreciation will be included in some of the expenses within the Statement of Profit or Loss. Depreciation is a non-cash item so it will need to be adjusted for.

Example

Expenses include a depreciation charge for £5,000. Total expenses are £14,000. All expenses are being settled on cash terms. Calculate the cash flow for expenses in the period.

Solution

The cash flow for expenses is: £14,000 – £5,000 = £9,000

Tax payments

Tax will be shown in both the Statement of Financial Position and the Statement of Profit or Loss.

It is normally a current liability in the Statement of Financial Position as tax is usually owing to HMRC at the end of the financial year. In the Statement of Profit or Loss the tax figure is the expense for the period. The tax expense is not always the tax paid. It may be necessary to calculate the cash paid to the HMRC.

Example

The tax payable at the start of the period shown on the Statement of Financial Position is expected to be £15,000 and at the end of the period it is expected to be £17,000. The tax expense show on the Statement of Profit or Loss is £16,000. Calculate the tax paid in the period

Solution

Tax liability

Cash paid	*14,000*	Opening balance	15,000
Closing balance	17,000	Statement of Profit or Loss	16,000
	31,000		31,000

Period expenses

There are some expenses that are paid as incurred. For example, wages tend to be paid in the month that they are earned by the employees so no adjustments are normally necessary to turn the Statement of Profit or Loss figure into a cash flow figure.

Activity 4

The Statement of Profit or Loss for L Boy's business for the quarter ended 31 March is as follows:

	£	£
Revenue		210,325
Less: Purchases		(32,657)
Gross profit		177,668
Less: Expenses		
Wages	50,100	
Rent of office	15,000	
Insurance of machinery	7,851	
Electricity	12,352	
Depreciation	8,687	
		(93,990)
Profit for the year		83,678

Extracts from the Statement of Financial Position at 1 January and 31 March show the following:

	1 January	*31 March*
	£	£
Receivables	18,695	15,985
Payables	965	1,054
Accruals – Electricity	550	450
Prepayments – Rent of office	1,200	1,350

Calculate the actual business cash receipts and cash payments for the quarter to 31 March.

	£
Sales receipts	
Purchases	
Wages	
Rent of office	
Insurance of machinery	
Electricity	
Depreciation	

4 Reconciling profit to cash flow

4.1 Introduction

As discussed there is a difference between profit and cash flow. It is possible to calculate cash flow from profit, or vice versa, using information from financial statements and other information.

Items added to profit to get to cash:

- depreciation (a non-cash item)
- loss on disposal (a non-cash item)
- a decrease in the receivables balance
- a decrease in the inventory balance
- an increase in the payables balance
- interest and tax payments

Items deducted from profit to get to cash:

- profit on disposal (a non-cash item)
- an increase in the receivables balance is deducted from profit
- an increase in the inventory balance
- a decrease in the payables balance

Note: the opposite would be applied to calculate profit from cash.

4.2 Change in receivables

Operating profit contains items included within the balances in the Statement of Financial Position. For example, revenue in the Statement of Profit or Loss includes **all** sales made, whether the cash has been received or not, so the **change** in the receivables balance is calculated to identify the necessary adjustment to change profit into cash.

The receivables account allows us to calculate the cash received, as seen in section 3.3, by completing the following calculation:

Cash receipts = sales + opening receivables – closing receivables

This can be rewritten as:

Cash received = sales adjusted for the change in receivables

The Statement of Profit or Loss already includes the sales in the operating profit so the adjustment to change profit into cash is simply the 'change in receivables'.

Example

A company believes that 90% of sales will be on credit terms. The balance of trade receivables at 1 April is £8,000 and the company expects trade receivables at the end of June to be 30% of the credit sales for the quarter. The sales for the quarter are £10,000.

Calculate the adjustment required.

Solution

The opening balance = £8,000

The closing balance = £10,000 × 90% × 30% = £2,700

The difference = £5,300 decrease in balance

An addition of £5,300 will adjust the operating profit for the period for the cash received in excess of the credit sales made already included in the revenue.

Receivables

Opening balance	8,000	Cash received	14,300
Credit sales	9,000	Closing balance	2,700
	17,000		17,000

£9,000 sales are already recorded in the Statement of Profit or Loss within the Sales revenue amount. £14,300 has been received from the receivables. This means that to fully account for the cash receipts profit needs to be increased by £5,300.

4.3 Change in inventory

If the balance on the inventory account has increased it indicates that more inventory has been purchased therefore more cash has been spent reducing the cash flow and vice versa. The profit needs to be adjusted for the movement in inventory to calculate the cash flow for the period.

Example

The opening inventory was £80,000 and the closing inventory is £90,000.

Calculate the adjustment required.

Solution

There has been an increase in the inventory balance. The difference is £10,000

Profit will need to be reduced by £10,000

4.4 Change in payables

Purchases in the Statement of Profit or Loss include all purchases made, whether the cash has been paid or not, so the change in the payables balance is calculated to identify the necessary adjustment to change profit into cash.

Example

All purchases are to be made on credit terms. Purchases for the quarter are £2,400. The balance of trade payables at 1 April is £1,200. Total payments for purchases during the quarter will be £2,000.

Calculate the adjustment required.

Solution

The opening balance = £1,200

The closing balance = £1,200 + £2,400 – £2,000 = £1,600

The difference = £400 increase in balance

An addition of £400 will adjust the operating profit for the period for the extra payment recorded in the Statement of Profit or Loss under Purchases.

Payables

Cash paid	2,000	Opening balance	1,200
Closing balance	1,600	Purchases	2,400
	3,600		3,600

£2,400 purchases are already recorded in the Statement of Profit or Loss within the Cost of sales. Only £2,000 has actually been paid to the payables. This means that to fully account for the cash paid, profit needs to be increase by £400.

Activity 5

The forecast Statement of Profit or Loss for A Business for the quarter ended June is as follows:

	£	£
Sales		7,500
Less: Cost of sales		
Opening inventory	600	
Purchases	1,200	
Closing inventory	(500)	
		(1,300)
Gross profit		6,200
Expenses		(940)
Operating profit		5,260
Tax		(1,350)
Profit after tax		3,910

Additional information

1 The company believes that 80% of sales will be on credit terms. 20% of total sales will be cash sales. The balance of trade receivables at 1 April is £5,000 and the company expects trade receivables at the end of June to be 30% of the credit sales for the quarter.

2 All purchases are to be made on credit terms. The balance of trade payables at 1 April is £600. Total payments for purchases during the quarter will be £1,000.

3 Expenses include a depreciation charge of £900. All other expenses are settled on cash terms.

4 The carrying amount of the non-current assets at 1 April is forecast to be £10,000 and the carrying amount at 30 June is forecast to be £12,000. The company will pay for any additions immediately by cash

5 The tax payable shown in the Statement of Financial Position is expected to be £1,300 at 1 April and £1,400 at 30 June.

6 The forecast cash position at 1 April is £15,000.

Calculate the closing cash position at 30 June. Use brackets or minus signs where appropriate.

	£
Operating profit	
Change in inventory	
Change in receivables	
Change in payables	
Adjustment for non-cash items	
Change in non-current assets	
Tax paid	
Net change in cash position	
Forecast cash position 1 April	
Forecast cash position 30 June	

Activity 6

Labet is an office and industrial furniture manufacturer.

The statement of financial position below is stated as at 31 October 20X6, which is followed by a summary of Labet's cash book for the year ended 31 October 20X7.

Labet's Statement of financial position at 31 October 20X6

		£000	£000
Non-current assets			
Property, plant and equipment	– cost	7,300	
	– depreciation	1,110	
			6,190
Current assets			
Inventory		1,200	
Trade receivables		753	
Cash and cash equivalents		82	
			2,035
			8,225
Equity			
Share capital		3,000	
Retained earnings		1,425	
			4,425
Non-current liabilities			
Loan notes		2,260	
Deferred tax		180	
			2,440
Current liabilities			
Trade and other payables		573	
Tax payable		670	
Interest payable		117	
			1,360
			8,225

Labet's summarised cash book for the year ended 31 October 20X7

	Note	*Receipts/ (Payment)* £000
Cash book balance at 1 November 20X6		82
Interest paid during the year	(ii)	(160)
Administration expenses paid		(500)
Income tax	(iii)	(690)
Purchase cost of property, plant and equipment	(iv)	(3,460)
Receipt for disposal of land	(v)	1,200
Cash received from customers		7,500
Payments to suppliers of production materials, wages and other production costs		(3,000)
Distribution and selling costs		(730)
Cash received from increase in loan notes		2,500
Cash book balance at 31 October 20X7		2,742

Notes:

(i) All sales and purchases are on credit terms.

(ii) Interest outstanding at 31 October 20X7 was £130,000.

(iii) The tax liability as at 31 October 20X7 was £502,000.

(iv) The property, plant and equipment balance at 31 October 20X6 was made up as follows:

	Land	*Premises*	*Plant & equipment*	*Total*
	£000	£000	£000	£000
Cost	2,000	1,500	3,800	7,300
Accumulated depreciation	0	350	760	1,110
Carrying value	2,000	1,150	3,040	6,190

During the year Labet purchased new premises at a cost of £1,600,000, and new plant and equipment for £1,860,000. Property, plant and equipment are depreciated on the straight line basis at 6% per year and are treated as a cost of sale. Labet charges a full year's depreciation in the year of acquisition.

(v) Land originally costing £1,000,000 was sold during the year for £1,200,000. Land is not depreciated.

(vi) Balances at 31 October 20X7:

Trade receivables	£620,000
Outstanding trade payables	£670,000
Inventory	£985,000
Deferred tax	£180,000

Prepare the Statement of Profit or Loss (all workings should be to the nearest £000.)

Labet's Statement of Profit or Loss for the year to 31 October 20X7

	£000
Revenue	
Cost of sales	
Gross profit	
Distribution costs	
Administrative expenses	
Disposal of land	
Operating profit	
Finance costs	
Profit before tax	
Income tax expense	
Profit for the period	

5 Summary

This chapter demonstrates the differences between cash and profit. It shows how to use the Statement of Profit or Loss and the Statement of Financial Position figures to calculate cash flows.

Answers to chapter activities

Activity 1

Type of receipt or payment	Description
Capital receipts	C
Capital payment	E
Regular revenue receipt	H
Exceptional payment	G
Exceptional receipt	B
Regular revenue payment	A
Annual disbursement	F
Drawings	D

Activity 2

Answer A

Non-current assets would require a large capital payment to be made.

Activity 3

Answer D

Income from an insurance claim would not be expected as part of day to day trading.

Activity 4

	Working	£
Sales receipts	18,695 + 210,325 – 15,985	213,035
Purchases	965 + 32,657 – 1,054	32,568
Wages	As per income statement	50,100
Rent of office	15,000 – 1,200 + 1,350	15,150
Insurance of machinery	As per Statement of Profit or Loss	7,851
Electricity	12,352 + 550 – 450	12,452
Depreciation	Non-cash item	0

Activity 5

	Working	£
Operating profit		5,260
Change in inventory	600 – 500 reduction	100
Change in receivables	7,500 × 0.8 × 0.3 = 1,800 5,000 – 1,800 reduction	3,200
Change in payables	600 + 1,200 – 1,000 = 800 600 – 800 increase	200
Adjustment for non-cash items	Depreciation charge	900
Change in non-current assets	12,000 + 900 – 10,000 = 2,900 for additions	(2,900)
Tax paid	1,300 + 1,350 – 1,400 = 1,250 paid	(1,250)
Net change in cash position		5,510
Forecast cash position 1 April		15,000
Forecast cash position 30 June		20,510

Activity 6

Labet's Statement of profit or loss for the year to 31 October 20X7

	£000
Revenue (W1)	7,367
Cost of sales (W2 – W4)	(3,838)
Gross profit	3,529
Distribution costs	(730)
Administrative expenses	(500)
Disposal of land (W5)	200
Profit from operations	2,499
Finance costs (W6)	(173)
Profit before tax	2,326
Income tax expense (W7)	(482)
Profit for the period	1,844

Workings

(W1) **Revenue**

	£000
Opening receivables	(753)
Cash received from receivables	7,500
Closing receivables	620
Revenue	7,367

(W2) **Depreciation**

	Premises	*Plant*	*Total*
	£000	£000	£000
Cost	1,500	3,800	7,300
Addition	1,600	1,860	3,460
	3,100	5,660	9,760
Depreciation charge for the year	186	340	526

(W3) **Purchases**

	£000
Opening payables	(573)
Cash paid	3,000
Closing payables	670
Purchases	3,097

(W4) **Cost of sales**

	£000
Opening inventory	1,200
Depreciation (W2)	526
Purchases (W3)	3,097
Closing inventory	(985)
	3,838

(W5) **Disposal of land**

	£		£
NBV	1,000,000	Accumulated depreciation	0
Gain	200,000	Proceeds	1,200,000
	1,200,000		1,200,000

(W6) **Interest charge**

	£000
Opening balance	117
Interest paid during the year	(160)
Closing balance	(130)
Statement of profit of loss charge	173

(W7) **Tax charge**

	£000
Opening balance	670
Tax paid during the year	(690)
Closing balance	502
Statement of profit of loss charge	482

6 Test your knowledge

Workbook Activity 7

Catherine Olivia owns a dance school. Catherine prepares quarterly statements of profit or loss and statements of financial position. These are prepared on an accruals basis.

Catherine buys costumes for shows put on by the school and keeps these in inventory. She gets credit from her suppliers as she uses them on a regular basis. The dancers who attend her classes pay on a regular basis, but in arrears, so Catherine is owed money by them all of the time.

The Statement of Profit or Loss for Catherine's business for the quarter ended June is as follows:

	£	£
Revenue		3,000
Less: Purchases		(1,400)
Gross profit		1,600
Less: Expenses		
Wages	300	
Advertising expenses	100	
Travel expenses	400	
Fees for competitions	150	
		(950)
		650

Extracts from the Statement of Financial Positions at 1 April and 30 June show the following:

Statement of Financial Position at	*1 April*	*30 June*
	£	£
Receivables	1,520	1,400
Payables	400	520
Accruals – travel costs	50	80
Prepayments – comp fees	80	110

Calculate the actual business cash receipts and cash payments for the quarter to 30 June.

	£
Sales receipts	
Purchase payments	
Wages paid	
Advertising expenses paid	
Travel expenses paid	
Competition expenses paid	

Forecasting cash flows

2

Introduction

This chapter considers methods that can be used to forecast cash payments and cash receipts. One of the most common of these methods is time series analysis which can be used to forecast sales for future periods. Cash flow forecasts might also be affected by changes in quantities of sales or production and by inflation of costs and prices.

ASSESSMENT CRITERIA

Prepare forecasts of income and expenditure using these statistical methods: moving averages; allowance for inflation; regression analysis (1.2S)

Ensure forecasts of future cash payments and receipts agree with known income and expenditure trends (1.4S)

CONTENTS

1 Information for cash budgets

1.1 Introduction

A lot of information is needed in order to produce a cash budget.

1.2 Sales information

The starting point for information for the cash budget will normally be sales quantities and prices, as this will be the basis for the production budget and expenses figures. The sales information will normally be provided by the **sales or marketing director or manager**. Both the quantity of sales and the price that will be charged are vital information for a cash budget.

1.3 Production information

Details such as the amount of production, the levels of closing inventories and the labour hours to be worked should all be available from the **production manager or director**. The production manager may also have information about variable and fixed expenses of the factory but equally that information may come from the accountant.

The production manager or director may also be able to provide information about any planned capital expenditure or any planned sales of non-current assets.

1.4 Accounting information

Further information will come from the **accounts department** in the form of materials prices, labour hour rates, variable and fixed costs, details of sales of non-current assets. The accounts department or the credit control department will also have the information required to determine the payment pattern of receivables and payables.

1.5 Forecast information

The information provided by the different departments will be current or past information. This information will need to be amended to allow for any adjustments or alterations foreseen for future periods.

There are a number of different techniques that can be used to produce forecasted figures:

- Time series analysis using moving averages – removes peaks and troughs in time series data to produce a trend that can be extrapolated.

- Regression analysis – calculates the line of best fit, in a set of data, which can then be extrapolated.
- Percentage change and index numbers – to adjust prices and quantities by known percentages and to apply changes due to inflation.
- Mark-ups and margins – to calculate costs and revenues when a desired return is known.

2 Time series analysis

2.1 Introduction

Definition

A time series is a set of values for some variable (e.g. monthly sales) which varies with time. A set of observations will be taken at specific times, usually at regular intervals.

Examples of figures which can be plotted as a time series are:

(a) train ticket sales each hour

(b) daily closing price of a share on the Stock Exchange

(c) weekly sales in a department store.

2.2 Time series graph

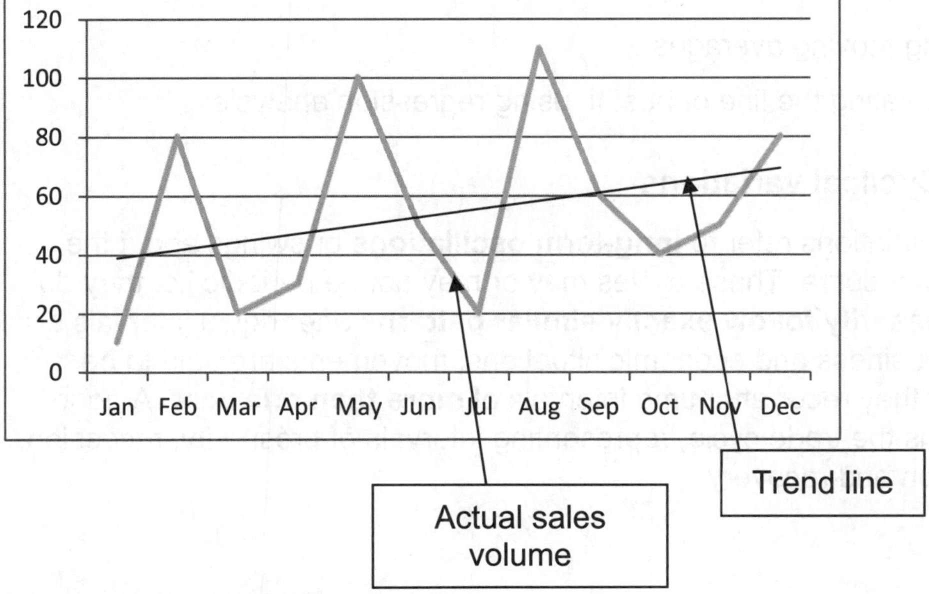

The graph shows the monthly sales volume for a year in a business. It can be seen that the sales have fluctuated month on month producing peaks and troughs in the data. For this graph to be useful for predicting cash flows the 'trend' or general movement of the data needs to be known – is it increasing, decrease or staying static?

The graph of a time series may be useful for investigating what happened in the past but the real value of producing a time series is to use it to forecast what will happen in the future. In other words the past information is recorded, analysed and projected into the future to help with production planning, staff recruitment, etc.

2.3 Components of a time series

Analysis of time series has revealed certain characteristic movements or variations. These movements are the components of the time series. Analysis of these components is essential for forecasting purposes.

The four main components are:

- basic trend or long-term movement
- cyclical movement
- seasonal movement
- residual or random movements.

2.4 Basic trend

The basic trend refers to the **general direction** in which the graph of a time series goes over a long interval of time. This movement can be represented on the graph by a trend curve or line.

One way of identifying the trend is simply to draw it in freehand on the graph. This is not usually good enough for forecasting purposes. Two more robust methods are:

- using moving averages
- calculating the line of best fit using regression analysis

2.5 Cyclical variations

Cyclical variations refer to **long-term oscillations** or swings about the trend line or curve. These cycles may or may not be periodic i.e. they do **not necessarily follow exactly similar patterns** after equal intervals of time. In business and economic situations, movements are said to be cyclical if they recur after time intervals of **more than one year**. A good example is the trade cycle, representing intervals of prosperity, recession, depression and recovery.

For cyclical variations to be apparent, data must be available over very long periods of time since the periods of oscillation are so long. This is impractical for cash flows and, for that reason, the **calculation of cyclical variations is ignored in this chapter** although you must, of course, realise that they exist.

2.6 Seasonal variations

Seasonal fluctuations are the **identical, or almost identical, patterns** which a time series follows during corresponding intervals of successive periods. Such movements are due to recurring events, such as the sudden increase in department store sales before Christmas. Although, in general, seasonal movements refer to a period of three months, this is not always the case and **periods of hours, days, week or, months**, may also be considered, depending on the type of data available.

2.7 Random variations

Random variations are the **sporadic motions** of time series due to chance events such as **floods, strikes, elections**.

By their very nature they are **unpredictable** and therefore cannot play a large part in any forecasting, but it is possible to isolate the random variations by calculating all other types of variation and removing them from the time series data. It is important to extract any significant random variations from the data before using them for forecasting.

3 Moving averages

3.1 Introduction

The analysis of a time series consists of:

Step 1 Breaking the series down into trend and seasonal variations

Step 2 Projecting the trend into the future.

Step 3 Applying the seasonal variation to the projected trend, to arrive at forecast figures.

3.2 Moving averages

By using moving averages, the **variations in a time series can be eliminated leaving a 'smoothed' set of figures** which is taken as the trend.

It is important that the correct cycle is chosen for the moving average; otherwise the result will not be as good as it should be. For instance, if there are seasonal variations present in a time series and the pattern is repeated every third period (quarterly), the moving average should be calculated based on three periods at a time to get the best results. It is possible to calculate a moving average based on any length of cycle.

3.3 Calculating moving averages

Example

The underlying trend is estimated using moving averages.

Month	*Actual sales*	*3 month moving total*	*Trend*
Jan	74		
Feb	100	267 (W1)	89 (W2)
Mar	93	279	93 (W3)
Apr	86	291	97
May	112	303	101
Jun	105	315	105
Jul	98	327	109
Aug	124	339	113
Sept	117	351	117
Oct	110	363	121
Nov	136	375	125
Dec	129		

Workings

(W1) Calculate the total of the sales for the first three months (month January to March).

74 + 100 + 93 = 267

(W2) Find the average sales for this three month period by dividing by 3.

267 ÷ 3 = 89

This represents the trend for February.

(W3) Repeat the process for the next three month period, moving on just one month (months February to April).

100 + 93 + 86 = 279

279/3 = 93

This represents the trend for March.

Repeat the calculation for each successive three-month period until the data has been fully analysed into three-month blocks.

Months March to May = 97 (trend for April).

Months April to June = 101 (trend for May).

Activity 1

The following represents monthly output of a product.

What are the trend figures that would be obtained by a 3 month moving average?

Month	*Output*	*3 month moving total*	*Trend*
Jan	12		
Feb	26		
Mar	19		
Apr	15		
May	29		
Jun	22		
Jul	18		
Aug	32		
Sept	25		

3.4 Centred moving averages

In the previous example the period for the moving average was an odd number i.e. a three month moving average. This meant that it was possible to place each moving average against the central month for each calculation.

However if the moving average is taken with an even number of periods e.g. a four month moving average, then there is no central period. Instead the moving average total must be shown in the middle of the period which will be between the second and third periods of each calculation.

Therefore a further average must be taken known as the **centred moving average**. This is done by taking each successive pair of moving average figures and finding their own average which is then placed in the middle of their figures. This is the trend figure.

Example

The underlying trend is estimated using moving averages.

Month	*Actual sales*	*4 month moving average*	*Centred moving average (trend)*
Jan	100		
Feb	118		
		120 (W1)	
Mar	125	→	121(W2)
		122	
April	137	→	123
		124	
May	108	→	125
		126	
Jun	126	→	127
		128	
Jul	133	→	129
		130	
Aug	145	→	131
		132	
Sept	116	→	133
		134	
Oct	134	→	135
		136	
Nov	141		
Dec	153		

Workings

(W1) Calculate the four month moving average for each successive period:

100 + 118 + 125 + 137 = 480   480/4 = 120

118 + 125 + 137 + 108 = 488   488/4 = 122

125 + 137 + 108 + 126 = 496   496/4 = 124

Place each of these figures in the central point of the four month period

(W2) Calculate the centred moving average by taking each successive pair of four month moving averages and finding their average:

120 + 122 = 242   242/2 = 121

122 + 124 = 246   246/2 = 123

Show each of these centred moving averages in the centre of the two four-month figures used.

The final column, the centred moving average, is the trend of the data.

Be sure that you have understood the positioning of the moving averages in the above table. Each average has been written exactly opposite the middle of the figures from which it has been calculated. This results in the moving averages for even numbers of values (four in this case) being suspended halfway between two of the original figures.

Where you have a moving average for an even number of values, it is necessary to realign the moving averages so that they fall opposite an original value by calculating a centred moving average for every two moving average values.

Activity 2

The table below provides details of Masham plc's quarterly sales in units.

Calculate the four quarter moving average of Masham's sales units

Year	*Quarter*	*Actual sales units*	*Moving average*	*Centred moving average (trend)*
1	1	120		
	2	168		
	3	140		
	4	172		
2	1	136		
	2	184		
	3	156		
	4	188		
3	1	152		
	2	200		
	3	172		
	4	204		

3.5 Seasonal variations

Once the trend has been calculated it is possible to calculate the **seasonal variation from the trend**. This is how much the actual data varies from the trend line. There are two ways of dealing with the seasonal variations:

(a) Using an **additive** model where variations are expressed in **absolute** terms with above and below average figures designated by plus and minus signs respectively.

(b) Using a **proportional** or **multiplicative** model where variations are represented in percentage terms with high and low figures being above or below 100%.

Both models can be used with a trend produced by any method.

The basic idea here will be to take a predicted trend figure and adjust it for an 'average' seasonal variation.

In an additive model, the seasonal effect is the same (roughly constant) in the same period over different years.

Example

The underlying trend has been estimated using a 4 quarterly moving average.

Using the **additive** model:

Year	*Quarter*	*Sales value*	*Trend*	*Seasonal variation*
1	1	74		
	2	100		
	3	94	100	–6
	4	127	102	25
2	1	84	106	–22
	2	106	111	–5
	3	120	114	6
	4	141	116	25

3	1	94	118	–24
	2	112	120	–8
	3	130	123	7
	4	147	126	21
4	1	112	129	–17
	2	118	134	–16
	3	148		
	4	169		

When using the **additive** model **absolute** numbers are calculated. The additive model calculates the difference between the actual data and the trend.

The seasonal variation is **from** the trend. Year 1 quarter 4's value is **greater than the trend** therefore the seasonal variation is **positive**. Year 2 quarter 1's value is **less than the trend** therefore the seasonal variation is **negative**. If this data is plotted on a graph February's sales value would lie above the trend line and April's would lie below.

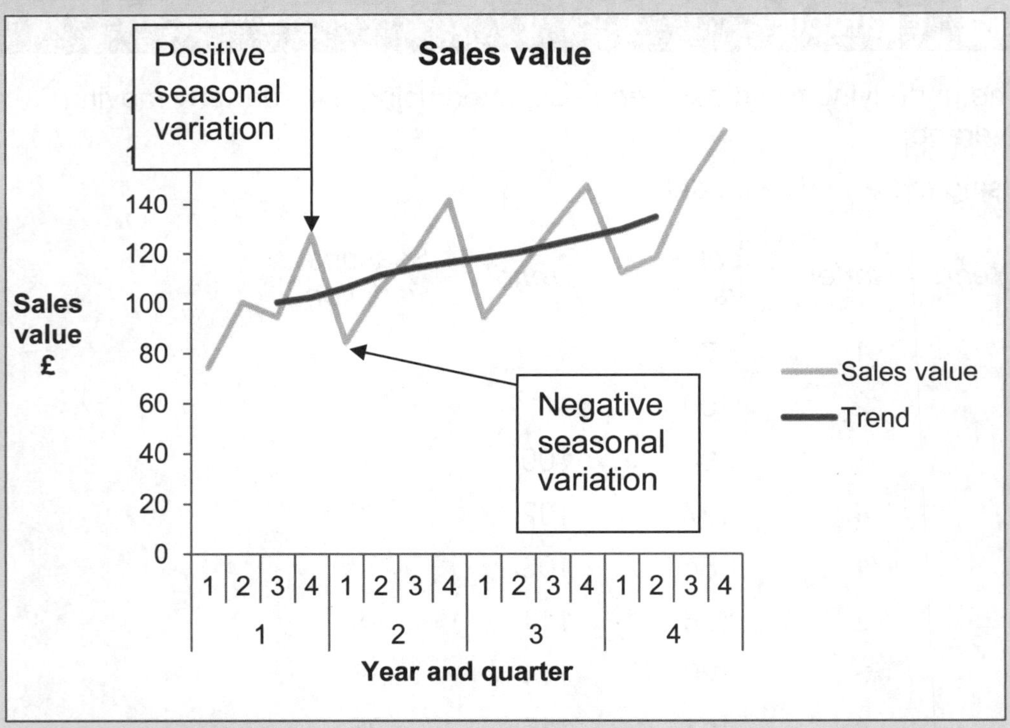

Activity 3

A company is preparing its forecast sales for next year. Identify the sales volume trend from this year's data using a 4 month moving average. Calculate the seasonal variation using the additive model.

Month	*Sales volume*	*Moving average*	*Centred average*	*Seasonal variation*
Jan	150			
Feb	310			
Mar	380			
Apr	420			
May	310			
Jun	470			
Jul	540			
Aug	580			
Sept	470			
Oct	630			
Nov	700			
Dec	740			
Jan	630			
Feb	790			
Mar	860			

Sometimes the seasonal variation is a **proportion** of the underlying trend value. It is then appropriate to use a **multiplicative model**. Using the **proportional** or **multiplicative** model the variations are represented in percentage terms with high and low figures being above or below 100%.

Example

The underlying trend has been estimated using a 4 quarterly moving average.

Using the **multiplicative** model:

Year	*Quarter*	*Value*	*Trend*	*Proportion of the trend % (rounded to nearest whole number)*
1	1	74		
	2	100		
	3	94	100	94 ÷ 100 × 100 = 94
	4	127	102	127 ÷ 102 × 100 = 125
2	1	84	106	84 ÷ 106 × 100 = 79
	2	106	111	106 ÷ 111 × 100 = 96
	3	120	114	105
	4	141	116	122
3	1	94	118	80
	2	112	120	93
	3	130	123	106
	4	147	126	117
4	1	112	129	87
	2	118	134	88
	3	148		
	4	169		

The seasonal variations in the proportional model are not true variations but percentage increases or decreases.

In some questions you may see multiplicative seasonal variations being stated as a positive or negative percentage from the trend.
For example:

- Year 1 quarter 3 would be referred to as 6% less than the trend
- Year 2 quarter 4 would be referred to as 22% more than the trend

Activity 4

A company is preparing its forecast sales for the first quarter of next year. Identify the sales volume trend from the data below using a 3 month moving average and calculate the monthly sales trend. Calculate the seasonal variation using the multiplicative model.

Month	*Sales volume*	*3 Month trend*	*Seasonal variation %*
Jan	4,000		
Feb	8,680		
Mar	5,260		
Apr	4,540		
May	9,220		
Jun	5,800		
Jul	5,080		
Aug	9,760		
Sept	6,340		
Oct	5,620		
Nov	10,300		
Dec	6,880		

3.6 Forecasting future cash flows

Once the seasonal variations have been calculated they can be used to forecast future values.

The trend line is extrapolated and the variations are applied to the trend.

Example

Using the **additive** model

Year	*Quarter*	*Trend*	*Seasonal variation*
1	3	100	–6
	4	102	25
2	1	106	–22
	2	111	–5
	3	114	6
	4	116	25
3	1	118	–24
	2	120	–8
	3	123	7
	4	126	21
4	1	129	–17
	2	134	–16

Step 1

Identify the trend. The increase in the trend is not constant so the average increase per quarter is calculated.

Total increase over range: 134 – 100 = 34.

Number of increases = 11 (i.e. 12 quarters but only 11 steps up).

Average increment per quarter = 34 ÷ 11 = 3.09.

Therefore the trend figure for the next quarter will be 134 + 3.09 = 137.09.

Step 2

Since the seasonal variations, in this example, change, an average adjustment is computed, by adding together each quarter's variations and dividing by the number of observations.

	Quarter			
Year	*1*	*2*	*3*	*4*
1	–	–	(6)	25
2	(22)	(5)	6	25
3	(24)	(8)	7	21
4	(17)	(16)	–	–
Sum	(63)	(29)	7	71
Average	(21)	(9.67)	2.33	23.7

These figures can then be applied to the extrapolated trend

Suppose we want to predict **year 5 quarter 3** sales. This would be done as follows.

Step 1 Trend figure

Starting from the last trend figure available, add on the appropriate number of trend increments.

Year 4	Quarter 2	=	134
Year 5	Quarter 3	=	134 + 5 movements
		=	134 + (5 × 3.09)
		=	149.45

Step 2 Adjust for average seasonal variation for quarter 3

Prediction = 149.45 + 2.33 = 151.78

Example

Using the **multiplicative** model:

Year	*Quarter*	*Trend*	*Seasonal variation %*
1	3	100	94
	4	102	125
2	1	106	79
	2	111	96
	3	114	105
	4	116	122
3	1	118	80
	2	120	93
	3	123	106
	4	126	117
4	1	129	87
	2	134	88

Step 1

Identify the trend. The increase in the trend is not constant so the average increase per quarter is calculated.

Total increase over range: 134 – 100 = 34.

Number of increases = 11 (i.e. 12 quarters but only 11 steps up).

Average increment per quarter = 34 ÷ 11 = 3.09.

Therefore the trend figure for the next quarter will be 134 + 3.09 = 137.09.

Step 2

Since the seasonal variations, in this example, change, an average adjustment is computed, by adding together each quarter's variations and dividing by the number of observations.

Year	*Quarter* 1	2	3	4
1	–	–	94	125
2	79	96	105	122
3	80	93	106	117
4	87	88	–	–
Sum	246	277	305	364
Average	82	92.3	101.7	121.3

These figures can then be applied to the extrapolated trend.

Suppose we want to predict **year 5 quarter 3** sales. This would be done as follows.

Step 1 Trend figure

Starting from the last trend figure available, add on the appropriate number of trend increments.

Year 4	Quarter 2	=	134
Year 5	Quarter 3	=	134 + 5 movements
		=	134 + (5 × 3.09)
		=	149.45

Step 2 Adjust for average seasonal variation for quarter 3

Prediction = 149.45 × 101.7% = 151.99

Exam tip

In the exam you may find that the trend increases by a constant amount each time and that the seasonal variations are cyclical. For example:

Using the **additive** model

Month	*Actual sales*	*Trend*	*Seasonal variation*
Jan	74		
Feb	100	89	11
Mar	93	93	0
Apr	86	97	–11
May	112	101	11
Jun	105	105	0
Jul	98	109	–11
Aug	124	113	11
Sept	117	117	0
Oct	110	121	–11
Nov	136	125	11

Step 1

Identify the trend. In this example the trend is increasing by 4 each month. Extrapolate the trend for future periods by adding 4 each time.

Step 2

Apply the seasonal variations. In this example the seasonal variations cycle 0, –11, 11, 0, –11, 11. We assume this continues for the forecast trend. The seasonal variation is **from** the trend so if there is a negative variation the forecast will be lower than the trend and a positive variation the forecast will be higher than the trend.

Forecast values			*Forecast*
Dec	129	0	129
Jan	133	–11	122
Feb	137	11	148
Mar	141	0	141

(This will not apply for the multiplicative model)

Activity 5

A company is preparing its forecast sales for the first quarter of next year. Identify the sales volume trend from this year's data using a 3 month moving average. Calculate the seasonal variation using the additive model. Use this information to predict March, April and May's sales volume for next year.

Month	*Sales volume*	*3 Month trend*	*Seasonal variation*
Jan	4,600		
Feb	5,300		
Mar	5,100		
Apr	5,050		
May	5,750		
Jun	5,550		
Jul	5,500		
Aug	6,200		
Sept	6,000		
Oct	5,950		
Nov	6,650		
Dec	6,450		

Month	*Forecast sales trend*	*Variation*	*Forecast sale volume*
Mar			
Apr			
May			

Activity 6

Below is the sales data for January to December 20X1 and January to March 20X2. Calculate the 5 month trend and monthly variation using the additive model.

Month	*Sales volume*	*5 Month trend*	*Seasonal variation*
Jan	150		
Feb	310		
Mar	400		
Apr	490		
May	750		
Jun	180		
Jul	340		
Aug	430		
Sept	520		
Oct	780		
Nov	210		
Dec	370		
Jan	460		
Feb	550		
Mar	810		

What will be the predicted sales volume for December 20X2?

A 610

B 476

C 526

D 482

3.7 Disadvantages of moving averages

- Values at the beginning and end of the series are lost; therefore, the moving averages do not cover the complete period.
- The moving averages may generate cycles or other movements that were not present in the original data.
- The averages are strongly affected by extreme values. To overcome this, a weighted moving average is sometimes used, giving the largest weights to central items and small weights to extreme values.

4 Regression analysis

4.1 Introduction

Regression analysis is concerned with establishing the relationship between two variables.

Regression analysis finds the line of best fit or trend using formulae. It seeks to minimise the distance between each data point and the trend line.

4.2 The regression equation

The general equation for the regression line is given as:

$y = a + bx$

Where:

x is the independent variable

y is the dependent variable

a is the intercept on the y axis

b is the gradient of the line

You will be required to use the regression equation to forecast future values. When the regression equation is used for time series data the time periods are changed to numbers rather than specified days, months or years.

You must understand that the independent variable (x) in some way causes the dependent variable (y) to have the value given by the equation. For example, if we were calculating the cost of producing cars the number of cars produced would be the independent variable (x) and the cost would be the dependent variable (y) i.e. volume of production causes production cost to change and not vice versa.

You may need to interpret a graph or use the high low method to calculate 'a' and 'b' in the regression equation.

Example

The following scatter graph has been prepared for the sales revenue received month by month by an organisation that delivers hot meals to the elderly in their homes.

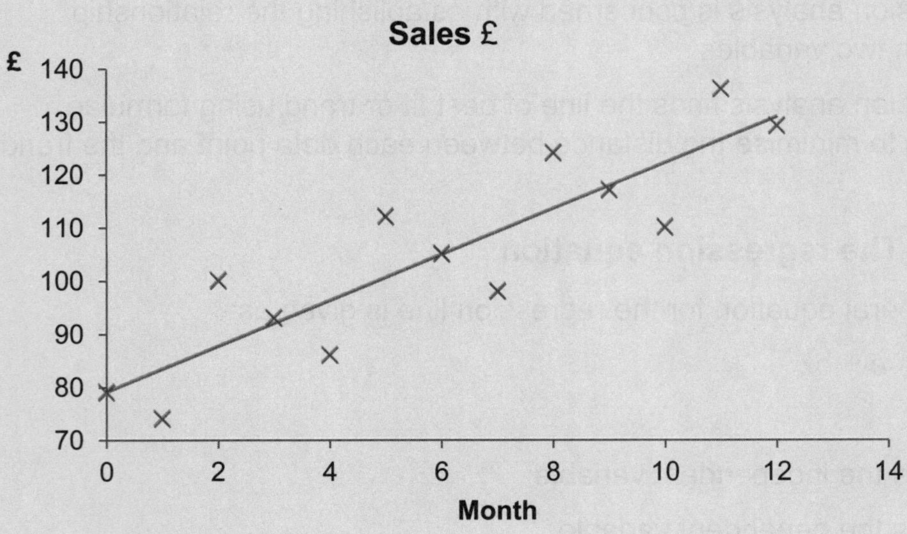

From the graph we can estimate the following:

a = £80 (the point where the trend line crosses the y axis)

b = the gradient of the line is calculated as:

$$\frac{\text{change in y}}{\text{change in x}}$$

b = (130 – 80)/(12 – 0) = £4.17

We can apply this to the regression equation to be able to predict future revenues

y = 80 + 4.17x

So the revenue in month 13 would be

y = 80 + (4.17 × 13) = £134.21

Example

The total cost incurred at various output levels in a factory have been measured as follows:

Output (units)	*Total cost* (£)
26	6,566
30	6,510
33	6,800
44	6,985
48	7,380
50	7,310

Using the high-low method we can estimate the regression equation:

To calculate b:

Take the highest and lowest levels of activity or output and their respective costs and put it into the following calculation.

b = change in cost ÷ change in output

b = (7,310 – 6,566)/(50 – 26) = £31

To calculate a:

a = total cost – (activity × b)

a = 7,310 – (50 × 31) = £5,750

Therefore: y = 5,750 + 31x

If planned output was 40 units the forecast cost would be:

y = 5,750 + (31 × 40) = £6,990

Activity 7

A company uses regression to forecast sales.

y = 220,000 + 500x

Where y is the sales value and x is the period. June 20X3 was period 18. The forecast value of sales for September 20X3 using the regression equation is:

A £229,000

B £230,500

C £230,000

D £229,500

4.3 The assumptions of regression analysis

Regression analysis is based on sample data and if we selected a different sample it is probable that a different regression equation would be constructed. For this reason, regression analysis is most suited to conditions where there is a relatively simple (and linear) relationship between cost and activity level.

Assumptions we are making:

- The relationship is a linear one.
- The data used is representative of future trends.

5 Inflation

5.1 Introduction

Once the trend and forecasted values have been calculated it may be necessary to adjust them for inflation.

Inflation is a rise in the general level of prices of goods and services in an economy over a period of time.

Adjustments for inflation can be done using:

- Percentages
- Index numbers

5.2 Percentage increases

One of the simplest ways of applying inflation to costs and revenues is to add a percentage increase that reflects the predicted level of inflation for the period compared to current figures.

Example

From past experience and knowledge of the market, a sales director predicts sales prices to rise by 2% due to inflation each month. So, if January sales are £100,000, then:

February sales will be	£100,000 × 1.02	=	£102,000
March sales will be	£103,000 × 1.02	=	£104,040
April sales will be	£104,040 × 1.02	=	£106,121

This can also be calculated using compounding. January sales are £100,000 by April interest will have been applied three times

April sales will be £100,000 × 1.02^3 = £106,121

Activity 8

If sales are forecast to be £3,000 in February and inflation is to be applied at 2.4% per month. What would be the forecast sales for June?

A £3,299

B £7,093

C £3,221

D £5,720

5.3 Percentage change

Calculating the percentage change from one period to another can also be used as a basis for forecasting. The difference between the two periods may be an indicator of the inflation rate that has been applied.

Example

A shop keeper received the following amounts from the sale of radios:

	£000
20X1	1,000
20X2	1,100

The shop keeper hopes to maintain the increase in revenue for the following years. Calculate the forecast revenue for 20X3, 20X4 and 20X5.

Solution

Step one

Calculate the difference in absolute figures:

1,100 – 1,000 = 100

Step two

Calculate the difference in percentage (relative) terms:

There has been a 10% increase from 20X1 to 20X2

100 ÷ 1,000 × 100 = 10%

Step three

Apply this percentage increase year on year:

20X2		1,100
20X3	1,100 + (1,100 × 10%)	1,210
20X4	1,210 + (1,210 × 10%)	1,331
20X5	1,331 + (1,331 × 10%)	1,464

Activity 9

The unit sales for a clock shop were as follows:

	Units
Jan	50
Feb	75
Mar	70
Apr	60
May	80

Calculate the percentage change month to month. Show a decrease in unit sales with a minus sign. Calculate to two decimal places.

	Percentage change
Jan to Feb	
Feb to Mar	
Mar to Apr	
Apr to May	

5.4 Index numbers

Index numbers can also be used to apply the effects of inflation.

Definition

An index number is a technique for comparing over time changes in some feature of a group of items (e.g. price or quantity) by expressing the change each year as a percentage of some earlier year.

An index is a useful method of comparing figures over time by simplifying data to a single index figure that can be compared to a base period (normally a year) which is given an index of 100. The index then shows the change in the figures each year compared to that base period.

5.5 Choosing a base year for an index

The year or period chosen for a base must be 'normal', e.g. if constructing an index to measure the number of tourists in London, England then the choice of the summer of 2012 would not be representative of normal tourist levels due to the Olympic games being held in London that year. It would give a misleading impression of the tourist levels as any year compared to 2012 is likely to show a lower numbers of tourists.

The base period may be a single date, a month or a year.

The index number for the base period is given the value 100 and this might be allocated to:

- a year – 20X5 = 100
- a month – August 20X5 = 100
- a single date – 16 August 20X5 = 100

5.6 Calculating an index number

An index number is calculated as $\frac{\text{Current costs}}{\text{Base costs}} \times 100$

Price could be used instead of cost in the calculation if sales prices are being considered.

Example

Given below are the production cost figures for a business for five months:

Month	*Cost*
	£000
May	138
June	149
July	158
August	130
September	136

You are required to calculate an index for these costs using May as the base month.

Solution

Month	*Cost*	*Calculation*	*Index*
	£000		
May	138	138/138 × 100	100.0
June	149	149/138 × 100	108.0
July	158	158/138 × 100	114.5
August	130	130/138 × 100	94.2
September	136	136/138 × 100	98.6

The indices that are above 100 show that the costs are higher than in May. The indices that are below 100 show that the costs are lower than in May.

We can see from the index figures that costs rose for two months then fell below May levels for two months.

The figures in the example above are the percentage change **from May** (the base month) e.g. the cost for July is 14.5% higher than that in May.

Activity 10

The price per unit of product is set on the first day of every month. The prices for the last three months were:

Month	5	6	7
Price	£52	£56	£50

The price in month 1 was £40. Create an index for the price per unit using month 1 as the base period.

Month	5	6	7
Price	£52	£56	£50
Index			

5.7 Using an index number

Index numbers can also be used to forecast future data to be in cash flows.

The formula for using an index is $\frac{\text{Current index}}{\text{Base index}} \times \text{base value}$

Example

It is January and Aerials plc is forecasting future production costs. Given below are the forecast index numbers for the next 8 months:

Month	*Index*
January	103
February	108
March	115
April	94
May	99
June	109
July	112
August	117

January's production cost is £129,000

Calculate the forecast production cost for April, May and June to the nearest £.

Solution

April's forecasted production cost will be:

$$\frac{94}{103} \times £129{,}000 = £117{,}728$$

May's forecasted production cost will be:

$$\frac{99}{103} \times £129{,}000 = £123{,}990$$

April's forecasted production cost will be:

$$\frac{109}{103} \times £129{,}000 = £136{,}515$$

Activity 11

A company uses an industry wage rate index to forecast monthly wage costs. Employees receive a pay rise in September each year. The current monthly cost of £7,800 was calculated when the wage index was 134. The forecast wage rate index for the next three months is:

August	152
September	162
October	168

What will the wage cost be for September, to the nearest £?

A £6,452

B £6,876

C £9,430

D £8,848

6 Mark-ups and margins

6.1 Introduction

It is also possible to predict sales and costs by using mark ups and margins.

6.2 Mark-ups

A mark-up is a percentage added to the cost of a sale to calculate the selling price. The following proforma can help you work back from the sales price to calculate the cost of sales or vice versa.

	£	%
Revenue	X	100 + mark up
(Cost of sales)	(X)	(100)
Gross profit	X	Mark up

Example

If **revenue** is £2,750 and the mark up is 10% what is the cost of sales?

	£	%
Revenue	2,750	100 + 10 = 110
(Cost of sales)	(??)	(100)
Gross profit	??	10

The revenue of £2,750 is the equivalent of 110%. Therefore to calculate the cost of sales we need to divide the 2,750 by 110 and multiply it by 100.

2,750 ÷ 110 × 100 = £2,500

If the **cost of sales** is £3,500 and the mark up is 10% what is the revenue?

	£	%
Revenue	??	100 + 10 = 110
(Cost of sales)	(3,500)	(100)
Gross profit	??	10

The cost of sales of £3,500 is the equivalent of 100%. Therefore to calculate the revenue we need to divide the 3,500 by 100 and multiply it by 110.

3,500 ÷ 100 × 110 = £3,850

6.3 Margins

A margin shows in percentage terms the amount of profit generated from revenue i.e. what percentage of the revenue eventually ends up as gross profit. The following proforma can help you work back from the sales price to calculate the cost of sales or vice versa.

	£	%
Revenue	X	100
(Cost of sales)	(X)	(100 – margin)
Gross profit	X	Margin

Example

If **revenue** is £10,000 and the margin is 5% what is the cost of sales?

	£	%
Revenue	10,000	100
(Cost of sales)	(??)	(100 – 5)
Gross profit	??	5

The sales value of £10,000 is the equivalent of 100%. Therefore to calculate the cost of sales we need to divide the 10,000 by 100 and multiply it by 100 – 5 which is 95, or multiply 10,000 by 95%

10,00 ÷ 100 × 95 = £9,500

If the **cost of sales** is £4,500 and the margin is 10% what is the revenue?

	£	%
Revenue	??	100
(Cost of sales)	(4,500)	(100 – 10)
Gross profit	??	10

The cost of sales of £4,500 is the equivalent of 90%. Therefore to calculate the revenue we need to divide the 4,500 by 90 and multiply it by 100.

4,500 ÷ 90 × 100 = £5,000

7 Forecasting inventory levels

7.1 Changes in inventory levels

It may be necessary to forecast the volume of inventory that is needed by a business. Inventory is needed to meet the sales demand and also the closing inventory level requirements of a business. Inventory may take the form of materials to be used in producing a product (raw material) or items ready to sell on (finished goods). The required volume of purchases is calculated based on sales demand.

If items are bought ready to sell:

The purchases budget is calculated as follows:

		Units
Sales		X
Less:	Opening inventory	(X)
Add:	Closing inventory	X
Purchases		X

If a business buys raw materials to use to make its own products, the production budget has to be calculated first.

		Units
Sales		X
Less:	Opening inventory of finished goods	(X)
Add:	Closing inventory of finished goods	X
Production		X

This is then used to calculate the raw material usage budget and purchases budget as follows:

		Units
Usage:	Production units × Raw material per unit	X
Less:	Opening inventory of raw materials	(X)
Add:	Closing inventory of raw materials	X
Purchases		X

Once the volume of purchases is calculated this is then converted into money by multiplying the purchase volume by price per unit.

Example

A business has planned sales of its product of 4,000 units in March which will be expected to increase by 200 units each month. Finished goods inventory at the start and end of March is anticipated to be 500 units and this is budgeted to increase to 600 units at the end of April and 700 units at the end of May.

Each unit of the finished product requires 2 kg of raw materials which are purchased in the month of production and cost £20 per kg. At the beginning of March there will be 1,000 kg of raw materials in inventory but these inventory levels are to be decreased by 100 kg at the end of March and by 100 kg at the end of each month thereafter.

What is the forecast cost of raw material for March, April and May?

Solution

(a) **Production budget in units**

	March *Units*	*April* *Units*	*May* *Units*
Sales	4,000	4,200	4,400
Less: Opening inventory (finished goods)	(500)	(500)	(600)
Add: Closing inventory (finished goods)	500	600	700
Production quantity	4,000	4,300	4,500

Note that the closing finished goods inventory at the end of each month is the opening inventory at the start of the following month.

Once the amount of production is known then the raw materials purchases can be determined in quantities first of all. Start with the materials needed for the actual production, then take into consideration the fact that there is 1,000 kg of material at the start of March and that inventory level is to decrease by 100 kg per month thereafter.

(b) **Materials purchases budget in kg**

	March *kg*	*April* *kg*	*May* *kg*
Production × 2 kg	8,000	8,600	9,000
Less: Opening inventory (raw materials)	(1,000)	(900)	(800)
Add: Closing inventory (raw materials)	900	800	700
Purchases in kg	7,900	8,500	8,900

The materials purchases in each month are therefore the number of kg required at the price of £20 per kg.

Materials purchases budget in £s

	March	*April*	*May*
	£	£	£
Purchases in kg × £20	158,000	170,000	178,000

8 Problems with forecasting

8.1 Problems with forecasting

Forecasting future cash flows has many problems which may limit their usefulness when producing a cash budget. These include:

- The assumption that past behaviour can be used as a basis for future activity.
- The volume of data available to base the forecast on may be limited this reduces the reliability of a forecast.
- The reliability of data provided. A supplier could change the selling price once the cash budget is completed. A competitor could drop their selling price leading to a decrease in the businesses selling price or volume.
- Data does not necessarily take into account outside influences on a business such as political, environmental, technological and social changes.

9 Summary

When preparing cash budgets a lot of forecast information is required.

There are various methods that can be used to try and predict future costs and revenues.

Answers to chapter activities

Activity 1

Month	*Value*	*3-month moving total*	*Trend*
Jan	12		
Feb	26	57	19
Mar	19	60	20
Apr	15	63	21
May	29	66	22
Jun	22	69	23
Jul	18	72	24
Aug	32	75	25
Sept	25		

Activity 2

Year	*Quarter*	*Actual sales value*	*Moving average*	*Centred moving average (T)*
	1	120		
	2	168		
			150	
1	3	140		152
			154	
	4	172		156
			158	
	1	136		160
			162	
	2	184		164
2			166	
	3	156		168
			170	
	4	188		172
			174	

Year	Quarter	Sales	Moving average	Centred average
	1	152		176
			178	
	2	200		180
3			182	
	3	172		
	4	204		

Activity 3

Month	Sales volume	Moving average	Centred average	Seasonal variation
Jan	150			
Feb	310			
		315		
Mar	380		335	45
		355		
Apr	420		375	45
		395		
May	310		415	–105
		435		
Jun	470		455	15
		475		
Jul	540		495	45
		515		
Aug	580		535	45
		555		
Sept	470		575	–105
		595		
Oct	630		615	15
		635		
Nov	700		655	45
		675		
Dec	740		695	45
		715		
Jan	630		735	–105
		755		
Feb	790			
Mar	860			

Activity 4

Month	*Sales volume (units)*	*3 Month trend*	*Seasonal variation %*
Jan	4,000		
Feb	8,680	5,980	45.2
Mar	5,260	6,160	–14.6
Apr	4,540	6,340	–28.4
May	9,220	6,520	41.4
Jun	5,800	6,700	–13.4
Jul	5,080	6,880	–26.2
Aug	9,760	7,060	38.2
Sept	6,340	7,240	–12.4
Oct	5,620	7,420	–24.3
Nov	10,300	7,600	35.5
Dec	6,880		

Activity 5

Month	*Sales volume*	*3 Month trend*	*Seasonal variation*
Jan	4,600		
Feb	5,300	5,000	300
Mar	5,100	5,150	–50
Apr	5,050	5,300	–250
May	5,750	5,450	300
Jun	5,550	5,600	–50
Jul	5,500	5,750	–250
Aug	6,200	5,900	300
Sept	6,000	6,050	–50
Oct	5,950	6,200	–250
Nov	6,650	6,350	300
Dec	6,450		

The monthly sales volume trend is an increase of 150 each month.

Month	*Forecast sales trend*	*Variation*	*Forecast sale volume*
Mar	6,950	–50	6,900
Apr	7,100	–250	6,850
May	7,250	300	7,550

The variation cycle is 300, –50, –250 therefore the variation for March is –50. The variation is negative therefore the sales will be less than the trend.

Activity 6

Month	*Sales volume*	*5 Month trend*	*Seasonal variation*
Jan	150		
Feb	310		
Mar	400	420	(20)
Apr	490	426	64
May	750	432	318
Jun	180	438	(258)
Jul	340	444	(104)
Aug	430	450	(20)
Sept	520	456	64
Oct	780	462	318
Nov	210	468	(258)
Dec	370	474	(104)
Jan	460	480	(20)
Feb	550		
Mar	810		

What will be the predicted sales volume for December 20X2?

A 610

480 + (6 × 11) + 64 = 610

Activity 7

Answer B

y = 220,000 + (500 × 21) = £230,500

Activity 8

Answer A

£3,000 × 1.024^4 = £3,298.53 rounded = £3,299

Activity 9

	Working	*Percentage change*
Feb	(75–50)/50	50.00%
Mar	(70–75)/75	–6.67%
Apr	(60–70)/70	–14.29%
May	(80–60)/60	+33.33%

Activity 10

Month	5	6	7
Price	£52	£56	£50
Index	130	140	125

Month 5 = 52 ÷ 40 × 100 = 130

Activity 11

Answer C

162 ÷ 134 × 7,800 = £9,430

10 Test your knowledge

Workbook Activity 12

The managers of a company are preparing plans for the first quarter of next year. The figures below refer to the sales volumes for the year just past. Complete the table to calculate the monthly sales volume trend, the monthly variations from the trend using the additive model and then the prediction for the January to March for next year.

Month	*Sales volume*	*3 Month trend*	*Seasonal variation*
Jan	49		
Feb	37		
Mar	58		
Apr	50		
May	38		
Jun	60		
Jul	51		
Aug	40		
Sept	61		
Oct	53		
Nov	41		
Dec	61		

Month	*Forecast sales trend*	*Variation*	*Forecast sale volume*
Jan			
Feb			
Mar			

Workbook Activity 13

A company is preparing its forecast sales and purchase information for October of the next financial year.

The sales volume trend is to be identified using a 3–point moving average based on the actual monthly sales volumes for the current year.

(a) Complete the table below to calculate the current monthly sales volume trend and identify any monthly variations, using the additive model.

	Sales volume (units)	*Trend*	*Monthly variation*
May	11,000		
June	11,850		
July	12,550		
August	11,900		
September	12,750		

Additional information

The trend is assumed to be a straight line and the seasonal variations are cyclical.

The selling price per unit has been set at £21.

Monthly purchases are estimated to be 60% of the value of the forecast sales.

(b) Using the trend and the monthly variations identified in part (a) complete the table below to forecast the sales volume, sales value and purchase value for October of the next financial year.

	Forecast trend	*Variation*	*Forecast sales volume*	*Forecast sales £*	*Forecast purchases £*
October					

Workbook Activity 14

The company uses an industry sector index to calculate the selling price of its product. The price to due to be revised in March, in line with the index. The current selling price of £45 was set when the index was 132. The forecast index is as follows:

January	145
February	152
March	154
April	157

What will be the selling price, to the nearest penny in March?

A £37.83

B £51.82

C £38.57

D £52.50

Workbook Activity 15

A company is planning to produce 2,000 shirts; each shirt requires $1m^2$ of material. There is currently $100m^2$ of material in inventory and the company wishes to increase inventory levels by 10%. How much material needs to be bought? (**Note:** There is no opening or closing inventory of shirts.)

A $1,790m^2$

B $2,000m^2$

C $2,010m^2$

D $2,210m^2$

Patterns of cash flow

3

Introduction

The preparation of a cash budget relies on identifying the expected payment patterns for receipts and payments by accounting for differences in timings arising from selling or purchasing goods and services on credit terms and on cash terms and deposits made in advance.

ASSESSMENT CRITERIA

Explain cash flows over the accounting period, and anticipate any exceptional receipts or payments (2.2S)

Explain the effects lagged receipts and payments upon an organisation's cash management (2.3K)

CONTENTS

1 Cash flows

1.1 The importance of cash flow

Cash is a business's most important asset as without cash it is not possible to pay for the running of the business. Managers must forecast and monitor cash flows to ensure the business does not become bankrupt.

Cash budgets are prepared:

- To show when cash surpluses are likely to occur
- To show where there is inadequate cash to finance any plans
- To act as an indicator of when extra finance will be needed
- To provide a basis of control for the forthcoming year

2 Receipts

2.1 Introduction

Sales are often made on credit and customers do not pay until subsequent periods. The credit terms offered to customers will be decided by the managers and a general pattern of receipts from these customers can therefore be established. The cash budget needs to show when the actual cash is expected to be received from receivables in the period rather than the actual sales made to receivables in the period.

2.2 Lagging of receipts

It will be necessary to use actual and forecast sales revenue and adjust it for the effects of lagging. This is the time it takes for receivables to pay off their debts. Lagging of receipts affects a business's cash inflow as it will not match the sales revenue shown in the financial accounts.

From past experience it will be possible to estimate how the receivables of a business tend to pay and this can be used to estimate cash inflows to a business.

Example

A business makes sales on credit. From past experience the credit controller expects cash to be received as follows:

- 20% in the month of sale
- 50% in the month after sale
- 30% two months after sale

Calculate the cash receipts for December to March.

	Dec £	*Jan* £	*Feb* £	*Mar* £
Sales revenue	10,000	12,000	14,000	16,000
In the month of sale (20%)	2,000	2,400	2,800	3,200
One month after sale (50%)	–	5,000	6,000	7,000
Two months after sale (30%)	–	–	3,000	3,600
Total receipts	2,000	7,400	11,800	13,800

The above example shows how receipts from receivables for a particular month are not the same as sales to receivables for that month.

2.3 Closing receivables

It is also possible to estimate the closing receivables figure for the period to be input into the Statement of Financial Position.

Example

Continuing from the previous example forecast the closing receivables balance as at 31 March.

	Dec £	*Jan* £	*Feb* £	*Mar* £
Sales revenue	10,000	12,000	14,000	16,000
Received in December	2,000			
Received in January	5,000	2,400		
Received in February	3,000	6,000	2,800	
Received in March		3,600	7,000	3,200
Amounts outstanding	0	0	4,200	12,800

The closing receivables balance as at 31 March is £17,000. This is made up of 30% of February's and 80% of March's credit sales.

2.4 Opening receivables

The closing receivables balance for one period becomes the opening receivables balance for the next period. When calculating the cash receipts from an opening balance, care must be taken to account for the proportion of cash that has already been received in prior months.

Example

Continuing with the previous example.

From past experience the credit controller expects cash to be received as follows:

- 20% in the month of sale
- 50% are received in the month after sale
- 30% two months after sale

		April	*May*	*June*
		£	£	£
Sales revenue		18,000	20,000	22,000
Opening balance £	17,000			
In the month of sale		7,800	4,000	4,400
One month after sale		8,000**	9,000	10,000
Two months after sale		4,200*	4,800***	5,400
Cash receipts		20,000	17,800	19,800

The opening receivables balance as at 31 March is £17,000. This is made up of 30% (£4,200) of February's and 80% (£12,800) of March's credit sales.

*February's outstanding balance will all be received in April as this is two months after sale.

March's outstanding balance will be split between April and May:

The outstanding balance from March is 80% of March's total credit sales so the calculations are:

**April receipts from March = £12,800 ÷ 80 × 50 = £8,000

***May receipts from March = £12,800 ÷ 80 × 30 = £4,800

Activity 1

Jason is preparing a cash budget. His credit sales are as follows.

	£
Opening receivables	24,000
May	30,000
June	20,000
July	25,000

His recent debt collection experience has been as follows:

In the month of sale	40%
One month after sale	60%

Required:

Forecast Jason's receipts from receivables for May to July and his closing receivables balance at the 31 July.

2.5 Sales volume and prices

It is also possible to calculate the forecast cash receipts when provided with information about sales volume and price. The total monetary amount of the sales revenue for the period is calculated and then the cash receipts can be forecast using the technique described above.

Example

Kelly Limited sold 3,000 units of a product in June 20X3 at a selling price of £45 each. Due to an increase in production costs, this price will increase to £48 with effect from 1 July 20X3 and this is expected to reduce demand for July to 2,900 units. Thereafter demand is expected to increase by 10% per month.

All sales are on credit and receivables pay as follows:

10% in the month of sale

60% in the month following sale

30% two months after sale

Opening receivables for June 20X3 were:

Balance from April £33,750

Balance from May £85,050

What are the budgeted cash receipts in June, July and August 20X3?

	June	*July*	*August*
	£	£	£
Sales units	3,000	2,900	3,190
Selling price per unit	45	48	48
Sales	135,000	139,200	153,120
10% in the month of sale	13,500	13,920	15,312
60% in month after sale	56,700**	81,000	83,520
30% 2 months after sale	33,750*	28,350***	40,500
Total cash receipts	103,950	123,270	139,332

Notes

*All of April's outstanding balance will be received in June

**60/90 × May's outstanding balance will be received in June

***30/90 × May's outstanding balance will be received in July

Activity 2

Major Inc has requested assistance with calculating sales receipts for entry into a cash budget

Actual sales values are available for January and February and forecast sales values have been produced from March to June.

	Actual		*Forecast*			
	January	*February*	*March*	*April*	*May*	*June*
Total sales	30,000	32,000	33,000	35,000	37,000	40,000

It is estimated that cash sales are 17% of the total sales, the remaining are on credit.

Major Inc estimates that 40% of credit sales are received in the month after sale with the balance being received two months after sales.

Complete the table using the information above to calculate the timing of sales receipts that would be included in a cash budget for Major Inc for the period of March to June.

	March £	*April* £	*May* £	*June* £
Cash				
Credit sales receipts:				
Month after sale				
2 months after sale				
Total cash received				

Activity 3

A company has supplied information regarding its forecast sales.

Sales volume has been forecast for periods 1 to 5. Each product sells for £20.

The company estimates that 10% of sales are made on a cash basis with the balance made on a credit basis. An analysis of historical data shows that credit customers settle their debts on the basis of 20% one month after the date of sale and 80% two months after the date of sale.

	Period 1	*Period 2*	*Period 3*	*Period 4*	*Period 5*
Sales volume (units)	8,000	8,300	8,500	7,500	7,000

Required:

Complete the table below to identify the total sales receipts forecast for periods 4 and 5. Identify the forecast trade receivables balance at the end of period 5.

	Period 4 £	*Period 5* £
Total sales receipts		

The trade receivables balance at the end of period 5 is forecast to be:

£ ______

2.6 Irrecoverable debts

It is possible that some debts will not be collected. These are known as irrecoverable debts.

Example

A business has found that 30% of customers pay in the month of sale, 40% of customers pay in the month after the sale and 20% of customers pay two months after the month of sale. From past experience it is known that 10% of the customers do not pay.

Credit sales for the business are as follows:

	Actual			*Budgeted*	
	February	*March*	*April*	*May*	*June*
	£	£	£	£	£
Credit sales	10,000	20,000	30,000	25,000	30,000

Required:

Calculate the total (closing) irrecoverable debt for the period from February to June to be written off to the Statement of profit or loss.

Solution

Total credit sales =

£10,000 + £20,000 + £30,000 + £25,000 + £30,000 = 115,000

Closing irrecoverable debt = £115,000 × 10% = £11,500

2.7 Discounts allowed

Settlement discounts or discounts allowed can be useful to improve the liquidity of a business in the short term, as cash should be received earlier, but in the long term less cash will be received from receivables.

When considering offering a settlement discount it is worth considering whether the cost outweighs the benefit i.e. the improvement in earlier cash flows outweighs the reduction in cash overall. This could be measured by the impact a settlement discount has on the overall cash balance of a business.

Example

A business is considering whether to offer a 3% discount for payment received from credit customers in the month of sale.

Credit sales for the business are as follows:

	February £	*March* £	*April* £	*May* £	*June* £
Credit sales	20,000	22,000	24,000	18,000	21,000

The business estimates that 60% of customers would take advantage of the settlement discount by paying in the month of sale, 30% of customers will pay in the month after the sale and 10% of customers will pay two months after the month of sale.

Required:

Calculate the value of the discount offered for February to June.

Solution:

Total credit sales =

£20,000 + £22,000 + £24,000 + £18,000 + £21,000 = £105,000

Total discount = £105,000 × 3% = £3,150

Activity 4

A company's budgeted accounts show a figure of £4,000 for discounts allowed and £50,000 for total credit sales.

Calculate the settlement discount percentage that has been offered.

3 Payments

3.1 Introduction

A business will incur lots of expenditure when running a business, for example:

- raw materials need to be purchased
- employees need a wage
- overheads, such as rent, will be incurred

Some of the payments for these will be made in the month the cost is incurred, whereas others will be lagged payments. Lagged payments are calculated in the same way as lagged receipts.

3.2 Lagging of payments

Businesses will buy goods on credit and take time to make the payment to the supplier (payable). To be able to complete the cash budget for payments the timing and value of the payments needs to be calculated.

The calculation for the payments to payables is similar to that for receipts from receivables – calculate the total cost to be paid and then lag the payments in line with forecast timings.

Example

A business estimates that its credit purchases for February and March will be £14,000 but will increase by 10% each month thereafter. Its payment pattern to payables is that 60% are paid in the month after the purchases and the remaining 40% two months after the purchase.

What are the payments to payables for the three months of March, April and May?

	February	*March*	*April*	*May*
	£	£	£	£
Purchases	14,000	14,000	15,400	16,940
Payments to payables				
One month after purchase		8,400	8,400	9,240
Two months after purchase			5,600	5,600
Cash payments		8,400	14,000	14,840

3.3 Closing payables

It is also possible to estimate the closing payables figure for the period to be input into the Statement of Financial Position.

Example

Continuing from the previous example forecast the closing receivables balance as at 31 May.

	February	*March*	*April*	*May*
	£	£	£	£
Purchases	14,000	14,000	15,400	16,940
Paid in March	8,400			
Paid in April	5,600	8,400		
Paid in May		5,600	9,240	
Amount outstanding	0	0	6,160	16,940

The closing payables balance as at 31 May is £23,100. This is made up of 40% of April's and 100% of May's credit sales.

3.4 Opening payables

The closing payables balance for one period becomes the opening payables balance for the next period. When calculating the cash paid from an opening balance, care must be taken to account for the proportion of cash that has already been paid in prior months.

Example

Continuing from the previous example.

From past experience the credit controller expects cash to be paid as follows:

- 60% in the month after purchase
- 40% two months after purchase

		June £	*July* £	*August* £
Purchases		18,600	20,500	22,550
Opening balance £	23,100			
One month after purchase		10,164**	11,160	12,300
Two months after purchase		6,160*	6,776***	7,440
Cash payments		16,324	17,936	19,740

The opening payables balance as at 31 May is £23,100. This is made up of 40% (£6,160) of April's and 100% (£16,940) of May's credit sales.

*April's outstanding balance will all be paid in June as this is two months after purchase.

May's outstanding balance will be split between June and July:

The outstanding balance from May is 100% of May's total credit purchases so the calculations are:

**June payments from May = £16,940 ÷ 100 × 60 = £10,164

***July payments from May = £16,940 ÷ 100 × 40 = £6,776

Activity 5

Remus's purchases in May were £100,000 and these are expected to increase by £10,000 per month for the next three months. All purchases are on credit terms. Payables are paid as follows:

- 50% in the month of purchase
- 30% in the month after purchase
- 20% two months after purchase.

Complete the table below to identify the total purchase payments forecast for July and August. Identify the forecast trade payables balance at the end of August.

	July £	*August* £
Total payments	113 000	123 000

The trade payables balance at the end of August is forecast to be:

£ 89000

Activity 6

A company pays its suppliers are follows:

- 30% one month after purchase
- 25% two months after purchase
- 45% three months after purchase.

At the end of period 3 the balance of trade payables is forecast to be:

	£
Balance from period 1	18,000
Balance from period 2	35,000
Balance from period 3	70,000
Trade payables at the end of period 3	123,000

Complete the table below to identify the value of trade payables at the end of period 3 that will be paid in periods 4 and 5.

	Period 4 £	*Period 5* £
Total payments	51500	40 000

3.5 Discounts received

It may be possible to receive a discount from a supplier for prompt payment. Payment must be made within a specified time frame for a discount to be applied to the amount due. This will reduce the overall amount paid to the payable but also reduces the length of time the money is in the bank gaining interest.

Example

A business has been offered a discount of 2% if payment is received in the month of sale. The business forecasts purchases to be:

April £43,000

May £45,000

June £50,000

How much money can the business save by paying early?

Solution

Total purchases = £43,000 + £45,000 + £50,000 = £138,000

Total saving = £138,000 × 2% = £2,760

Activity 7

One supplier has offered a discount to Box Co of 2% on an invoice for £7,500, if payment is made within one month, rather than the three months normally taken to pay. If Box's overdraft rate is 10% p.a., calculate if it is financially worthwhile for them to accept the discount and pay early?

3.6 Purchases expressed in terms of sales value

In some cases the information supplied about purchases will be expressed in terms of the sales value which has been budgeted for i.e. sales figures will be provided together with the anticipated gross profit margin. The purchases each month will then be calculated using the gross profit percentage given to find the cost of purchases. Once the purchases are known then the cash payments to the suppliers can be calculated.

Example

A business has the following budgeted sales:

	February	*March*	*April*	*May*	*June*	*July*
	£	£	£	£	£	£
Budgeted sales	38,000	40,000	44,000	46,000	45,000	50,000

The business operates at a gross margin of 40% and its policy is to make purchases on credit each month which are enough to cover the following month's sales. Payables are paid two months after the month of purchase. What are the payments to payables for each of the four months of April, May, June and July?

Solution

The first step is to calculate the cost of purchases incurred in each month.

If there is a gross profit margin of 40% then purchases are 60% of sales.

	Feb	*March*	*April*	*May*	*June*	*July*
	£	£	£	£	£	£
Budgeted sales	38,000	40,000	44,000	46,000	45,000	50,000
Purchases (60% of following month's sales)	24,000	26,400	27,600	27,000	30,000	

The next step is to apply the timing of the payment.

	Feb	*March*	*April*	*May*	*June*	*July*
Payments (two months after purchase)			24,000	26,400	27,600	27,000

3.7 Inventory levels

Another method of expressing information about purchase quantities is to include plans for any increases or decreases in inventory levels during the period.

Example

A business generally has purchases of £80,000 each month on credit. These are paid for in the month following the purchase. However, it is budgeted to increase inventory levels at the end of May by £20,000 and that inventory levels will then remain at that value. There is no anticipated increase in sales.

What are the cash payments to payables for each of the three months of April, May and June?

Solution

Again the first step is to calculate the amount of purchases each month. This will generally be £80,000 but in May must be £100,000 in order to increase the inventory levels. As there is no anticipated increase in sales levels then purchases in June can revert to £80,000.

	March	*April*	*May*	*June*
	£	£	£	£
Purchases	80,000	80,000	100,000	80,000

As payments are made in the month following the purchase then the cash payments will be as follows:

	April	*May*	*June*
	£	£	£
Purchases	80,000	80,000	100,000

Inventory levels may also be used if we are calculating how much needs to be purchased or produced to meet sales demand. This is calculated by subtracting the opening inventory and adding the closing inventory to the sales demand for the period. This is calculated as follows:

		Units
Sales		X
Less:	Opening inventory of finished goods	(X)
Add:	Closing inventory of finished goods	X
Production or purchases		X

If production is calculated then it will be necessary to convert this to purchases by calculating the total material needed for production and then how much these purchases are going to cost.

3.8 Labour costs

Labour costs are **normally** paid in the month in which they are incurred. Labour cost can be calculated based on units produced (piecework), standard hours worked and/or an annual salary. Overtime payments/ premiums may also be incurred in labour costs.

Example

Labour costs include hourly paid employees and four weekly paid employees. The labour costs for hourly paid employees are calculated based on the number of hours worked multiplied by a standard hourly rate of £10. Hourly paid employees are paid an overtime rate of £12 per hour. The company also employs two supervisors who are paid every four weeks. They are paid an annual salary of £20,800. The year is divided into 13 four week periods.

Hourly paid employees are paid their standard hours in the period incurred and overtime hours in the following period. The supervisors are paid on the last day of each period.

The forecast standard and overtime hours are given below.

	Period 1	*Period 2*	*Period 3*	*Period 4*	*Period 5*
Forecast standard hours	1,200	1,340	1,720	1,370	1,400
Forecast overtime hours	100	150	135	105	90

Complete the table below to identify the total payments for labour costs forecast for periods 4 and 5.

	Period 4	*Period 5*
Supervisors	£20,800/13 × 2 = £3,200	£20,800/13 × 2 = £3,200
Standard hours	1,370 × £10 = £13,700	1,400 × £10 = £14,000
Overtime hours	135 × £12 = £1,620	105 × £12 = £1,260
Total labour cost	£18,520	£18,460

Activity 8

The production budget for a company shows the following monthly production:

	April Units	*May* Units	*June* Units
Production	6,200	6,800	7,000

Each unit of production requires two labour hours and the wage rate is £7.00 per hour for April and May increasing to £7.40 per hour in June. Normal working hours are 12,000 hours and, after that overtime is paid at time and a half. Overtime is paid in the following month.

Complete the table below to identify the total payments for labour costs for May and June.

	May £	*June* £
Total labour costs		

3.9 Other costs

Care should be taken with other costs, for example administration or distribution costs, as they may include a certain amount which relates to depreciation. **Depreciation is not a cash flow and therefore this amount should be excluded from the cash budget.**

Activity 9

Housing plc is preparing cash payment figures to include in a cash budget. The following information was provided by the production manager.

- Purchases are 35% of next month's forecast sales and are paid two months after the date of purchase.

	Actual			*Forecast*		
	February	*March*	*April*	*May*	*June*	*July*
Total sales	70,000	72,000	77,000	80,000	83,000	85,000

- Wages are paid in the month that they are incurred and expenses are paid in the month after they are incurred. The figures are:

	Actual			*Forecast*		
	February	*March*	*April*	*May*	*June*	*July*
Wages	15,000	17,000	17,000	18,000	18,000	18,500
Expenses	6,000	6,500	6,750	7,000	7,000	7,750

- Expenses include £3,000 each month for depreciation
- A new machine is to be purchased in May at a total cost of £40,000. Payment for the machine is to be made in 8 equal instalments starting in June. This machine is to be depreciated monthly on a straight line basis at 25% per annum.

Complete the table below for the payments section of the cash budget for Housing plc for the three months ended July.

	May £	*June* £	*July* £
Purchases	26950	28000	29050
Wages	18000	18000	18500
Expenses	3750	4000	4000
New machine	–	5000	5000
Total payments	48700	55000	56550

4 Mark ups and margins

As seen in Chapter 2 it is possible to predict sales or costs by using mark ups and margins. This can also be used to determine either sales price or purchase price which could then be used to calculate the expected cash receipts and/or cash purchases.

4.1 Mark ups

A business may wish to add a mark up to the cost of purchases to calculate the selling price of a product or the selling price might have been determined due to competitor pricing strategy so a target cost needs to be calculated.

Example

Hall plc makes a single product. The total cost of the product is £30. Hall plc wishes to add a mark up of 20%.

Calculate the selling price of the product.

Solution

A mark up is calculated by taking the required percentage of the cost of the product to calculate the required profit. This is then added to the cost to calculate the selling price.

£30 × 20% = £6

Selling price = £30 + £6 = £36

Example

Stairs plc makes a single product which is also made by Landing plc. Landing plc sell their product at £50. Stairs plc wish to sell their product at £40 and to add a mark up of 25% to any production costs to produce a profit.

Calculate the target cost for the product.

Solution

A mark up is calculated by taking the required percentage of the cost of the product to calculate the required profit. The selling price is the equivalent of 100% plus the mark up %.

	%	£
Selling price	125	40
(Cost)	(100)	40 ÷ 125 × 100
Profit	25	8

The target cost = 40 ÷ 125 × 100 = £32

4.2 Margins

A business may wish to have a certain amount of profit generated from sales – this is a margin. The selling price might have been determined due to competitor pricing strategy so a target cost needs to be calculated based on achieving a certain profit margin. The purchase price may be known and a margin is calculated to set the selling price.

Example

George makes a single product which is also made by William. William sells his product for £75. George wishes to sell his product at £60 and to make a profit of 25%.

Calculate the target cost for the product.

Solution

A margin is calculated by taking the required percentage of the selling price. This is then deducted from the selling price to calculate the target cost:

£60 × 25% = £15

The target cost = £60 – £15 = £45

Example

Catherine makes a single product. The total cost of the product is £30. Catherine wishes to make a profit based on a margin of 20%.

Calculate the selling price of the product.

Solution

A margin is calculated by taking the required percentage of the selling price. This is then deducted from the selling price to calculate cost. The cost is the equivalent of 100% less the margin %.

	%	£
Selling price	100	30 ÷ 80 × 100
(Cost)	(80)	(30)
Profit	20	7.50

Selling price = £30 ÷ 80 × 100 = £37.50

5 Summary

Forecast sales revenue and purchases do not necessarily reflect the cash in and out flows required for a cash budget. This is because of a possible delay in receiving receipts from receivables and delays in paying payables. This **lagging** needs to be taken into account when producing the figures for inclusion into a cash budget.

Answers to chapter activities

Activity 1

The opening receivables balance will be 60% of April's credit sales as 40% of April's credit sales will have been collected in April. Any previous credit sales will have already been collected. For example March's credit sales will be collected 40% in March and 60% in April therefore none should be outstanding.

	Opening	*May*	*June*	*July*
	£	£	£	£
Sales	24,000	30,000	20,000	25,000
40% in month of sale		12,000	8,000	10,000
60% 1 month after sale		24,000	18,000	12,000
Total cash receipts		36,000	26,000	22,000

Closing receivables at 31 July = £25,000 × 60% = £15,000

Activity 2

	March	*April*	*May*	*June*
	£	£	£	£
Cash	5,610	5,950	6,290	6,800
Credit sales receipts:				
Month after sale 40%	10,624**	10,956	11,620	12,284
2 months after sale 60%	14,940*	15,936 ***	16,434	17,430
Total cash received****	31,174	32,842	34,344	36,514

*January £5,100 is cash, £24,900 is credit. Of the credit sales 40% will be received in February leaving 60% in March £24,900 × 60% = £14,940

February £5,440 is cash, £26,560 is credit. 40% will be received in March £26,560 × 40% = £10,624** and 60% in April £26,560 × 60% = £15,936***

**** total cash received includes cash sales

Activity 3

	Period 1	Period 2	Period 3	Period 4	Period 5
	£	£	£	£	£
Sales	160,000	166,000	170,000	150,000	140,000
Receipts					
Cash sales	16,000	16,600	17,000	15,000	14,000
Credit sales	*144,000*	*149,400*	*153,000*	*135,000*	*126,000*
One month after sale		28,800	29,880	30,600	27,000
Two months after sale			115,200	119,520	122,400
Total cash receipts				165,120	163,400

Closing receivables

80% of P4 = £108,000

All of P5 = £126,000

Total = £234,000

Activity 4

Settlement discount % = £4,000 ÷ £50,000 × 100 = 8%

Activity 5

	May	June	July	Aug
	£	£	£	£
Purchases	100,000	110,000	120,000	130,000
In the month of purchase	50,000	55,000	60,000	65,000
One month after purchase		30,000	33,000	36,000
Two months after purchase			20,000	22,000
Cash payments			113,000	123,000

Closing payables

July 20% × £120,000 = £24,000

August 50% × £130,000 = £65,000

Total = £89,000

Activity 6

	Period 4 £	*Period 5* £
Total payments	51,500	40,000

Workings

Period 4

All of Period 1's outstanding amount = £18,000

Period 2 = 25 ÷ 70 × £35,000 = £12,500

Period 3 = 30 ÷ 100 × £70,000 = £21,000

Total = £51,500

Period 5

Period 2 = 45 ÷ 70 × £35,000 = £22,500

Period 3 = 25 ÷ 100 × £70,000 = £17,500

Total = £40,000

Activity 7

Discount saves 2% of £7,500 = £150

Financed by overdraft for extra two months in order to pay £7,350 early:

$$\text{Cost} = 10\% \times \frac{2}{12} \times £7{,}350 = £122.50$$

Net saving = £27.50

It is worth accepting the discount.

Activity 8

	April	*May*	*June*
Time taken (hours)	12,400	13,600	14,000
Standard hours	12,000	12,000	12,000
Overtime hours	400	1,600	2,000
Forecast standard cost £	84,000	84,000	88,800
Forecast overtime cost £	4,200	16,800	22,200
Forecast labour cost		84,000 + 4,200 = **£88,200**	88,800 + 16,800 = **£105,600**

Activity 9

	May £	*June* £	*July* £
Purchases (W1)	26,950	28,000	29,050
Wages	18,000	18,000	18,500
Expenses (W2)	3,750	4,000	4,000
New machine	0	5,000	5,000
Total payments	48,700	55,000	56,550

Workings

(W1) **Purchases**

May – payment is for purchases made in March based on the April forecast sales figures.

77,000 × 35% = £26,950

(W2) **Expenses**

Remove the depreciation as this is a non-cash item and then payment occurs in the following month.

May – April expenses less £3,000

£6,750 – £3,000 = £3,750

6 Test your knowledge

Workbook Activity 10

The following data and estimates are available for ABC Ltd:

	April	*May*	*June*	*July*	*August*
	£	£	£	£	£
Sales	30,000	37,000	45,000	50,000	60,000

Notes:

(1) 10% of sales are for cash.

(2) The remainder is received 30% in the month following the sale and 70% two months after the sale.

Task

Prepare the cash receipts budgets for June, July and August.

	June	*July*	*August*
	£	£	£
Receipts of cash			
Cash sales			
Credit sales			

Workbook Activity 11

Shirley Ltd has been trading for a number of years. Shirley's owner, Kelly, has asked for help calculating their cash and credit sales.

Actual sales values achieved are available for October and November and forecast sales values have been produced for December to March.

Kelly estimates that cash sales account for 20% of the total sales. The remaining 80% of sales are made on a credit basis.

(a) Complete the table below to show the split of total sales between cash sales and credit sales.

	Actual		*Forecast*			
	Oct	*Nov*	*Dec*	*Jan*	*Feb*	*Mar*
Total sales	11,000	14,000	16,000	18,500	19,900	22,100
Cash sales	2200	2800	3200	3700	3980	4420
Credit sales	8800	11200	12800	14800	15920	17680

Kelly estimates that 25% of credit sales are received in the month after sale with the balance being received two months after sale.

(b) Using your figures from part (a) calculate the timing of credit sales receipts that would be included in a cash budget for Shirley Ltd's for the period December to March.

	Dec £	*Jan* £	*Feb* £	*Mar* £
Monthly credit sales receipts	9400	11600	13300	15080

75% 6600 8400 9600 11,100

25% 2800 3200 3700 3980

Workbook Activity 12

XYZ Ltd has the following forecast sales for the nine months to 29 February 20X2:

June	£40,000	September	£48,000	December	£44,000
July	£44,000	October	£40,000	January	£42,000
August	£50,000	November	£45,000	February	£50,000

60% of the company's sales are on credit, payable in the month after sale. The remainder are cash sales.

Calculate the cash receipts for November to February.

	Nov	*Dec*	*Jan*	*Feb*
Receipts:	£	£	£	£
Cash sales	18000	17600	16,800	20000
Credit sales	24000	27000	26400	25200
	42000	44600	43200	45200

Purchases amount to 40% of sales. XYZ buys and receives inventory to meet the following month's sales and these are paid for two months after delivery.

Wages comprise a fixed sum of £2,000 per month.

Fixed costs amount to £7,500 per month, payable one month in arrears, of which £1,500 is depreciation.

Calculate the cash payments for November to February.

	Nov	*Dec*	*Jan*	*Feb*
Payments:	£	£	£	£
Purchases	16000	18000	17600	16800
Wages	2000	2000	2000	2000
Fixed costs	6000	6000	6000	6000
	24000	26000	25600	24800

Preparing cash budgets

4

Introduction

Once a cash flow forecast has been prepared it has a variety of uses to management. By changing individual assumptions within the forecast it is possible to see what effect this might have on the eventual cash balance.

ASSESSMENT CRITERIA

Estimate cash flows over the accounting period and anticipate any exceptional receipts or payments (2.2S)

Prepare cash budgets in accordance with the organisation's preferred format and clearly indicate net cash requirements (2.4S)

Undertake sensitivity analysis on elements within the cash budget and quantity the effects of possible changes in assumptions (2.5S)

CONTENTS

1 Preparation of cash budgets

1.1 Cash budget

A cash budget or cash flow forecast is an **estimate of all of the cash inflows and outflows for the period**. When these are applied to the opening cash figure, the closing cash balance at the end of each period can be estimated and management can plan to take any necessary action. For example:

- if there is a cash deficit then agreement with the bank can be sought for an overdraft facility
- if there is a cash surplus then the treasury department may look into short-term investment

1.2 Proforma receipts and payments cash budget

Cash budget for the three months to September 20X4

	July £	*Aug* £	*Sept* £
RECEIPTS			
Cash sales			
Cash from receivables			
Capital introduced			
Total receipts			
PAYMENTS			
Fixed costs			
Payments to payables			
Purchases of non-current assets			
Total payments			
Net cash flow			
Opening cash balance			
Closing cash balance			

Example

At 1 March 20X4 Apple Ltd expects to have a cash balance of £2,000. It is estimated that cash from sales in March, April and May will be £24,000 each month. Cash payments for expenses each month are estimated to be £21,000 but some new equipment must be purchased at a cost of £12,000 paid for in May.

Prepare the cash budget for the next three months and determine the net cash position at the end of each of the three months.

Solution

Cash budget	*March*	*April*	*May*
	£	£	£
Cash inflows	24,000	24,000	24,000
Cash outflows:			
Expenses	(21,000)	(21,000)	(21,000)
Capital expenditure			(12,000)
Net cash inflow/(outflow)	3,000	3,000	(9,000)
Opening cash balance	2,000	5,000	8,000
Closing cash balance	5,000	8,000	(1,000)

The closing cash balance at the end of each month is derived by adding or deducting the net cash flow for the month to or from the cash balance at the start of the month. The closing cash balance of one month therefore becomes the opening cash balance the following month.

This indicates to management that although there will be cash in the bank at the end of March and April, there is expected to be a shortage at the end of May. Management can then use this information to plan for this eventuality by, for example, arranging for a bank overdraft or bank loan or selling some surplus assets.

Each cash budget has to be **amended to reflect** the particular circumstances of the business.

For example, other sources of income may arise, such as proceeds from the sale of non-current assets. There are many sorts of cash payments; possibly cash purchases as well as credit purchases, wages and salaries to employees or the drawings of a proprietor, and each must be detailed line by line under the payments heading.

Remember that a cash budget monitors cash – do not include any non-cash items i.e. depreciation.

2 Interest received or payable

2.1 Introduction

One of the purposes of a cash budget is to identify the cash balance at the end of each month and to determine whether any interest is due to the business from the bank from a positive balance or whether an overdraft facility is required due to a negative balance. If an overdraft is agreed with the bank and the facility is used then the bank will charge interest on the amount of the overdraft.

2.2 Interest received

In practice the amount of the interest will be calculated on a daily basis. However for cash budgeting purposes the amount of interest will normally be calculated on the basis of the amount of the credit balance at the end of the month. The figure for interest will then be included in the following month's cash receipts.

Example

A business anticipates having a credit balance of £2,000 at the end of March. The budgeted cash receipts and payments (excluding interest) for the following three months are expected to be as follows:

	April	*May*	*June*
	£	£	£
Cash receipts	16,500	18,000	17,200
Cash payments	17,400	17,500	17,000

Interest is received at 0.5% per month on the balance at the start of each month.

Prepare the completed cash budget including the amount of interest.

Solution

		April	May	June
		£	£	£
Cash receipts		16,500	18,000	17,200
interest	(2,000 × 0.5%)	10		
	(1,110 × 0.5%)		6	
	(1,616 × 0.5%)			8
Cash payments		(17,400)	(17,500)	(17,000)
Net cash flow		(890)	506	208
Opening balance		2,000	1,110	1,616
Closing balance		1,110	1,616	1,824

2.3 Overdraft interest

In practice the amount of the overdraft interest will be calculated on a daily basis. However for cash budgeting purposes the amount of overdraft interest will normally be calculated on the basis of the amount of the overdraft outstanding at the end of the previous month. This figure for interest will then be included in the following month's cash payments.

Example

A business anticipates having an overdraft of £2,000 at the end of March. The budgeted cash receipts and payments (excluding overdraft interest) for the following three months are expected to be as follows:

	April	May	June
	£	£	£
Cash receipts	16,500	18,000	17,200
Cash payments	17,400	17,500	17,000

Overdraft interest is charged at 0.5% per month on the overdraft balance at the start of each month.

Prepare the completed cash budget including the amount of overdraft interest.

Solution

		April	*May*	*June*
		£	£	£
Cash receipts		16,500	18,000	17,200
Cash payments		(17,400)	(17,500)	(17,000)
Overdraft interest	(2,000 × 0.5%)	(10)		
	(2,910 × 0.5%)		(15)	
	(2,425 × 0.5%)			(12)
Net cash flow		(910)	485	188
Opening balance		(2,000)	(2,910)	(2,425)
Closing balance		(2,910)	(2,425)	(2,237)

Note that you can only calculate the overdraft interest month by month once you have calculated the opening cash balance of the relevant month.

3 VAT

3.1 Introduction

If a business is registered for VAT it must:

- charge VAT on its sales or services to its customers
- recover the VAT charged on its purchases and expenses rather than having to bear these costs as part of the business.

In such cases, as the VAT charged and incurred is neither revenue nor expense, the revenues and costs of the business are entered in books at their net of VAT value, and the VAT is entered in the VAT account.

3.2 Output VAT

Definition

The VAT charged on sales or taxable supplies is called **output VAT.**

3.3 Input VAT

When a business buys goods or pays expenses (inputs), then it will also be paying VAT on those purchases or expenses.

Definition

VAT paid by a business on purchases or expenses is called **input VAT.**

Businesses are allowed to reclaim their input tax. They do this by deducting the input tax they have paid from the output tax which they owe, and paying over the net amount only. If the input tax exceeds the output tax, then the balance is recoverable from HMRC.

3.4 Standard rated activities

Any taxable supply which is not charged at the zero or reduced rates is charged at the standard rate. There will only be standard rated activities in the CSHM exam.

This is calculated by taking the VAT exclusive amount and multiplying by 20%.

If you are given the VAT inclusive rate then calculate the VAT amount by 20/120.

The following VAT structure can also be used to calculate VAT, VAT inclusive or VAT exclusive figures.

	£
VAT inclusive (gross)	120
VAT	20
VAT exclusive (net)	100

It may be necessary to calculate the VAT payment or refund from the HMRC for inclusion in the cash budget.

Example

Suppose that a business makes sales on credit of £2,000 and purchases on credit of £800 (both amounts exclusive of any VAT). How much cash will be paid to or received from HMRC?

Solution

Sales account

	£		£
		Receivables	2,000

Receivables account

	£		£
Sales and VAT	2,400		

Purchases account

	£		£
Payables	800		

Payables account

	£		£
		Purchases	960

VAT control account

	£		£
Payables	160	Receivables	400
Balance c/d	240		
	400		400
		Balance b/d	240

The amount due to HM Revenue and Customs is the balance on the VAT account, £240.

If a business is registered for VAT then it will charge VAT on its sales, although they will be recorded as sales at their net amount, and its expenses will also be recorded at the net amount. The output and input VAT is recorded in the VAT account and the difference paid over to HM Revenue and Customs.

Activity 1

A business that is registered for VAT makes credit sales of £220,000 in the period and credit purchases of £150,000. Each of these figures is net of VAT at the standard rate of 20%.

Calculate how much VAT is due to or from HM Revenue and Customs.

4 Loans

4.1 Loans

A business may take out a bank loan to be able to pay for new purchases. The receipt of the loan would be included in the receipts section of the cash budget. A loan will need to be paid back to the bank. There are 2 parts to a loan repayment – the **capital (principal) repayment** and the **interest charged** on the loan – these will both feature in the payments section of the cash budget.

Activity 2

The cash budget for Sampras Construction for the three months ended May has been partially completed. The following information needs to be included to complete the cash budget.

- A bank loan of £60,000 has been arranged and it is to be received by Sampras Construction in March.
- The principal element is to be repaid in 60 equal monthly instalments beginning in April. This has been arranged as Sampras Construction is purchasing some new machinery for £58,000 in April.
- The loan has a 5% interest charge per annum calculated on the principal amount of the loan. The interest is to be payable from March and should be rounded to the nearest £.
- There is a 2% monthly interest charge if Sampras uses its overdraft. The charge is calculated on the previous month end balance. Interest is rounded to the nearest £.
- On the 28 February the cash balance was £3,400 overdrawn.

Complete the cash budget below. Use positive figures for cash inflows and negative figures are cash outflows. Enter zero where appropriate.

	March £	*April* £	*May* £
RECEIPTS			
Cash sales	6,200	6,700	7,500
Credit sales	35,000	38,000	39,000
Bank loan			
Total receipts			
PAYMENTS			
Purchases	–15,000	–10,000	–13,000
Wages	–10,000	–11,000	–10,500
Expenses	–5,600	–6,200	–6,800
Capital expenditure			
Bank loan principal repayments			
Bank loan interest			
Overdraft interest			
Total payments			
Net cash flow			
Opening cash balance			
Closing cash balance			

5 Exchange rates

5.1 Introduction

A change in exchange rates might affect a business in the following ways:

- Exchange rate changes can increase or reduce the price of a product sold abroad
- The price of imported raw materials may change
- The price of competitors' products may change in the home market

5.2 Converting foreign currency to sterling

An exchange rate is the value of one currency expressed in terms of another. So, for example, £1 may be worth $1.50 in America and €1.39 in France.

Example

A business buys $4,000 of raw materials.

If the exchange rate is £1:$1.5000 then the sterling value of the raw materials is $4,000 ÷ 1.5000 = £2,667

If the exchange rate is $1:£0.6667 then the sterling value of the raw material is $4,000 × £0.6667 = £2,667

(rounded to the nearest whole £)

Activity 3

An English company is to purchase materials costing $100,000. You have the following information:

£1:$1.9000

What is the value of the purchase in £ (to the nearest whole £)?

6 Sensitivity of the cash budget

6.1 Introduction

Once a cash budget is produced it is important to know how much cash inflows and cash outflows are able to change before they affect the cash balance position. The cash flows could change due to:

- A change in price or volume in goods bought or sold or a change in another income or expense.
- A change in payment or collection periods.
- The introduction of a settlement discount.
- Irrecoverable debts.

Computer spreadsheets can be used, not only to speed up the preparation of cash budgets, but also to easily carry out a variety of forms of sensitivity analysis.

7 Percentage changes

7.1 Percentage changes

In many cases managers may need to consider how the cash position will alter if there is a change in any of the receipt or expenditure items. What may seem a healthy positive cash position could change with a 1% increase in wages or a 2% fall in sales. It is therefore advisable to assess the sensitivity of the balance to such changes.

Example

Consider the following cash flow.

	January £	*February* £	*March* £
Receipts			
Sales	10,000	20,000	15,000
Payments			
Payables	10,000	10,000	20,000
Wages	2,000	3,000	2,000
Sundry	500	500	500
	12,500	13,500	22,500
Net cash flow	(2,500)	6,500	(7,500)
Opening cash balance	4,000	1,500	8,000
Closing cash balance	1,500	8,000	500

What would be the net cash position each month if:

(i) wages increased by 5% or

(ii) sales increased by 4%?

Solution

(i) If wages increase by 5% the impact on the cash balance is as follows:

	£	£	£
Wages	2,100	3,150	2,100
(increase)/decrease	(100)	(150)	(100)
New net cash flow	(2,600)	6,350	(7,600)
Opening cash balance	4,000	1,400	7,750
Closing cash balance	1,400	7,750	150

Thus, although wages have increased, the cash balance is still positive and corrective measures are not yet required.

(ii) If sales increase by 4% the impact on the cash balance is as follows:

	£	£	£
Sales	10,400	20,800	15,600
Increase/(decrease)	400	800	600
New net cash flow	(2,100)	7,300	(6,900)
Opening cash balance	4,000	1,900	9,200
Closing cash balance	1,900	9,200	2,300

Activity 4

	April £	*May* £	*June* £
Sales	2,600	3,100	1,600
Payables	1,300	1,550	700
Wages	1,000	1,000	1,000
Power	200	200	200
	2,500	2,750	1,900
Net cash flow	100	350	(300)
Opening cash balance	100	200	550
Closing cash balance	200	550	250

In the above cash flow, how sensitive is the cash balance at the end of June to a 1% increase and a 2% decrease in sales?

(a) **1% increase**

	April	May	June
	£	£	£
Sales			
Increase/(decrease)			
New net cash flow			
Opening cash balance	100		
Closing cash balance			

(b) **2% decrease**

	April	May	June
	£	£	£
Sales			
Increase/(decrease)			
New net cash flow			
Opening cash balance	100		
Closing cash balance			

8 Changes in receipts from receivables

8.1 Introduction

The cash flows that appear in the cash budget are heavily dependent upon the payment patterns of receivables. Managers may need information about the effect that a change in those payment patterns would have on the net cash position.

The cash received from receivables could change due to a number of reasons:

- Change in volume
- Change in price
- Change in timing of receipts
- Offering a settlement discount
- Occurrences of irrecoverable debts

8.2 Changes in volume, price and/or timing

Example

A business is producing its cash budget for the next three months. Credit sales in February and March were £50,000 and £58,000. Credit sales are forecast as £60,000, £70,000 and £50,000 respectively for each of the months of April, May and June. Credit customers are currently offered one month's credit and they all pay in the month after the sale.

Cash outflows in each month are estimated to be:

April	*May*	*June*
£48,000	£57,000	£60,000

At the end of March there is an overdraft of £10,000.

What would be the effect on the net cash position at the end of each month if credit customers were given two months' credit?

Solution

Current policy cash budget (one month credit)

	April £	*May* £	*June* £
Receipts from receivables (previous months sales)	58,000	60,000	70,000
Cash outflows	(48,000)	(57,000)	(60,000)
Net cash flow	10,000	3,000	10,000
Cash balance b/f	(10,000)	–	3,000
Cash balance c/f	–	3,000	13,000

New policy cash budget (two months credit)

	April £	May £	June £
Receipts from receivables (sales from two months ago)	50,000	58,000	60,000
Cash outflows	(48,000)	(57,000)	(60,000)
Net cash flow	2,000	1,000	–
Cash balance b/f	(10,000)	(8,000)	(7,000)
Cash balance c/f	(8,000)	(7,000)	(7,000)

The effect of receivables paying two months after the sale rather than one month has been to reduce a positive cash balance to an overdraft balance at the end of each month.

Activity 5

A cash budget has been prepared for Maximillian Ltd for the next 4 periods for a new product. The budget was prepared based on the following sales volumes and a selling price of £12 per item.

	March	*April*	*May*	*June*
Sales volume units	1,300	1,500	1,700	1,900

The pattern of cash receipts used in the budget assumed 50% of sales were received in the month of sale and the remaining 50% in the month following sale.

	March	*April*	*May*	*June*
Original forecast sales receipts £	7,800	16,800	19,200	21,600

In the light of current economic trends Maximillian Ltd needs to adjust its cash budget to take account of the following:

- The selling price will be reduced by 5% per item
- The pattern of sales receipts changes to 25% of sales received in the month of sale, 30% in the month following sale and the remaining 45% two months after sale.

Complete the table below to show the effect of the changes in values and timing of receipts for March to June:

	Revised forecast sales £	*Sales receipts*				
		March £	*April* £	*May* £	*June* £	*Total* £
March sales						
April sales						
May sales						
June sales						
Revised forecast sales receipts						

Complete the sentence below:

Receipts from sales in March to June will *increase/decrease* by ___% if the sales price and timing of receipts change.

8.3 Settlement discounts

The payment pattern of receivables can also be altered by offering settlement discounts to credit customers. Settlement discounts should encourage earlier payment of debts as customers who pay earlier pay less.

Example

A business has the following budgeted credit sales and budgeted cash payments:

	Actual		*Forecast*			
	Jan £	*Feb* £	*Mar* £	*Apr* £	*May* £	*Jun* £
Credit sales in £000s	100	120	130	140	150	160
Payments in £000s	80	94	108	110	120	135

The current credit terms for customers are 60 days and the current payment pattern is that 20% of customers pay during the month following sale, 70% pay two months after the sale and 10% three months after the date of sale.

The company is considering introducing a settlement discount of 2% for payment during the month after sale. This is anticipated to result in 60% of customers paying in the month after sale, 30% two months after the date of sale and 10% three months after the date of sale.

The company anticipates a cash overdraft of £20,000 at the start of April.

(i) Determine the net cash balance at the end of each of the months of April, May and June under the existing credit terms.

(ii) Calculate the effect on the net cash balance at the end of each of the three months if the new policy of offering a settlement discount were introduced for credit sales made from 1 March onwards.

(iii) Comment on how the new policy affects the net cash balance for each of the three months.

Solution

Under existing policy	*April* £	*May* £	*June* £
RECEIPTS			
Cash from receivables in one month 20%	26,000	28,000	30,000
Cash from receivables in two months 70%	84,000	91,000	98,000
Cash from receivables in three months 10%	10,000	12,000	13,000
Total receipts	120,000	131,000	141,000
PAYMENTS			
Payment to payables	110,000	120,000	135,000
Total payments	110,000	120,000	135,000
Net cash flow	10,000	11,000	6,000
Opening cash balance	(20,000)	(10,000)	1,000
Closing cash balance	(10,000)	1,000	7,000

Under new policy	*April* £	*May* £	*June* £
RECEIPTS			
Cash from receivables in one month 60% × 98%	76,440	82,320	88,200
Cash from receivables in two months 30%	36,000	39,000	42,000
Cash from receivables in three months 10%	10,000	12,000	13,000
Total receipts	122,440	133,320	143,200
PAYMENTS			
Payment to payables	110,000	120,000	135,000
Total payments	110,000	120,000	135,000
Net cash flow	12,440	13,320	8,200
Opening cash balance	(20,000)	(7,560)	5,760
Closing cash balance	(7,560)	5,760	13,960

Under the new policy of offering the settlement discount, the overdraft is removed by the end of May which is the same as the original policy. The overall cash balance has increased more rapidly under the new policy.

The cash budget may need to be expanded to ensure that the 2% reduction in actual cash received does not have a negative effect later on.

Activity 6

A business is considering whether to offer a 3% discount for payment received from credit customers in the month of sale. This will only be offered to sales made after 1 April.

Credit sales for the business are as follows:

	Actual		*Budgeted*		
	February £	*March* £	*April* £	*May* £	*June* £
Credit sales	20,000	22,000	24,000	18,000	21,000

The current receivables collection forecast is:

- 15% in month of sale
- 75% in month after sale
- 10% two months after sale

	April £	*May* £	*June* £
Original forecast sales receipts	22,100	22,900	19,050

The business estimates that 60% of customers would take advantage of the settlement discount by paying in the month of sale, 30% of customers will pay in the month after the sale and 10% of customers will pay two months after the month of sale.

Calculate the cash receipts for April, May and June if the settlement discount is offered.

	April £	*May* £	*June* £
New forecast sales receipts			

Should this business offer a settlement discount?

8.4 Irrecoverable debts

It is possible that some debts will become irrecoverable debts i.e. the cash will not be received. The cash flows will need to be adjusted for this.

It may be that a business predicts that a certain percentage of outstanding amounts will not be received or that there is a specific receivable that will not be able to pay.

Example

A business has found that 30% of customers pay in the month of sale, 40% of customers pay in the month after the sale and 20% of customers pay two months after the month of sale. From past experience it is known that 10% of the customers do not pay.

Credit sales for the business are as follows:

	Actual		*Budgeted*		
	February	*March*	*April*	*May*	*June*
	£	£	£	£	£
Credit sales	10,000	20,000	30,000	25,000	30,000

	April	*May*	*June*
	£	£	£
The cash receipts will be:			
30% in month of sale	9,000	7,500	9,000
40% in subsequent month	8,000	12,000	10,000
20% two months after sale	2,000	4,000	6,000
10% irrecoverable debt	0	0	0
Giving:			
Total cash receipts	19,000	23,500	25,000

Irrecoverable debts are not recovered therefore no cash is received.

Example

It has come to the attention of the credit control manager that one of the credit customers is going into liquidation. The customer bought £14,000 worth of goods in June. The credit manager has decided it is necessary to write off the outstanding amount as an irrecoverable debt. The current credit sales budget is as follows:

	Actual			*Forecast*		
	April	*May*	*June*	*July*	*August*	*September*
Total sales	82,000	84,000	85,000	90,000	92,000	95,000

The pattern of sales receipts are 30% in the month of sale, 45% in the month following sale and 25% two months after sale.

	June	*July*	*August*	*September*
Original value of sales	85,000	90,000	92,000	95,000
30% in month of sale	25,500	27,000	27,600	28,500
45% in subsequent month	37,800	38,250	40,500	41,400
25% two months after sale	20,500	21,000	21,250	22,500
Original timing of receipts	83,800	86,250	89,350	92,400
Revised value of sales	71,000	90,000	92,000	95,000
30% in month of sale	**21,300**	27,000	27,600	28,500
45% in subsequent month	37,800	**31,950**	40,500	41,400
25% two months after sale	20,500	21,000	**17,750**	22,500
Revised timing of receipts	79,600	79,950	85,850	92,400
Change in receipts	–4,200	–6,300	–3,500	0

Note how the irrecoverable debt effects 3 months of the forecasted cash inflow due to the payment pattern of the receivables.

9 Changes in payments to payables

9.1 Introduction

The cash flows that appear in the cash budget are heavily dependent upon the payment patterns to payables. Managers may need information about the effect that a change in those payment patterns would have on the net cash position.

The cash paid to a payable could change due to a number of reasons:

- Change in volume
- Change in price
- Change in timing of payments
- Receiving a settlement discount

9.2 Changes in volume, price and/or timing

Example

A business is producing its cash budget for the next three months. Credit purchases are forecast to be:

February	*March*	*April*	*May*	*June*
£50,000	£58,000	£48,000	£57,000	£60,000

Suppliers currently offer two month's credit.

Cash inflows in each month are estimated to be:

April	*May*	*June*
£58,000	£60,000	£70,000

At the end of March there is an overdraft of £10,000.

What would be the effect on the net cash position at the end of each month if the suppliers reduced the credit to one month from February?

Solution

Current policy cash budget (two months credit)

	April	*May*	*June*
	£	£	£
Cash inflows	58,000	60,000	70,000
Payments to payables	(50,000)	(58,000)	(48,000)
Net cash flow	8,000	2,000	22,000
Opening cash balance	(10,000)	(2,000)	–
Closing cash balance	(2,000)	–	22,000

New policy cash budget (one month credit)

	April	*May*	*June*
	£	£	£
Cash inflows	58,000	60,000	70,000
Payment to payables	(58,000)	(48,000)	(57,000)
Net cash flow	–	12,000	13,000
Opening cash balance	(10,000)	(10,000)	2,000
Closing cash balance	(10,000)	2,000	15,000

The effect of paying the payables one month earlier has meant that the positive cash balance has been reduced.

Activity 7

Maximillian Ltd has managed to negotiate extended payment terms with its suppliers. The original budget was to pay in the month after purchase.

	March	*April*	*May*	*June*
Forecast purchases	8,000	8,200	8,400	8,600
Original forecast payment		8,000	8,200	8,400

The settlement is now split over the 2 months after purchase, 50% is paid in the month after purchase and the remainder the month after that.

Complete the table below to show the new payments for April to June:

	April	*May*	*June*
Revised forecast payments			

9.3 Receiving a settlement discount

The payment pattern of payables can also be altered by receiving a settlement discount from the supplier.

Activity 8

A company has managed to negotiate new payment terms with its suppliers. The original budget was prepared on the basis of paying suppliers in the month following purchase. The revised payment terms allow for settlement of 40% in the month of purchase with a 5% settlement discount, 30% in the month following purchase with the remaining 30% two months after purchase.

The budgeted purchases figures are:

	Period 1 (£)	*Period 2* (£)	*Period 3* (£)	*Period 4* (£)	*Period 5* (£)
Purchases	8,700	8,000	6,800	10,900	11,000

Complete the table to show the effect of the changes on the timing of purchase payments for periods 3, 4 and 5:

	3	4	5
Original forecast payments			
Revised forecast payments			
Increase/(decrease) in cash			

10 Summary

The figures in the cash budget are all estimates based upon projected figures and assumptions regarding factors such as the payment pattern of receivables and payables.

Management will be interested in how the net cash position would change if these estimates or assumptions change. This can be determined by various forms of sensitivity analysis.

Answers to chapter activities

Activity 1

Sales account

	£		£
		SLCA	220,000

Sales ledger control account

	£		£
Sales + VAT (220,000 + 44,000)	264,000		

Purchases account

	£		£
PLCA	150,000		

VAT control account

	£		£
PLCA (150,000 × 20/100)	30,000	SLCA (220,000 × 20/100)	44,000
Balance c/d	14,000		
	44,000		44,000
		Balance b/d	14,000

Purchases ledger control account

	£		£
		Purchases + VAT (150,000 + 30,000)	180,000

The amount due to HM Revenue and Customs is the balance on the VAT control account, £14,000.

Activity 2

	March £	*April* £	*May* £
RECEIPTS			
Cash sales	6,200	6,700	7,500
Credit sales	35,000	38,000	39,000
Bank loan	60,000	0	0
Total receipts	101,200	44,700	46,500
PAYMENTS			
Purchases	–15,000	–10,000	–13,000
Wages	–10,000	–11,000	–10,500
Expenses	–5,600	–6,200	–6,800
Capital expenditure	0	–58,000	0
Bank loan principal repayments	0	–1,000	–1,000
Bank loan interest	–250	–250	–250
Overdraft interest	–68	0	0
Total payments	30,918	86,450	31,550
Net cash flow	70,282	–41,750	14,950
Opening cash balance	–3,400	66,882	25,132
Closing cash balance	66,882	25,132	40,082

Activity 3

$100,000 ÷ 1.9000 = £52,632

Activity 4

(a) **1% increase in sales**

	April	*May*	*June*
	£	£	£
Sales (× 1.01)	2,626	3,131	1,616
Increase/(decrease)	26	31	16
New net cash flow	126	381	(284)
Opening cash balance	100	226	607
Closing cash balance	226	607	323

A 1% increase in sales results in the cash balance increasing from £250 to £323. This is an increase of £73 (i.e. 29%).

(b) **2% decrease in sales**

	April	*May*	*June*
	£	£	£
Sales (× 0.98)	2,548	3,038	1,568
Increase/(decrease)	(52)	(62)	(32)
New net cash flow	48	288	(332)
Opening cash balance	100	148	436
Closing cash balance	148	436	104

A 2% decrease in sales has not caused the cash balance to become overdrawn but cash has fallen to £104. This is a £146 (i.e. 58%) fall.

Activity 5

	Revised forecast sales £	*Sales receipts*				
		March £	*April* £	*May* £	*June* £	*Total* £
March sales	14,820	3,705	4,446	6,669	0	
April sales	17,100	0	4,275	5,130	7,695	
May sales	19,380	0	0	4,845	5,814	
June sales	21,660	0	0	0	5,415	
Revised forecast sales receipts		3,705	8,721	16,644	18,924	47,994

Receipts from sales in March to June will *decrease* by 26.6% if the sales price and timing of receipts change.

Activity 6

	April £	*May* £	*June* £
Cash from receivables in month of sale	13,968	10,476	12,222
Cash from receivables in month after sale	16,500	7,200	5,400
Cash from receivables in two months after month of sale	2,000	2,200	2,400
Total receipts	32,468	19,876	20,022

This business should offer a settlement discount of 3% as cash receipts have increased by 13% over the 3 months in question.

Original total receipts £64,050

New total receipts £72,366

Activity 7

	April	*May*	*June*
Revised forecast payments £	4,000	8,100	8,300

Activity 8

	3	*4*	*5*
Original forecast payments £	8,000	6,800	10,900
In month of purchase 40% with 5% discount	2,584	4,142	4,180
Month following purchase 30%	2,400	2,040	3,270
2 months following purchase 30%	2,610	2,400	2,040
Revised forecast payments £	7,594	8,582	9,490
Increase/(decrease) in cash	406	(1,782)	1,410

11 Test your knowledge

Workbook Activity 9

Refer to the memos from Mark Bennett and Victoria Bartlett to prepare the cash flow forecast for the first 3 months of next year.

MEMO

To: John Parker

From: Mark Bennett

Date: 12 December

Subject: Next Year

Further to our conversation I have put together the forecast cash expenditure for next year:

- new equipment will cost a total of £200,000. We need to buy it in January and put down a deposit of £50,000 on 1 January. I have negotiated instalments for the remainder; three equal instalments payable on 1 February, 1 May and 1 September next year. We can get a grant for part of the cost (10% of total cost) and this will be received on 1 January;
- rent for premises will amount to £5,000 per quarter payable in advance, with the first payment being 1 January;
- wages will be £6,000 per month, payable on the last day of the month worked;
- purchases are currently £10,000 each month, but will be increasing by 2% every two months for the rest of the year from March. Purchases will be paid for two months after they have been received.
- The opening cash balance should be assumed to be £40,000.
- The bank charges 1% interest on any overdraft at the end of a month. Payable in the following month.

I look forward to seeing the cash flow forecast and discussing it further.

With regards.

Mark

MEMO

To: John Parker

From: Victoria Bartlett

Date: 13 December

Subject: Future sales

I have put together some forecast sales for the first three months of next year for the new division. I have been quite conservative so these figures should be achieved with relative ease.

	December	*January*	*February*	*March*
	£	£	£	£
Cash sales	16,000	18,000	18,500	20,000
Credit sales	7,000	6,000	7,000	6,000
Total	23,000	24,000	25,000	26,000

Credit sales will be payable by the end of the month after the sale was made. Selling and administration costs will amount to 10% of the sales made in the month and they are payable in cash as incurred.

With regards.

Victoria

Cash flow forecast

	January £	*February* £	*March* £
CASH RECEIVED Sales: cash credit			
Grant			
Total			
CASH PAID Equipment: deposit			
Equipment: instalment			
Rent			
Wages			
Purchases			
Selling/administration			
Overdraft interest			
Total			
Net cash flow			
Opening cash balance			
Closing cash balance			

Workbook Activity 10

Using the cash flow predictions, in the 2 memos below, produce a cash flow forecast for the first three months of next year for the new division.

MEMO

To: John Powell

From: Mark Bennett

Date: 12 January

Subject: New Division

Further to our conversation I have put together the forecast cash expenditure for the new division next year:

- new equipment will cost a total of £200,000. We need to buy it in January and put down a deposit of £50,000 on 1 January. I have negotiated instalments for the remainder; three equal instalments payable on 1 February, 1 May and 1 September next year. We can get a grant for part of the cost (10%) and this will be received on 1 January also;
- rent for premises will amount to £5,000 per quarter payable in advance, with the first payment being 1 January;
- wages will be £6,000 per month, payable on the last day of the month worked;
- purchases will amount to £10,000 in each of the first two months, then £12,000 in the next two months, increasing by £2,000 every two months for the rest of the year. Purchases will be paid for two months after they have been received.

I look forward to seeing the cash flow forecast and discussing it further.

With regards

Mark

MEMO

To: John Powell

From: Victoria Bartlett

Date: 13 January

Subject: Future sales from new division

I have put together some forecast sales for the first three months of next year for the new division. I have been quite conservative so these figures should be achieved with relative ease.

	January	*February*	*March*
	£	£	£
Cash sales	12,000	12,500	13,000
Credit sales	12,000	12,500	13,000
Total	24,000	25,000	26,000

Credit sales will be payable by the end of the month after the sale was made.

Selling and administration costs will amount to 10% of the sales made in the month and they are payable in cash as incurred.

With regards

Victoria

Workbook Activity 11

A cash budget has been prepared for Loadzmonie Ltd for the next 4 periods. The budget was prepared based on the following sales volumes and a selling price of £15 per item.

	January	*February*	*March*	*April*
Sales volume	2,000	3,000	3,400	3,800

The pattern of cash receipts used in the budget assumed 40% of sales were received in the month of sale and the remaining 60% in the month following sale.

In the light of current economic trends Loadzmonie Ltd needs to adjust its cash budget to take account of the following:

- The selling price from period 1 will be reduced by 4% per item.
- The pattern of sales receipts changes to 20% of sales received in the month of sale, 30% in the month following sale and the remaining 50% two months after sale.

Complete the table below to show the effect of the changes in values and timing of receipts:

	January £	*February* £	*March* £	*April* £
Original value of sales				
Original timing of receipts				
Revised value of sales				
Revised timing of receipts				
Increase/(decrease) in receipts				

Loadzmonie Ltd has managed to negotiate extended payment terms with its suppliers. The original budget was to pay in the month of purchase. The settlement is now split over the 2 months after purchase – 40% is paid in the month after purchase and the remaining the month after that.

	January £	*February* £	*March* £	*April* £
Purchases	4,000	4,200	4,400	4,600

Complete the table below to show the effect of the changes in timing of the payments:

	January £	*February* £	*March* £	*April* £
Original timing of payments				
Revised timing of payments				
(Increase)/decrease in payment				

Using the information above on receipts and payments complete the table below to show the revised budgeted cash balance for the months of February, March and April.

	February £	*March* £	*April* £
Original net cash flow	20,000	20,300	20,800
Changes in receipts			
Changes in payments			
Revised net cash flow			
Opening cash balance	7,500		
Closing cash balance			

Workbook Activity 12

MEMO

To: Henry Naem

From: James Powell

Date: 14 January

Subject: Work for this week

Henry

I have left a copy of the cash flow forecast for the next three months for a new venture. Please can you calculate the effect on the balance if the receivables were given an extra months grace.

The original data was as follows:

	December £	*January* £	*February* £	*March* £
Cash sales	16,000	18,000	18,500	20,000
Credit sales	7,000	6,000	7,000	6,000
Total	23,000	24,000	25,000	26,000

Credit sales are currently payable by the end of the month after the sale was made.

November's credit sales were £10,000.

Cash flow forecast for the first three months of next year

	January £	*February* £	*March* £
CASH RECEIVED			
Sales: cash	18,000	18,500	20,000
Sales: credit	7,000	6,000	7,000
Grant	20,000	0	0
Total Receipts	45,000	24,500	27,000
Total Payments	–73,400	–68,500	–18,924
Net cash flow	–28,400	–44,000	8,076
Opening cash balance	40,000	11,600	–32,400
Closing cash balance	11,600	–32,400	–24,324

Impact on cash balance if receivables pay one month later

	January £	*February* £	*March* £
CASH RECEIVED			
Sales: cash			
Sales: credit			
Grant			
Total			
CASH PAID			
Net cash flow			
Opening cash balance			
Closing cash balance			

Workbook Activity 13

Marchtitch Ltd's latest statement of financial position is attached. After examining this and the memos from the Production Manager, Sales Manager and Chief Accountant, you are required to carry out the following tasks:

(a) Prepare a cash flow forecast for each of the three months ending 31 December 20X3.

(b) Calculate what effect a 10% reduction in the price charged to the other retailers would have. Suggest two courses of action the company could take to lessen the adverse impact this would have on the cash flow.

Marshtitch Ltd – Statement of Financial Position at 30 September 20X3

	£	£
Non-current assets		
Land and buildings		75,000
Plant and machinery	315,000	
Less: Depreciation	150,000	
		165,000
		240,000
Current assets		
Inventory		
Raw materials	72,000	
Finished goods	152,000	
Receivables	432,000	
Cash in hand at shop	1,000	
	657,000	
Total assets		897,000

Equity		
Share capital		250,000
Retained earnings		363,400
		613,400
Current liabilities		
Bank overdraft	190,000	
Trade payables for raw materials	93,600	
	283,600	
Total equity and liabilities		897,000

MEMO

To: Accounting Technician

From: Production Manager

Subject: Budget data

Date: 2 October 20X3

You requested the following information recently:

1 The raw material cost of each 'Rose Bowl' is 90 pence. We have contracted for the next 6 months supplies at this price.

2 It takes 10 minutes for one member of staff to make each 'Rose Bowl' and we currently pay our staff £6.00 per hour.

3 Currently our fixed production overheads are running at £20,000 per month including depreciation of £4,000.

4 On 30 September we were carrying sufficient raw material inventory to make 80,000 'Rose Bowls'. We also held 40,000 'Rose Bowls' in inventory at that date.

5 We are anticipating an increasing demand for our product so I plan to increase our inventory of finished goods by 5,000 per month while maintaining raw material inventory at their present level.

M E M O

To: Accounting Technician

From: Sales Manager

Subject: Budget data

Date: 2 October 20X3

You requested the following information recently:

1 We expect to sell 100,000 'Rose Bowls' to the retail trade in October, 110,000 in November and 120,000 in December. We also expect to sell 4,000 per month in our own shop.

2 We intend to sell the 'Rose Bowl' to the retail trade for £2.40 each and for £3.50 each from our own shop.

3 The cost of running the sales department is currently fixed at £10,000 per month including depreciation of £500 per month.

4 The fixed running costs of the shop are £8,000 per month including £1,000 in depreciation.

MEMO

To: Accounting Technician

From: Chief Accountant

Subject: Budget data

Date: 30 September 20X3

While preparing the budgeted cash flow to 31 December, please include the following assumptions:

1 Our credit policy for all trade customers is for payment in 30 days. For budgetary purposes please assume that 25% of retail trade customers pay one month after sale, 70% two months after sale and the remainder three months after sale.

2 You should assume that the debtors at 30 September will pay as follows:

	£
October	240,000
November	180,000
December	12,000
	432,000

3 Purchases of all raw materials will be paid for one month in arrears as at present. All other costs are paid in the month in which they occur.

4 All sales from our own shop will be made for cash.

5 Budget administration overheads at £20,000 per month.

6 The bank is charging us interest on the overdraft at a monthly rate of 0.75% of the balance at the end of the previous month.

Workbook Activity 14

Michael George Ltd is a new company with no trading history. They intend to sell plastic garden gnomes and have approached their bankers who have insisted on a cash flow forecast for the first 6 months to 30 June 20X6. The following data is predicted by the directors.

(a) They expect that 10% of sales will be settled in the month of sale, 50% in the month following, 35% two months after with 5% not collected.

(b) In January they only expect sales of £2,000 but these are expected to rise to £5,000 in February, £8,000 in March, £10,000 in April and peak at £15,000 in May and June.

(c) Purchases are 50% of the value of sales.

(d) The company has already bought, in December, sufficient gnomes to meet the January sales. It intends to continue to buy sufficient gnomes each month to cover the following month's sales. The December purchases are not due to be paid for until February, but all subsequent purchases are to be paid for in the month following purchase.

(e) The company will pay salaries of £1,500 per month, rent of £2,000 per quarter paid in advance commencing January, and general expenses of £750 per month.

(f) The company has been offered a government grant of £10,000 but it will not be received until June 20X6. The shareholders will pay £5,000 for their shares with the money being received in January. A truck costing £6,000 will be purchased in January and paid for on delivery.

(g) The bank has indicated that it would charge interest on any borrowing at the rate of 6% per annum. It should be calculated on the balance at the month end and paid in the following month.

Draw up the cash flow budget for the first 6 months of 20X6 and suggest what overdraft facility should be requested.

Monitoring cash flows

5

Introduction

This chapter considers how cash flows will be monitored, how the cash flow forecast will be compared to the actual cash flows, and the importance of this area for management.

ASSESSMENT CRITERIA
Monitor cash receipts and payments against budgeted cash flow (3.1S)
Identify significant deviations from the cash budget and take corrective action within organisational policies (3.2S)

CONTENTS

1 Monitoring cash flow

1.1 Introduction

Once a cash budget has been drawn up, the management of the business are in a position to plan their working capital requirements. Knowing the business's projected cash position, it is possible to estimate:

- the need for cash and the ability to finance this
- the possible sources from which any shortfall can be financed
- what to do with any surplus cash.

As well as using the cash budget to identify any anticipated surplus or deficit in future periods, it is also important to monitor the actual performance of the business compared to the budgeted performance. This is part of the management process of control whereby the actual cash flows are compared to the budgeted cash flows and any significant variances between the two are highlighted and investigated.

1.2 Comparison of actual to budgeted cash flows

For each item in the cash budget the actual cash flow can be compared to the budgeted cash flow. Any significant differences should be investigated to determine why the variance happened and to consider how this can be dealt with in terms of future operations or future budgeting.

Example

Given below are the actual and budgeted cash flows for the month of April:

	Budget	*Actual*
	£	£
Cash sales	9,000	6,400
Receipts from receivables	34,000	27,800
Payments to payables	(16,700)	(20,500)
Production wages	(3,600)	(3,600)
Administration costs	(2,000)	(2,100)
Capital expenditure	–	(14,000)
Net cash flow	20,700	(6,000)

Calculate the percentage change from the budget and state what the most significant variance is?

Solution

- Cash sales are £2,600 less than budgeted, a drop of nearly 29% from budget.
- Receipts from receivables are £6,200 less than budgeted, a drop of just over 18% from budget.
- Payments to payables are £3,800 more than budgeted, an increase of nearly 28% on budget.
- Production wages have matched budget.
- Administration costs are £100 more than budget, an increase of 5%.
- There is capital expenditure of £14,000 which was not budgeted for.

The most significant variance is the omission of the capital expenditure from the budget. This needs to be investigated.

Other significant variances include the reduction in cash sales with a 29% decline from budget and the payments to payable with an increase of 28% on budget.

1.3 Reconciliation of budgeted cash balance to actual cash balance

After determining the variances between the actual and budgeted cash flows for the period then it should be possible to use these differences to reconcile the budgeted cash balance at the end of the period to the actual cash balance. This provides a useful summary, to the management of the business, of the causes of the unexpected actual position.

Example

Given below are the actual and budgeted cash flows for April:

	Budget	*Actual*
	£	£
Cash sales	9,000	6,400
Receipts from receivables	34,000	27,800
Payments to payables	(16,700)	(20,500)
Production wages	(3,600)	(3,600)
Administration costs	(2,000)	(2,100)
Capital expenditure	–	(14,000)
Net cash flow	20,700	(6,000)
Opening cash balance	3,200	3,200
Closing cash balance	23,900	(2,800)

Prepare a reconciliation of the budgeted cash balance of £23,900 to the actual overdraft figure of £2,800 at the end of the month

Reconciliation of budgeted cash balance to actual cash balance.

	£
Budged cash balance at 30 April	23,900
Shortfall in cash sales	(2,600)
Shortfall in receipts from receivables	(6,200)
Additional payments to suppliers	(3,800)
Additional administration costs	(100)
Unbudgeted capital expenditure	(14,000)
Actual overdraft at 30 April	(2,800)

Activity 1

Following are the budget and actual figures for the last quarter.

	Budgeted £	*Actual* £
Receipts from receivables	94,875	98,214
Cash sales	10,250	9,750
Payments to payables	(52,741)	(56,254)
Cash purchases	(6,985)	(7,594)
Capital expenditure	–	(15,000)
Wages and salaries	(15,000)	(16,000)
General expenses	(19,584)	(18,745)
Net cash flow	10,815	(5,629)
Opening bank balance	8,800	8,800
Closing bank balance	19,615	3,171

Prepare the reconciliation below, selecting the appropriate description for each entry:

	£
Budgeted closing bank balance	
Surplus/shortfall in receipts from receivables	
Surplus/shortfall in cash sales	
Increase/decrease in payments to payables	
Increase/decrease in cash payments	
Increase/decrease in capital expenditure	
Increase/decrease in wages and salaries	
Increase/decrease in general expenses	
Actual closing bank balance	

Activity 2

Fastinfo Ltd

MEMO

To: Henry Naem

From: John Powell

Date: 14 January

Subject: Work for this week

Henry

I have left a copy of the cash flow forecast and actual cash flow for the final three months of last year on my desk. Please calculate the differences between actual and budget for the whole 3 months to reconcile the budgeted closing bank balance with the actual closing bank balance.

Cash flow forecast

	October	*November*	*December*
	£000	£000	£000
CASH RECEIVED			
Cash sales	1,200	1,100	1,100
Credit sales	1,100	1,150	1,200
TOTAL	2,300	2,250	2,300
CASH PAID			
Rent	250	250	250
Wages	38	35	37
Purchases	1,600	1,600	1,800
Selling/administration	28	29	29
TOTAL	1,916	1,914	2,116
Net cash flow	384	336	184
Opening cash balance	20	404	740
Closing cash balance	404	740	924

Actual cash flow

	October £000	*November* £000	*December* £000
CASH RECEIVED			
Cash sales	1,100	1,300	1,250
Credit sales	1,000	1,000	1,050
TOTAL	2,100	2,300	2,300
CASH PAID			
Rent	275	275	275
Wages	40	38	40
Purchases	1,500	1,650	1,750
Selling/administration	25	25	25
TOTAL	1,840	1,988	2,090
Net cash flow	260	312	210
Opening cash balance	20	280	592
Closing cash balance	280	592	802

Reconciliation of actual to budget

	Actual £	*Budget* £	£
Budgeted closing cash balance			
Cash sales			
Credit sales			
Rent			
Wages			
Purchases			
Selling/administration			
Actual closing cash balance			

1.4 Cause of variances between budget and actual cash flow

Variances between budget and actual cash flows can occur for a number of reasons. There are also a variety of courses of action available to minimise adverse variances or benefit from favourable variances.

Listed below are possible causes for adverse variances with possible courses of action.

Reduced receipts from receivables

Cause	Possible courses of action
Lower volume of sales than budgeted	• Increase marketing/advertising • Reduce price to be competitive • Offer deals e.g. Buy one get one free • Improve the product
Lower selling price than budgeted	• Check the deals being offered by salesmen • Check competition for their prices
Receipts taking longer to be collected from receivables	• Improve credit control/outsource debt collection • Change payment terms in contract • Offer a settlement discount for early payment

Increased payments

Cause	Possible courses of action
Higher price paid for raw materials	• Negotiate an early payment discount • Negotiate a trade or bulk discount • Change supplier
More materials required for production	• Change manufacturing techniques • Offer bonuses to employees for meeting usage targets • Investigate product requirement

Increase in labour costs	• Reduce overtime working • Offer bonuses to employees for meeting efficiency targets • Inexperienced staff take longer so look to increase training • Investigate the possibility of mechanisation/ computerisation of some tasks or processes
Increase in other costs i.e. electricity, rent etc	• May be little action that can be taken as these are not very controllable by the business. It may be that the original budget did not take into account price rises
Capital expenditure/receipts	
Payment or receipt made	• Make sure that all large items of expenditure are communicated to the budget manager

On the whole, favourable variances indicate that a working practice has improved i.e. labour costs are lower than budget; staff are working more efficiently therefore not working as much overtime to meet production or sales demand.

Unfortunately sometimes a favourable variance may mean that there has been an adverse variance somewhere else in the business. For example, labour costs are lower than expected (favourable); this could be caused by sales demand being lower than expected (adverse) so staff are not required to work as many hours. The favourable labour variance was not due to more efficient staff but due to a reduced demand for the product.

Example

Given below are the actual and budgeted cash flows for the month of April, along with the variance:

	Budget £	*Actual* £	*Variance* £
Cash sales	9,000	6,400	2,600A
Receipts from receivables	34,000	27,800	6,200A
Payments to payables	(16,700)	(20,500)	3,800A
Production wages	(3,600)	(3,600)	0
Administration costs	(2,000)	(2,100)	100A
Capital expenditure	–	(14,000)	14,000A
Net cash flow	20,700	(6,000)	

What may have caused these variances? How might the company have improved the cash flow for the period?

Solution

The most significant variance is the reduction in cash sales; this may be because more customers have taken credit. Receipts from credit sales have also declined so if more customers have taken credit sales then the collection of debts needs looking into.

Both cash and credit sales may have declined due to a drop in sales revenue.

Payments to payables have also increased, either due to increased purchase volume or cost or because payment is being demanded by the suppliers.

The combination of a reduction in receipts and an increase in payments may cause this business to have serious cash flow problems.

Production wages and administration costs are less of a concern.

Capital expenditure has occurred in the period that was not budgeted for. This may have been an oversight during budget creation or perhaps a machine failure occurred meaning that funds had to be spent to buy a replacement.

The company could have improved cash flow in the following ways:

- Better credit control and collection procedures leading to higher receipts from receivables.
- More advertising to keep the product in the public eye.

- Improvements to the products to increase the desirability of the product.
- Delaying payments to payables.
- Negotiating a settlement discount for prompt payments or longer credit terms with the suppliers.
- Postponing the capital expenditure.
- Purchasing the capital items using a lease or hire purchase terms rather than outright.
- Finding specific finance for the capital expenditure such as a bank loan.

Activity 3

Match each cause of a variance listed on the left with a possible course of action from the list on the right.

Cause	Course of action
Receipts are not coming in as planned	Check the competition
Payments are being made late to suppliers	Change supplier
Sales volume has decreased	Outsource credit control
Payments to suppliers have increased in value	Improve staff efficiency
Labour costs have increased	Negotiate an early settlement discount

Activity 4

Variances between budget and actual cash flows can occur for number of reasons. Match the variance below with the possible course of action.

Variance	Course of action
Labour costs have increased	Negotiate early settlement discount
Prices of raw materials have increased	Improve the product
Payments to suppliers are being made earlier	Buy in bulk to achieve discounts
Sales volumes have decreased	Reduce overtime working

Activity 5

Variances between budget and actual cash flows can occur for number of reasons. Match the variance below with the possible course of action.

Variance	Course of action
Suppliers are insisting on earlier payments	Improve communication
Customers are insisting on longer credit periods	Improve credit control
A new machine was bought that was not in the budget	Negotiate early settlement discount
Receipts from receivables is less than budget	Reduce discounts available

2 Summary

As well as using cash budgets in order to plan for anticipated deficits or surpluses, management will also need to compare the actual cash flows for a period to the budgeted cash flows as part of the process of control. Useful information for management will be a reconciliation between the budgeted cash balance at the end of the period and the actual cash balance, in order to highlight areas that can be improved in terms of operations or budgeting.

Answers to chapter activities

Activity 1

	£
Budgeted closing bank balance	19,615
Surplus in receipts from receivables	3,339
Shortfall in cash sales	–500
Increase in payments to payables	–3,513
Increase in cash payments	–609
Increase in capital expenditure	–15,000
Increase in wages and salaries	–1,000
Decrease in general expenses	839
Actual closing bank balance	3,171

Activity 2

Reconciliation of actual to budget

	Actual £000	*Budget* £000	£000
Budgeted closing bank balance			924
Cash sales	3,650	3,400	250
Credit sales	3,050	3,450	–400
Rent	825	750	–75
Wages	118	110	–8
Purchases	4,900	5,000	100
Selling/administration	75	86	11
Actual closing bank balance			802

Activity 3

Receipts are not coming in as planned	Outsource credit control
Payments are being made late to suppliers	Negotiate an early settlement discount
Sales volume has decreased	Check the competition
Payments to suppliers have increased in value	Change supplier
Labour costs have increased	Improve staff efficiency

Activity 4

Labour costs have increased	Reduce overtime working
Prices of raw materials have increased	Buy in bulk to achieve discounts
Payments to suppliers are being made earlier	Negotiate early settlement discount
Sales volumes have decreased	Improve the product

Activity 5

Suppliers are insisting on earlier payments	Negotiate early settlement discount
Customers are insisting on longer credit periods	Reduce discounts available
A new machine was bought that was not in the budget	Improve communication
Receipts from receivables is less than budget	Improve credit control

3 Test your knowledge

Workbook Activity 6

Given below are the actual and budgeted cash flows for the month of October for a business:

	Actual £	*Budget* £
Receipts from receivables	106,000	132,400
Payments to suppliers	(79,000)	(70,000)
Production wages	(17,500)	(17,000)
Production expenses	(1,500)	(1,000)
Selling expenses	(3,400)	(4,000)
Administration expenses	(4,100)	(4,100)
Dividend	(20,000)	
Net cash flow	(19,500)	36,300
Opening cash balance	10,000	10,000
Closing cash balance	(9,500)	46,300

(a) Reconcile the actual cash balance at the end of October to the budgeted cash balance at that date.

	£
Budgeted closing bank balance	
Surplus/(Shortfall) in receipts from receivables	
(Increase)/decrease in payments to suppliers	
(Increase)/decrease in production wages	
(Increase)/decrease in production expenses	
(Increase)/decrease in selling expenses	
Other –	
Actual closing bank balance	

(b) What one action could the organisation have taken to avoid an overdrawn bank balance?

A Chased customers to pay sooner

B Delayed payments to suppliers

C Avoided dividend payment

D Reduced selling expenses

Workbook Activity 7

Variances between budget and actual cash flows can occur for number of reasons. Match the variance below with the possible course of action.

Variance	Course of action
Customers are buying lower value products	Improve credit control by agreeing invoices before they are posted
Customers are taking more days to settle their debts	Actively market more expensive product lines
Electricity cost increases	Offer a settlement discount
Customers are delaying payments due to invoice queries	Install energy saving lights

Liquidity management

6

Introduction

The effective management of cash is not something that can be undertaken in isolation or without an awareness of the general financial environment in which organisations operate.

ASSESSMENT CRITERIA

Explain how government monetary policies affect an organisation's treasury functions (4.1K)

Identify the principles of liquidity management (4.2K)

Describe how an organisation's principles of cash management will be determined by their specific financial regulations, guidelines and security procedures (4.3K)

Identify statutory and other regulations relating to the management of cash balances in different types of organisations (4.4K)

CONTENTS

1 Liquidity

1.1 Liquidity

Liquidity is the measure of surplus cash and near cash, over that level required to meet obligations. The main sources of liquidity are usually:

- cash in the bank
- short term investments that can be cashed in easily and quickly
- cash inflows from normal trading operations (cash sales and payments by receivables for credit sales)
- an overdraft facility or other ready source of extra borrowing

2 Working capital cycle

2.1 Working capital

Definition

Working capital is the short-term net assets of the business made up of inventory, receivables, payables and cash.

Working capital is the capital available for conducting the day to day operations of an organisation. It is normally expressed as the excess of current assets over current liabilities.

Working capital management is the management of all aspects of both current assets and current liabilities, to minimise the risk of insolvency whilst maximising the return on assets.

2.2 Working capital cycle

The working capital cycle or the **cash operating cycle** is the length of time between the company's outlay on raw materials, wages and other expenditures and the inflow of cash from the sale of goods. The faster a firm can 'push' items around the cycle the lower its investment in working capital will be.

Working capital is an investment which affects cash flows:

When inventory is purchased, cash is paid to acquire it

Receivables represent the cost of selling goods or services to customers, including the costs of materials and the labour incurred.

The cash tied up in working capital is reduced to the extent that inventory is finance by trade payables. If suppliers give a firm time to pay, the firm's cash flows are improved and working capital is reduced.

The working capital cycle:

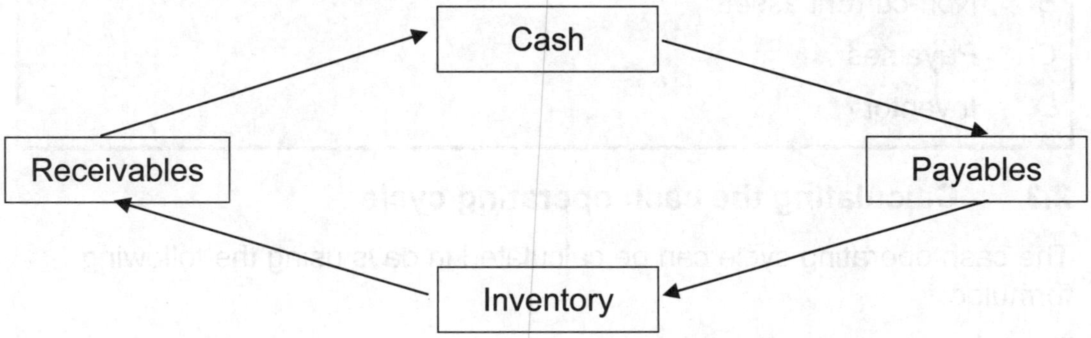

Time line:

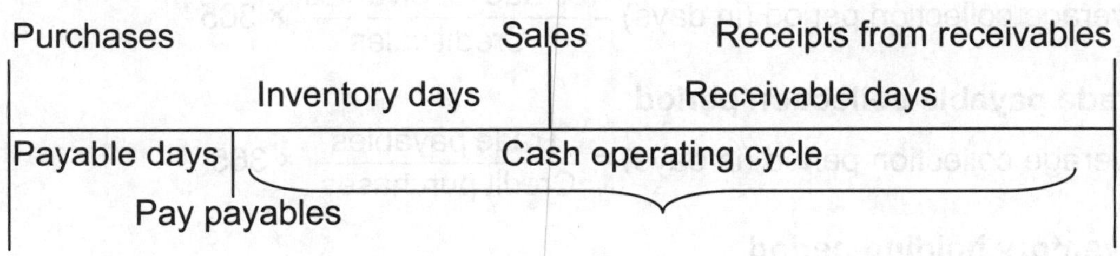

The length of the cycle depends on:

- how the balancing act between liquidity and profitability is resolved
- the efficiency of management
- the nature of the industry

The optimum level is the amount that results in no idle cash or unused inventory, but that does not put a strain on liquid resources. Trying to shorten the cash cycle may have detrimental effects elsewhere, with the organisation lacking the cash to meet its commitments and losing sales since customers will generally prefer to buy from suppliers who are prepared to extend trade credit, and who have items available when required.

Additionally, any assessment of the acceptability or otherwise of the length of the cycle must take into account the nature of the business involved. A supermarket chain will tend to have a very low or negative cycle – they have very few, if any, credit customers, they have a high inventory turnover and they can negotiate quite long credit periods with their suppliers.

Activity 1

Which of the following is not part of the working capital cycle?

A Receivables

B Non-current assets

C Payables

D Inventory

2.3 Calculating the cash operating cycle

The cash operating cycle can be calculated in days using the following formulae:

Trade receivable collection period

$$\text{Average collection period (in days)} = \frac{\text{Trade receivables}}{\text{Credit sales}} \times 365$$

Trade payable collection period

$$\text{Average collection period (in days)} = \frac{\text{Trade payables}}{\text{Credit purchases}} \times 365$$

Inventory holding period

$$\text{Average holding period (in days)} = \frac{\text{Inventory}}{\text{Cost of sales}} \times 365$$

Note: In some instances it may not be possible to locate the figures for credit sales or credit purchases in which case the next best item is used i.e. sales or revenue for receivable days and purchases or cost of sales for payable days.

The cash operating cycle is then calculated as:

Inventory holding period + Receivable days – Payable days

Example

Below are the relevant details from the statement of financial position and statement of profit or loss from Josh plc. Calculate the cash operating cycle.

Statement of financial position

	£000	£000
Current assets		
Inventories	500	
Trade receivables	1,000	
Cash and cash equivalents	200	
	1,700	
Trade payables	(900)	
		800

Statement of profit or loss

	£000
Revenue	5,000
Cost of sales	(3,000)
Gross profit	2,000
Operating expenses	(500)
Profit for the year	1,500

$$\text{Inventory days} = \frac{\text{inventory}}{\text{cost of sales}} \times 365 = \frac{500}{3{,}000} \times 365 = 60.8 \text{ days}$$

$$\text{Receivable days} = \frac{\text{receivables}}{\text{credit sales}} \times 365 = \frac{1{,}000}{5{,}000} \times 365 = 73 \text{ days}$$

$$\text{Payable days} = \frac{\text{payables}}{\text{credit purchases}} \times 365 = \frac{900}{3{,}000} \times 365 = 109.5 \text{ days}$$

Working capital cycle = 60.8 + 73 – 109.5 = 24.3 days

Activity 2

Which is the correct formula for the working capital cycle?

A Receivable days – inventory days – payable days

B Receivable days – inventory days + payable days

C Receivable days + inventory days – payable days

D Receivable days + inventory days + payable days

Activity 3

A business has an average inventory holding period of 45 days receives payment from its customers in 30 days and pays its payables in 38 days. What is the cash operating cycle in days for the business?

A 23 days

B 53 days

C 37 days

D 113 days

Activity 4

A business has an average inventory holding period of 100 days, received payment from its customers in 60 days and pays its payables in 80 days. What is the cash operating cycle in days for the business?

A 120 days

B 80 days

C 40 days

D 240 days

Activity 5

A business provides the following information:

Trade receivables	£4m
Trade payables	£2m
Inventory	£4.3m
Sales (80% on credit)	£30m
Material purchases (all on credit)	£18m
Cost of sales	£25m

Calculate the businesses cash operating cycle?

Activity 6

(a) If a business has an average inventory holding period of 30 days, a trade payable payment period of 45 days and a trade receivables collection period of 40 days, what is the cash operating cycle?

(b) If the business above increased its inventory holding period by 3 days and increased the time it takes to pay its payables by 5 days, what is the impact on the cash operating cycle?

3 Overtrading

3.1 Overtrading

Overtrading usually occurs when a company tries to **expand too quickly** and **over-stretches its working capital** due to inadequate financing for its growth rate. If **sales increase too rapidly**, then working capital requirements may increase as **more money is tied up in inventories** of raw materials to support the increased sales levels; **receivables will also rise**. This can lead to a situation in which the company is operating at a profit but suffers a liquidity crisis as it has insufficient cash to pay its bills and expenses.

This problem happens over a period of time, with the working capital gradually being stretched and without the managers of the company realising what is happening as the company continues to be profitable. The statement of financial position eventually reveals the problem.

3.2 Identifying signs of overtrading

Signs of overtrading can be identified as follows:

- sharply and rapidly increasing sales volumes
- falling profit margins despite increased sales as higher discounts are given to attract more customers and production costs increase due to overtime costs, etc
- greater reliance on short-term funding such as overdrafts
- longer receivable/payable collection ratios.

3.3 Controlling overtrading

Planned overtrading is not dangerous; it is the unmanaged and undetected overtrading that causes company downfalls.

If, however, the symptoms of unmanaged overtrading are detected, then the problem may be averted by:

- issuing new share capital or loan stock
- taking out long-term loans rather than overdrafts
- reducing the operating cycle by controlling receivables and payables
- slowing down the company's expansion.

3.4 Over-capitalisation

The opposite of overtrading is over-capitalisation. There is too much cash. Consequently profit is suppressed in relation to the capital investment in the company and earnings per £ of capital are low. Unless this surplus can be invested by the company to earn a good return, it could be distributed to shareholders through a higher dividend or a buyback of shares.

Activity 7

Overtrading can occur when working capital levels are too high.

True or false?

Over-capitalisation can occur when working capital levels are too low.

True or false?

Which of the following are signs of overtrading?

A Rapidly decreasing sales volumes

B Rapidly increasing sales volumes

C Increased profit margins

D Falling profit margins

E Short receivable collection periods

F Longer receivable collection periods

G Shorter payable payment periods

H Longer payable payment periods

I Greater reliance on short term funding

J Less reliance on short term funding

4 The treasury function and the Government

4.1 Introduction

Many large companies have a separate **treasury department** which deals with **investing of surplus funds and the raising of finance**. In smaller companies this role normally falls to the accounts department. Whoever is in charge of this function, care must be taken to ensure that although **surplus cash is invested profitably**, excessive risks are not taken. There are many highly speculative and highly risky financial instruments on the market which although they may yield very high returns, can lead to huge losses.

The aim of the treasury activities in a trading company is to earn a **reasonable return on any surplus cash, but not to speculate**.

4.2 The treasury function

In order to manage the cash balance effectively, the treasury manager needs information about both the **long-term** and **short-term** cash flow figures. From the cash budget, the future can be predicted. However, the day-to-day balance needs to be monitored and controlled to ensure the actual balance approximates to the budgeted figures and is not in deficit.

The company's systems need to be looked at every day to ensure sufficient funds are available. The timing of the cash flows needs to be ascertained day by day to ensure money is banked quickly and prior to large payments being made to suppliers, etc. Short-term daily cash flows are as important to the company's liquidity as the longer-term forecasts.

The department will usually follow the **company's rules and procedures**.

4.3 The Government and the Bank of England

The Government can affect an organisation's treasury function by controlling the supply of money, interest rates and the availability of credit. Governments have two main ways of affecting the economy:

- Fiscal policy refers to the government's taxation and spending plans.
- Monetary policy refers to the management of the money supply (the total amount of money, including currency in circulation and deposited in banks and building societies) in the economy.

The Bank of England is the UK's central or national bank charged with overall control of the banking system in the interest of the nation.

In particular, monetary policy involves the changing of interest rates or varying of the amount of money that banks need to keep in reserve.

The Government and the Bank of England will want to try to maintain a stable economy and will change tax rates and interest rates to try to balance out any boom and bust periods.

Example

2008 global recession

VAT reductions

During the global recession of 2008, the UK government temporarily reduced the level of VAT to 15%. This had the effect of making consumer's purchases cheaper, increasing their confidence and meaning that their wages were able to buy more goods.

This was used as a way of stimulating the economy and boosting demand in a period when the UK economy was struggling.

Interest rates

Meanwhile, the Bank of England started significantly reducing interest rates. This was an attempt to make it cheaper for businesses to borrow funds.

The additional investment in businesses that this caused was also designed to boost demand.

The Bank of England is in the control of the UK government. The Governor, Deputy Governor and 16 directors are appointed by the Sovereign on the recommendation of the Prime Minister. Consequently, the Treasury is able to implement government policies through:

(a) the use of **monetary policy** – actions that determine the size and rate of growth of the money supply, which in turn affects interest rates. The aim of any monetary policy is to keep the economy stable.

(b) the Bank's overall control of the **banking system**, and

(c) the Bank's influence over the financial institutions.

The Bank of England acts as the government's bank in the widest possible sense, i.e. examining and anticipating banking problems.

4.4 The Bank of England and the treasury function

The Bank of England has control over interest rates which will influence what an organisations treasury function may wish to do with any surplus funds.

When **interest rates** are **low**:

- Money is less expensive to **borrow** so people will spend more.
- This can create employment opportunities and expansion within businesses that require capital investment.
- It will also create **inflation**.

Definition

Inflation is the rise in the prices of goods and services within an economy over time. It reduces the purchasing power of money, meaning that each £ sterling buys fewer goods and services.

Most governments want stable prices and low inflation. This is because high levels of inflation tend to have the following problems:

- As prices rise, consumers may purchase fewer goods, reducing growth in the economy.
- Employees will push for higher pay rises, in order to match price rises. This can lead to problems for businesses.

- Other costs (such as raw materials) will also rise for businesses, possibly leading to reductions in investment and production.
- Consumer confidence may be damaged due to uncertainty in the future prices of goods and services.
- People on fixed incomes (such as students or pensioners) may find themselves worse off, as their income will not rise even though the cost of goods has increased.

When **interest rates** are **high:**

- Money is more expensive to borrow which leads to higher levels of **saving or investing**.
- The government will reduce inflation rates to try to encourage people to spend money.

The interest rate position will impact on what a business decides to invest in as this will impact on the cost of capital and thus the level of return an investment makes.

If interest rates are low the treasury function is likely to invest less in external opportunities as the surplus funds may be required to meet internal expansion or requirements. If interest rates are high then the treasury function is more likely to invest any surplus funds to receive a return for the future.

4.5 Quantitative easing

Quantitative easing is a relatively unconventional monetary policy that involves Bank of England buying financial assets (such as government and corporate bonds) using money that it has generated electronically. Put more simply, the central bank has essentially printed itself new money that it can spend (although in practice it is unusual for the money to actually be printed). This has the effect of increasing the amount of cash within the economy, hopefully increasing aggregate demand. However, it can cause increased inflation and exchange rates.

> **Note**: It is important that you are aware of how the banking sector is structured, the relationship between different financial institutions and understand that legal relationships exist between lenders and borrowers.
>
> The CSHM assessment tasks may contain some technical financial terms to add reality to a task. The rest of this chapter aims to explain some of the more common terms.

5 The UK banking system

5.1 Introduction

There will always be individuals, partnerships, companies and governments with surplus funds. They will want to invest their excess funds to earn a return.

Similarly, there will always be entities without enough funds. For example, an individual might want to buy a car or a house, a company might want to undertake an ambitious expansion project, or a government might want to buy an expensive weapons system.

The financial system brings both groups together; its intermediaries act as links in the chains joining savers and borrowers. The system is seen at its simplest when individuals deposit their savings at the bank, which then lends the money on to others, but the path can get much more complicated.

5.2 Financial intermediation

Why are the intermediaries needed? Why don't the savers and borrowers get together directly and save the costs which the intermediaries involve? The reason is that financial intermediation brings benefits as follows.

- **'Maturity transformation'** occurs, in which deposits by customers, usually short term, and are lent out to borrowers for much longer periods of time.
- The **risk profile** of a saver is reduced. If financial intermediaries did not exist, a person or organisation with money to lend would have to seek out a potential borrower, who might eventually default. An intermediary is likely to aggregate the deposits of individual depositors for the purpose of granting fewer but more substantial advances, whilst reducing or eliminating the risk of default to savers.
- Intermediaries also provide **considerable benefits to borrowers**, who might otherwise have difficulty locating potential savers who are willing to lend appropriate amounts of funds at reasonable interest rates. Moreover, the use of a financial institution will provide **greater flexibility for borrowers** in that they almost certainly will be permitted to repay loans earlier than originally specified if circumstances permit, or reschedule debts if they have cash flow problems. It is unlikely that, with direct saving and lending, these provisions would be possible.

5.3 Types of financial institutions

There are many different types of financial institutions that play some role in the operation of securities and other capital markets. Some act solely in the role of intermediary, collecting money from investors and passing it on to borrowers; others act as investors/borrowers in their own right. We shall now look at some of the most common types of institution:

- brokers – stock and money
- banks – clearing and merchant
- institutional investors – pension funds, insurance companies, investment and unit trusts
- venture capitalists.

5.4 Brokers

Brokers, in their purest form, act as **agents for investors** who wish to buy or sell shares or funds. They seek out a source or outlet for the required shares or funds and act as a go between in settling price and other terms of the deal. Their profits are generally made by commission and fees.

5.5 Banks

There are two main types of banks in the UK: primary and secondary banks. **Primary banks** are those which operate the **money transmission service** in the economy, the banks which operate cheque accounts and deal with cheque clearing. These are often known as the **commercial banks, retail banks or clearing banks.**

The **secondary banks** consist of a wide range of **merchant banks**, other British banks and foreign banks in the UK. They do not tend to take part in the cheque clearing system.

5.6 Types of deposit

Banks take deposits from customers.

The banks offer a variety of deposit facilities to their customers, one useful distinction being between retail deposits and wholesale deposits.

5.7 Retail deposits

Those banks which operate an extensive branch network obtain a substantial proportion of their sterling resources as retail deposits: **current account deposits** held by individuals or organisations in connection with their ordinary payments and receipts, and other **interest-bearing deposits** held as a supplementary store of liquidity.

Retail banking is the **traditional high street banking** with relatively small deposits from and loans to customers.

5.8 Wholesale deposits

Wholesale deposits are **large interest-bearing deposits** – usually of at least £50,000 – on which the interest rate is negotiated. Deposits may be received directly from customers or indirectly through money brokers. The market is very competitive and the rate paid for funds is generally identical for institutions of the same standing. Sources of wholesale deposits include institutions at home and abroad, large companies, non-bank financial institutions and other banks with temporary surplus funds.

The **certificate of deposit (CD) is a particular type of wholesale deposit**. The CD is a document issued by a bank certifying that a deposit has been made with that bank which is repayable to the bearer on surrender of the certificate at maturity. A CD is a negotiable instrument so that, while the bank has a deposit for a fixed term, the depositor has the option of obtaining cash before maturity by selling the certificate in the market.

5.9 Lending facilities

The banks offer a variety of lending facilities to their customers with terms varying according to the type of lending and customer involved.

(a) Companies are offered overdraft and term lending, syndicated loan finance and services such as instalment credit, leasing and factoring which are often provided through subsidiaries.

(b) Personal customers get overdraft and bridging finance, personal loans, revolving credit and budget accounts, instalment credit (often through subsidiaries) and credit card finance.

5.10 Relationship of the banker and customer

There are **four main contractual relationships** between the banker and the customer.

The **debtor/creditor relationship** where the customer deposits his money with the bank and the bank becomes the debtor and the customer, the creditor. If the customer's account is overdrawn, however, the bank becomes the creditor and the customer the debtor.

There are a number of essential areas in this element of the contract:

- The bank must receive cheques for the customer's account.
- The bank borrows the customer's deposits and undertakes to repay them.
- The bank will only cease to do business with the customer with reasonable notice.
- The bank is not liable to pay until the customer demands payment.
- The customer exercises reasonable care when writing cheques.

The **bailor/bailee relationship** concerns the bank accepting the customer's property for storage in its safe deposit. The bank undertakes to take reasonable care to safeguard the property against loss or damage and then re-deliver it only to the customer or someone authorised by the customer.

The **principal/agent relationship** where, for example, the customer pays a crossed cheque into the bank, the bank acts as agent when presenting the cheque for payment and paying the proceeds into the customer's account.

The **mortgagor/mortgagee relationship** exists where the bank asks the customer to secure a loan with a charge over the customer's assets. If the customer does not repay the loan then the bank can sell the asset and use the proceeds to pay off the loan.

5.11 Services offered by merchant banks

Merchant banks may be subsidiaries of clearing banks, part of a large financial group of companies, or independent. Their main functions include:

- **Provision of financial advice** – mainly to larger commercial companies, on such aspects as the raising of finance, the investment of cash surpluses, and merger and acquisition activities. Such assistance can contribute significantly to a firm's financial management strategy.
- **Provision of finance** – merchant banks specialise in the provision of large, longer term lending through the money markets. They also have specialised 'issuing houses' that handle share and other security issues.

5.12 Institutional investors

Only about 20–25% of quoted company shares in the UK are currently held by private individuals.

The vast majority of equity finance for quoted companies comes from institutional investors, in particular the pension funds.

The most important types of institutional investors are:

Pension fund – buys securities with the pension contributions it receives. These produce income to pay current pensioners, and provide for the need to pay future pensioners.

Insurance company – buys securities with the insurance premiums it receives. These produce income to pay for claims (for example, when life assurance policies mature) and provide for future claims.

Investment trust – buys securities with the money raised by selling shares in the trust. The income and capital gains produced are distributed amongst the shareholders in the trust.

Unit trust – buys securities with the money raised by selling units in the trust. These produce income and capital gains to give the unit holders a return on their investment.

5.13 Venture capitalists

Venture capital is a **source of long-term (mainly equity) finance** where the investor relies on growth rather than income and is prepared to accept much greater risk.

It is normally provided under the condition of 'hands-on', the venture capitalist having a continuing involvement in the business of the company.

It is not subject to repayment on demand at a specified time, and realisation occurs only on the sale of the company or on flotation.

Venture capital is therefore a potentially valuable source of capital for small companies which would not prove attractive to the average investor on the Stock Exchange.

6 The Bank of England

6.1 The Bank of England's role as a banker

The Bank acts as banker:

(a) to the government

(b) to foreign central banks and international organisations.

All commercial banks have a bank account with the Bank which is used to settle debts between each other and to pay amounts due to the government.

6.2 The Bank of England's operations in the markets

- The Bank ensures implementation of government policy to control the economy by controlling the money market for short-term loans by the issue of Treasury bills.
- The Bank issues long-term government debt, referred to as gilt-edged securities or gilts.
- The Bank sets interest rates via a committee appointed by the government.
- The Bank manages the exchange rate to protect the pound. If sterling's value is too high the Bank sells sterling for foreign currencies, if its value is too low the Bank will buy sterling with its foreign currency reserves.
- The Bank meets the government's long-term borrowing requirements by open market operations on the Stock Exchange. The Bank is a lender of last resort and will provide funds for banks which are short of cash.

7 The money markets

7.1 Introduction

The term money markets covers a vast array of markets **buying and selling different forms of money or marketable securities**, which are short-term highly liquid investments that are readily convertible into cash. The money markets provide the financial institutions with a means of borrowing and investing to deal with short-term fluctuations.

The main traders in the money markets are banks, the government through the Bank of England, local authorities, brokers, jobbers and other intermediaries in the market.

7.2 Money market financial instruments

The main types of financial instrument that are traded in the money markets are:

- **Bills** – short-term financial assets that can be converted into cash by selling them in the discount market.
- **Deposits** – money in the bank accounts of banks and other financial intermediaries.
- **Commercial paper** – IOUs issued by large companies which can be either held to maturity or sold to third parties.
- **Certificates of deposit** (CDs) – a certificate for deposits of £50,000 or more for a fixed term which can be sold earlier than maturity in the CD market.

7.3 The primary market

This market consists of the **banks and securities firms and the Bank of England**. The primary market is used by the Bank to smooth out fluctuations in cash balances by buying bills and other short-term financial instruments from the financial institutions in order to provide more cash, and selling government bills to deal with any surplus cash.

7.4 The local authority market

In this market the local authorities borrow short-term funds by issuing local authority bills with a maturity of about one year.

7.5 The inter-bank market

This is a market for very short-term borrowing, often overnight, between the banks. It is used to smooth fluctuations in the banks' receipts and payments.

7.6 The foreign exchange market

Like the money market, the foreign exchange market operates through the general offices of its constituent banks. The aim of the foreign exchange dealers is to **secure supplies of foreign currency** as required to finance international trade.

The price of foreign currency is determined by demand and supply i.e. the demand for the country's goods and services by foreigners, and the supply of overseas goods and services which its own home nationals wish to buy.

7.7 The capital market

Many institutions apart from banks are used to provide capital, such as:

(a) **Issuing houses** who issue new shares or debentures for expanding firms.

(b) **Building societies** that collect funds for those wishing to purchase their own home.

(c) **Finance houses** who deal in the more risky but more profitable hire purchase field for financing purchase of consumer goods (e.g. cars).

(d) **Investment trusts and unit trusts** which accumulate small amounts from many individuals and purchase a balanced portfolio of investments, thus providing a good source of fixed capital for industry.

(e) **Insurance companies** who have large sums to invest from premiums received from insuring the public.

(f) The **Stock Exchange** which raises long-term capital not only via the provision of a market for existing stocks and shares but also by issuing new shares.

7.8 The Stock Exchange

Stock exchanges are based in many of the world's financial centres – such as New York, Tokyo and Paris. The function of such exchanges is to provide a **market place for the buying and selling of stocks and shares** so that companies can raise long-term finance and investors can buy or sell shares.

The Stock Exchange also provides a market for **government bonds or gilts.**

8 Summary

In this chapter we have looked at how important the management of cash and liquid funds are the running and maintenance of a business. Mis-management of working capital can lead to a business overtrading and possibly going out of business due to a lack of cash to pay for debts.

The chapter has also covered the main operations of the banks, the money markets and the Bank of England. The primary or retail banks deal in the transmission of money as high street banks, whereas the secondary banks deal with the wholesale business.

The Bank of England plays an important role in controlling the banking system and operating the government's monetary policy and regulation of interest rates. Interest rates are controlled by the Bank in the primary market and short-term finance is provided to banks, financial institutions and large commercial organisations through the secondary market which is made up of the local authority market, the inter-bank market, the CD market, the inter-company market and the commercial paper market.

Answers to chapter activities

Activity 1

Answer B

Non-current assets are not part of the working capital cycle – current assets are.

Activity 2

Answer C

Receivable days + inventory days – payable days

Activity 3

Answer C

45 + 30 – 38 = 37 days

Activity 4

Answer B

100 + 60 – 80 = 80 days

Activity 5

Receivable days = 4/(30 × 0.8) × 365 = 61 days

Inventory days = 4.3/25 × 365 = 63 days

Payable days = 2/18 × 365 = 41 days

Operating cycle = 61 + 63 – 41 = 83 days

Activity 6

(a) 30 days + 40 days – 45 days = 25 days

(b) 33 days + 40 days – 50 days = 23 days

The cash operating cycle will decrease by 2 days – the increase in inventory holding days increases the length of the cycle, the increase in the payment period decreases the length of the cycle – the net effect is a decrease of 2 days.

Activity 7

Overtrading can occur when working capital levels are too high.

False

Over-capitalisation can occur when working capital levels are too low.

False

Which of the following are signs of overtrading?

B Rapidly increasing sales volumes

D Falling profit margins

F Longer receivable collection periods

H Longer payable payment periods

I Greater reliance on short term funding

9 Test your knowledge

Workbook Activity 8

Fill in the blanks in the diagram of the working capital cycle below:

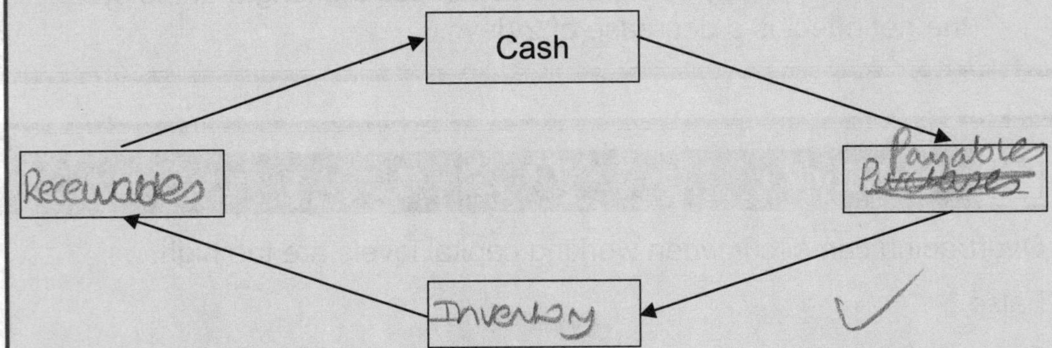

Workbook Activity 9

Overtrading can occur when working capital levels are too low.

True or false?

Over-capitalisation can occur when working capital levels are too high.

True or false?

7 Raising finance

Introduction

In an earlier chapter we saw that one of the purposes of preparing a cash flow forecast was in order for the management of a company to be able to forecast whether there is likely to be any cash surplus or cash deficit in the future periods.

If a cash deficit is forecast then management will need to make arrangements well in advance for how to deal with that deficit. In this chapter we consider different ways that finance can be raised.

ASSESSMENT CRITERIA

Take account of trends in the economic and financial environment in managing cash balances (4.5S)

Observe the organisation's financial regulations and security procedures (4.6S)

Manage cash, overdrafts and loans in order to maintain an adequate level of liquidity in line with cash forecasts (4.7S)

Explain how an organisation can raise finance and the basic terms and conditions associated with each of these types of financing (5.1K)

Anticipate cash requirements and arrange overdraft and loan facilities on the most favourable terms available (5.2S)

CONTENTS

1 Raising finance

1.1 Introduction

Any business will have an initial amount of capital which is either contributed by the owner or, in the case of a company, is issued share capital. However at various stages in the business life cycle the management may find that there is a need to raise additional finance.

1.2 Reasons for additional finance

There are many reasons why a business may need to raise additional finance but the most common are:

- to fund working capital
- to increase working capital
- to reduce payables
- to purchase non-current assets
- to acquire another business.

The need to raise the finance may be highlighted by a deficit in the cash budget, by management decisions regarding investment in non-current assets, or by the business strategy of growth by acquisition.

1.3 Funding working capital

One of the most common reasons for additional finance which is normally highlighted by a deficit in the cash budget is in order to fund working capital. The working capital of a business will have an operating cycle which is effectively the period between the payment of money for goods and the receipt of money from receivables. If payables are being paid more quickly than money is being received from receivables then at some time it is likely that the business will require funds to tide them over until the money from the receivables is received.

1.4 Increasing working capital

After a period of operating, a business may find that it needs an increase in its working capital. This may be due to **increased sales turnover** which in turn requires **increases in inventories and receivables**. The business may be able to gain additional credit from its trade payables but in the absence of that may have to raise funds to finance this increase. Care should be taken in such circumstances to ensure that the business is not overtrading.

Alternatively the additional finance required might be due to an increase in receivables. This might be due to inefficiencies in the credit control of the business or it may be that increased credit has had to be offered to customers in order to keep their custom in a competitive market or to increase market share and sales turnover.

Often additional finance might be required due to an increase in inventory levels which is not associated with a general increase in turnover. Such an inventory increase will normally only be temporary and could be due to:

- taking advantage of an attractive price by placing a bulk order
- building up inventories in advance of a peak period in a seasonal business
- receipt of a large order from a customer

1.5 Reduction of payables

A business may need to reduce its trade payables either in order to **take advantage of settlement discounts** or due to the fact that trade payables may be pressing the business for quicker payment for their own reasons. This reduction in trade credit will need to be funded by some other source of finance. If payables are to be paid earlier, then the cash to do this will have to be found.

Equally additional finance might be required for the short term to fund payments such as **quarterly VAT payments** or the **annual Corporation Tax payment**.

1.6 Purchase of non-current assets

Not only will a business require enough cash to pay its payables and expenses, such as wages, when they fall due, but most businesses will also need to **invest in additional or replacement non-current assets** on a fairly regular basis. In many cases a business will not have enough cash to purchase the non-current assets required to maintain or expand operations and will therefore need to raise finance in order to fund the purchase.

1.7 Acquisition of another business

Many businesses have a policy of growth by acquisition of other businesses. Such a major amount of expenditure will almost always require funding by some form of external finance.

1.8 Controls on the raising of finance

Public organisations are organisations that are funded by the Government e.g. Schools, NHS trusts (hospitals etc), Local Government. These organisations have **strict funding** (cash) controls. They are required by Government to **balance their budgets** i.e. only spend the cash they have been granted and no more. Public organisations that fall into deficit are not allowed to source their own external finance.

Private organisations are allowed to source their own finance but they still have regulations to adhere to through the **Companies Act**.

1.9 The form of finance required

As we will see in the rest of this chapter many forms of external finance are available to a business. What is important is that the most appropriate form of finance is sought for the purpose for which the finance is required. Regard should therefore be had to the purpose of the finance and also to any internal regulations within the business regarding financing. For example the business may have a policy of ensuring a cash balance or undrawn overdraft facility of £20,000 is always available as a back-up. Such policies should always be adhered to.

In general terms the types of finance available can be categorised as:

- short term – anything up to 3 years
- medium term – 3–10 years
- long term – over 10 years

In the rest of this chapter we will consider all three of these types of finance but as a rule of thumb the time scale of the finance should match the time scale of the reason for the finance. Therefore if the finance is required for working capital reasons then the finance should be short term whereas if the finance is required for longer term investment in non-current assets or another business then the appropriate finance may be medium or long term.

2 Short term debt finance

2.1 Introduction

Short term debt finance is used for:

(a) temporary working capital

(b) bridging finance for assets being financed from the sale of existing assets

(c) purchase of short-lived assets.

The most common type of short term finance is a bank overdraft.

2.2 Bank overdraft

Bank overdrafts are most often negotiated for a **fixed period** in terms of a maximum available facility. In other words, the bank undertakes to advance anything up to, say £50,000, and the business can take advantage of the facility as and when it needs to. The **interest** will generally be at a **variable** rate, calculated on a day-to-day basis with reference to the bank's base rate. Although the interest rate on an overdraft may be higher than that which could be negotiated on a loan, the important point about overdraft interest is that it is calculated daily on the amount of the actual overdraft rather than on a fixed amount as would be the interest on a loan.

The principal advantage of an overdraft is **flexibility**. The business only pays interest on the amount actually drawn, although there may be an additional flat charge of perhaps 0.25% on the maximum facility.

Overdrafts are (technically) **repayable on demand** and should never be regarded as substitutes for adequate medium term finance.

Activity 1

Which of the following best describes the main features of an overdraft?

A Interest rates are low; it is repayable on demand; it is useful for capital purchases

B Interest rates are high; it is repayable on demand; it is useful for capital purchases

C Interest rates are low; it is repayable on demand; it is a short term form of finance

D Interest rates are high; it is repayable on demand; it is a short term form of finance

2.3 Short term bank loan

A term loan with a bank is a loan for a fixed amount, for an agreed period on pre-arranged terms. The loan can be tailored to meet the requirements of the borrower. It can be taken out for a period which matches the assets which it is financing and the repayment terms can be negotiated to match with the cash flows from the asset or the other business cash flows. The loan will be governed by formal documentation which will include:

- The term of the loan.
- The interest rate.
- The way in which the interest is charged.
- The repayment date/dates.
- Any security required for the loan.
- Any covenants attached to the loan.

Term loans can be for virtually any period and the repayment terms can be negotiated with the bank:

- Interest rates may be fixed or variable and they tend to be lower than that on an overdraft.
- There are a variety of methods of repaying interest and capital.
- The loan can be drawn upon in stages, e.g. 50% now and 50% in three months time.

Activity 2

Which of the following best describes the main features of a bank loan?

A Interest rates are low; repayments can be negotiated; it is useful for capital purchases

B Interest rates are high; repayments can be negotiated; it is useful for capital purchases

C Interest rates are low; repayments can be negotiated; it is a short term form of finance

D Interest rates are high; repayments can be negotiated; it is a short term form of finance

2.4 Debt factoring

A further method of raising short term finance without resorting to an overdraft or a bank loan is a debt factoring service. Debt factoring is a continuing arrangement by which the factoring company purchases all the trade receivables due to a business as they arise. The business will be paid up to 80% of the value of invoices as they are raised, with the balance coming on the date the invoice is settled. The factoring may be with recourse or without recourse.

Definition

With recourse factoring means that the business is liable to the factoring company if a debtor defaults.

Definition

Without recourse factoring means that the factor takes over all responsibility for bad debts as well as collected amounts.

In a factoring arrangement the factoring company will generally take over responsibility for debt collection and sales ledger accounting. The factoring company will obviously make a charge which is proportional to the services it provides and the risk which it assumes.

2.5 Invoice discounting

Invoice discounting is another service provided by factoring companies. It is similar to factoring, in that debts are assigned to the factoring company as they arise, but whereas a factoring arrangement applies to all receivables, discounting is generally negotiated piecemeal for particular selections of invoices. When a batch of debts is assigned, the factoring company will advance up to 75% of the gross invoice value. The payments from customers are forwarded to the factoring company as and when the business receives them (debt collection remains the responsibility of the business) and at the end of the month the balance of the purchase price (less charges) is received from the factoring company.

Invoice discounting is simple and flexible, it can be used as and when short-term funds are needed and it enables the business to maintain a normal relationship with its customers (who need not know about the third party involvement).

2.6 Hire purchase

If a non-current asset is to be purchased by the business, but there is not enough cash available for outright purchase, one simple method is to purchase the asset on a hire purchase scheme.

Hire purchase and instalment credit arrangements can be set up quickly and can generally offer fairly flexible repayment terms. The security for the 'advance' is clearly provided by the asset being purchased. If payment is not completed then the assets is re-possessed by the finance company.

The main disadvantage of a hire purchase agreement is that the total payment for asset can far outweigh the cash purchase price.

2.7 Trade credit

Trade credit, in the form of extending the time taken to pay trade payables, can be used to provide finance which is apparently free of cost and easy to obtain (as the payables' permission is not sought). However, the company runs the risk of losing suppliers and ultimately prices will rise. If the company extends the payment period beyond 60 days without the supplier's prior agreement, then the supplier is entitled to charge interest.

Increasing the payables payment period is often the first reaction to a cash deficit but it must be appreciated that it is not without its costs and it does have limits beyond which the credit period cannot be extended without loss of supplies.

Activity 3

A business has produced its cash budget for the following six months. The cash budget shows that from month 4 onwards the current overdraft facility will be exceeded, largely due to the extension of additional credit to receivables in order to maintain market share in the face of stiff competition.

List the options the business has in dealing with this situation.

3 Medium term debt finance

3.1 Introduction

On the whole, medium term debt finance should be used to fund the purchase of assets with a 3 to 10 year life such as plant and machinery. However it can also be useful to fund a medium term deficit in working capital.

3.2 Bank loans

An obvious source of finance for say the purchase of major non-current assets is a medium term bank loan. The **term** of the loan should not exceed the **life of the asset** being purchased and will normally be approximately the same as the asset's useful life. The **interest** on the loan will either be **fixed or variable**. If the interest is variable then the interest charged will depend upon market rates of interest and will normally be a certain percentage above the bank's base rate or the London Inter-Bank Offered Rate (LIBOR).

How the interest is charged will depend upon the method of repayment of the loan. With a bullet repayment loan the borrower does not pay off any of the loan capital during the repayment period. The entire loan capital amount is repaid at the end of the term of the loan. Therefore the interest that is charged each year is based upon the full loan amount.

With an amortising loan each periodic repayment is made up of interest and repayment of the capital of the loan in such a way that when the final repayment is made there is no capital amount outstanding. Interest on this type of loan is based upon the amount of the loan outstanding during the period since the last repayment.

3.3 Medium term loan and working capital

In most cases a bank loan is most appropriate for the purchase of major assets which will hopefully provide income over the loan period out of which the loan interest and repayments can be made. However in some cases it may be necessary to raise a medium term loan to finance a working capital deficit.

For example suppose that a company has consistently had an overdraft of between £20,000 and £30,000 for the last two years. This would appear to be part of the permanent working capital of the business and is known as the hardcore overdraft. Overdraft finance tends to be at a higher rate of interest than loan finance as it is harder to monitor from the bank's perspective and is more volatile. Therefore this company might convert the hardcore overdraft into say a £20,000 five-year loan which will be paid off over the period but which should reduce the amount of additional overdraft finance required.

3.4 Leasing

If a business is to buy a non-current asset such as plant and machinery or motor vehicles it may find that leasing the asset is a cheaper option than taking out a bank loan and purchasing the asset outright. Many financial intermediaries such as banks and insurance companies provide lease finance for a wide range of assets.

There are two types of lease, an operating lease and a finance lease.

Operating leases

> **Definition**
>
> An operating lease is one where the lessor hires out the asset to the lessee for a short period which is normally substantially less than the asset's total life.

The asset is not treated as if it is owned, and lease payments are an expense in the statement of profit or loss, rather like rental payments.

Once the lease period is over then the lessor may lease the same asset to another lessee. The lessor is responsible for servicing and maintaining the asset and the lessee simply gets the use of the asset for the lease period in return for the lease payments.

This type of lease might be useful for example if a particular specialised type of equipment is only required for a fairly short time period. However if an asset is required for substantially its entire useful life then a finance lease would be required.

Finance leases

> **Definition**
>
> A finance lease is one where the lessee assumes all the risks and rewards associated with the asset.

Under a finance lease the lessee has the use of the asset for most, if not all, of its useful life. The lessee may even be able to sell the asset at the end of its life with only a proportion of the sale proceeds being returned to the lessor. However the lessee, although having use of the asset, never actually gains legal title to the asset.

The lessee will be responsible for the upkeep and maintenance of the asset and to all intents and purposes owns the asset. The lessee will treat the asset in the statement of financial position as if it is owned i.e. it will charge depreciation against the value of the asset. The finance lease charges will reflect the repayment of the value of the asset and the finance charge to the lessor which may make the cost of purchasing using a finance lease more expensive than outright purchase.

This may often be a cheaper form of financing the purchase of an asset than taking out a loan to purchase the asset outright.

Activity 4

A business has produced its cash budget for the following six months. The cash budget shows that from month 4 onwards the current overdraft facility will be exceeded, largely due to the necessity to replace the fleet of delivery vans in month 4.

List the options the business has in dealing with this situation.

4 Long term debt finance

4.1 Introduction

Long term debt finance is typically used for the purchase of long life, major non-current assets and for acquisitions of other businesses.

4.2 Loan stock and debentures

Any loan raised by the issue of a series of negotiable units could be described as 'loan stock' (the term is not used with a precise meaning) and the word **debenture** itself merely describes the document which acknowledges the indebtedness. All company borrowing could be referred to as debentures or debenture stock. In practice, the term debenture is usually restricted to **secured loans**.

Loan stock commonly has a **fixed** rate of **interest**, although in recent years a number of companies have issued floating rate debentures. They are repaid at a specified date.

Advantages of debentures

Advantages of debenture finance are as follows.

(a) It is generally cheaper to raise than a new issue of equity.

(b) Full repayment of the debenture is deferred until the end of the life of the loan.

(c) It may be cheaper to finance than equity since debenture-holders suffer less risk and may be satisfied by a lower return. However, this must be tempered by the fact that shareholders may perceive there to be a greater gearing risk if the company is already highly geared and may therefore require a higher return.

(d) The existing shareholders will retain the same degree of control.

(e) The interest paid will be allowable for corporation tax.

Disadvantages of debentures

Disadvantages of debenture finance include the following.

(a) The company may be committed to the fixed interest payments and will therefore have less flexibility than with equity.

(b) The manner in which future finance may be raised could be affected, as future lenders will consider the level of gearing already in existence.

(c) In the event of any default on the interest payments, the debenture-holders would have the power to appoint a receiver to run the company.

4.3 Mortgages

Mortgage loans are loans for specific assets and for which these specific assets (land or buildings) are the security. They are most commonly for 20 or 25 years, but can sometimes be for as long as 35 years. Interest rates on such loans can be fixed, but are more usually variable, at say 1.75% above base rate. The specialists in such loans for businesses are pension funds and insurance companies, who prefer a lower limit of at least £50,000, although smaller loans have been arranged with policy-holders.

4.4 Sale and leaseback

Sale and leaseback arrangements most commonly relate to property and (less likely) large items of capital equipment. The company sells such an asset to the financial institution (perhaps an insurance company) which then leases it back to the company for a term of, generally, between 20 and 25 years.

4.5 Convertible loan stock

Definition

Convertible loan stock is a debenture loan of a company which can be converted by the holder at some point in the future into equity shares of the company.

Convertible loan stock carries, as one of the terms of issue, the option for the holder to convert his stock, within a given time period, into equity shares at a specified price. If the option is not exercised, the loan stock will continue its normal term to redemption. If a majority of stockholders decide to convert, the company may take powers to convert the remaining stock or to repay it at a pre-determined price.

Advantages of convertibles

The advantages of a convertible loan stock issue from the company's point of view are as follows:

(a) In many cases it will be possible to offer convertible loan stock at a lower interest rate than ordinary debentures. This can be particularly useful for a business which is just starting up or is developing a new product, because the conversion date can be planned to coincide with the growing availability of profits sufficient to pay acceptable dividends.

(b) The incentive of a future share in profits may encourage lenders who would not otherwise invest in the company.

(c) If the company is in need of permanent capital but the market price of shares is currently depressed, the issue of convertible loan stock can be used as a delaying tactic in the hope that the conversion period will coincide with higher share prices, thus giving the company a higher amount per share issued.

The big advantage from the point of view of the investor is that he can wait to see how the share price of the company moves before deciding whether to invest in the equity i.e. whether or not to convert his convertible debentures, or simply redeem or exchange them for cash.

4.6 Bonds

Just as the total equity of a company is split into shares, loans may be broken down into smaller units (e.g. one bond may have a face or par value of £100). Different varieties include debentures and loan stock and may be issued by companies, local authorities and governmental organisations.

Corporate bonds are used by many companies to raise funding for large-scale projects – such as business expansion, takeovers, new premises or product development. They can be used to replace bank finance, or to provide long-term working capital.

Bonds will normally have a nominal value (e.g. £1,000), a coupon rate (e.g. 5%) and redemption terms (e.g. redeem at par in 2015). The annual interest is the product of the nominal value and the coupon rate (e.g. £1,000 × 5% = £50 per annum).

The main features of a corporate bond are:

- the nominal value – the price at which the bonds are first sold on the market e.g. £1,000
- the interest (coupon) rate paid to the bond owner – this is usually fixed e.g. 5% the annual interest is the nominal value × coupon rate
- the redemption terms – when the nominal value of the bond must be repaid to the bond holder e.g. redeem at par in 2015

Bonds can be sold on the open market to investment institutions or individual investors, or they can be sold privately. If bonds are sold on the public market, they can be traded – similar to shares. Some corporate bonds are structured to be convertible, which means they can be exchanged for shares at some point in the future.

Advantages of issuing corporate bonds

Bonds can be a very flexible way of raising debt capital. They can be secured or unsecured, and you can decide what priority they take over other debts. They can also offer a way of stabilising your company's finances by having substantial debts on a fixed-rate interest. This offers some protection against variable interest rates or economic changes.

Other advantages of using bonds to raise long-term finance include:

- not diluting the value of existing shareholdings – unlike issuing additional shares
- enabling more cash to be retained in the business – because the redemption date for bonds can be several years after the issue date

Disadvantage of issuing corporate bonds

There are also some disadvantages to issuing bonds, including:

- regular interest payments to bondholders – though interest may be fixed, the interest will usually have to be paid even if you make a loss
- the potential for your business' share value to be reduced if your profits decline – this is because bond interest payments take precedence over dividends

- bondholder restrictions – because investors are locking up their money for a potentially long period of time, they can impose certain covenants or undertakings on your business operations and financial performance to limit their risk
- ongoing contact with investors can be somewhat limited so changes to terms and conditions or waivers can be more difficult to obtain compared to dealing with bank lenders, who tend to maintain a closer relationship

5 Equity finance

5.1 Shares

Companies issue shares to raise capital, usually in the form of cash although shares may be issued in exchange for assets.

A shareholder is a member of the company and therefore, depending on the class of shares held, has voting rights. They are also entitled to dividends depending on the availability of profits. There are two main types of shares that can be sold to raise finance:

	Preference shares	**Ordinary shares (equity)**
Voting rights	None, or restricted	Full
Dividend rights	Fixed dividend paid in priority to other dividends	Paid after the preference dividend and the value can vary

Both preference and ordinary shares can be redeemable shares; this means that after a period of time the company buys them back.

When deciding whether to issue preference shares or not, the directors have a range of choices as they can issue different types of preference shares. If they wish to raise capital for a period of time and then repay it, as an alternative to borrowing they could offer redeemable preference shares. These will be issued for a specified period of time and then bought back by the company at the time agreed.

In times of high interest rates redeemable preference shares may be particularly attractive to companies. This is because if a company borrows money, interest at the agreed rate must be paid whether or not the company is making a profit. However, dividends to the preference (and ordinary) shareholders are only paid if the company has available profits.

6 Choosing the form of finance

6.1 Introduction

As we have seen, there is a variety of forms of finance available to a business from the very short term to the long term. Each of these forms of finance have different characteristics and different costs and it is vital that the most appropriate and cheapest form of finance is chosen to meet the funding requirements of each situation.

In some situations a specific form of finance will be clearly the most appropriate, for example, the acquisition of a fleet of salesmen's cars under a leasing arrangement. However, in many cases, the choice that must be made by the accounting function is that the choice between financing by bank overdraft or by taking out a term loan.

6.2 Which type of finance?

In general terms the financing method should be matched to the reason the cash is required or to life of the asset that is being purchased. Therefore, in most cases, an overdraft is most suitable for increased working capital requirements but it may be possible to use debt factoring or invoice discounting to inject cash into the business when needed. A loan or other longer term finance option is more suitable for the purchase of non-current assets or another business.

However, you do need to appreciate the advantages and disadvantages of each of the sources of finance to be able to make an informed decision. Consideration should be made of:

- Cost – interest, fees, early redemption penalties
- Timescale – how long will the cash be required for
- Security – fixed and floating charges
- Impact on the gearing of the company

6.3 Considering the finance options

If a company is unable to raise money by the mainstream methods, then more desperate options may have to be considered. Companies performing badly may not be able to borrow further money from their bank, nor raise money from capital disposals.

(a) The sale/leaseback of assets as previously mentioned is often the first of the more desperate options to be considered. This may realise funds in the short term, although freehold rights will be lost.

(b) A company might consider running its inventory levels down to a very minimum quantity or alternatively not holding any inventory at all. The disadvantages of this step are considerable:

- The company runs the risk of a stock-out, i.e. customer demand exceeds the goods in inventory, so goodwill and customers are lost.
- The production cycle will have to be altered and staff possibly made redundant.
- Bulk purchase discounts will no longer be available.
- The company's scale of operation usually has to be reduced.
- Consequently, this is a step which is only taken when no other finance is available and the directors are trying to keep the business operating.

7 Interest rates

7.1 Introduction

There are different forms of interest that need to be considered when looking at the different options available when needing to raise finance:

- Base interest rate – the lowest interest rate a bank will charge. The rate is set by the **Bank of England**. Banks usually charge interest at 'an amount above base rate'. If the base rate rises, then usually the rate of interest charged on the loan will rise by the same amount. If it falls, so will the rate on the loan.
- Fixed interest rate – provides an **unchanging** interest rate over the length of the borrowing/investing period.
- Variable interest rate – the rate **changes** in line with an agreed indicator (usually in line with base interest rate but it can be another agreed index).
- Flat rate interest – is calculated based on the **loan principal** or capital amount. It is applied to the whole of the loan every year and **does not** take into account any **repayments**. The flat rate of interest can seem to be a lower option but in reality can be quite expensive.
- Capped interest rate – an interest rate that has an upper limit.

- Simple interest – can be calculated by taking the **total interest** as a **percentage** of the original **principal**.
- Annual percentage rate (APR) – The APR is an annual rate that is charged for borrowing (or made by investing), expressed as a single percentage number. It is calculated on the loan principal outstanding so that the interest charge reduces each monthly in line with the reduction in the amount outstanding. It represents the actual yearly cost of funds over the term of a loan. This includes any fees or additional costs associated with the transaction. This is the **effective interest rate** that a borrower will pay on a loan.

This is also applicable when considering how to invest surplus funds (Chapter 8).

7.2 Interest charged

It is worth considering the interest rate charges in both percentage and type to try to work out the cheapest form of finance.

Fixed rate borrowing may be cheaper if the base rate is rising thus affecting the variable rate. Variable rate borrowing may be cheaper if the base rate is falling.

Example

The base rate is currently 1%.

It is possible to get a loan at a fixed rate of 5% or a variable rate of 2% above base rate.

The base rate would need to rise by more than 2% to make the fixed rate cheaper. The likelihood of this happening would have to be considered.

It is also necessary to consider costs other than interest rates, such as fees and other charges that maybe incurred.

Example

A one year loan of £30,000 is required. Two options are available:

A loan with a fixed rate of 6.9%, with set up fees of 1% of the loan or a loan with an APR of 8%. Which is cheaper?

The total cost of the loan with fixed rate is

£30,000 × 6.9% = £2,070

£30,000 × 1% = £300

Total cost £2,370

The total cost of the loan with an APR of 8% is

£30,000 × 8% = £2,400

The fixed rate loan is cheaper.

It is possible to use both an overdraft and a loan to meet a cash deficit. It may be that doing so actually reduces cost and meets the organisation's guidelines and regulations.

Activity 5

Steinburgs are planning to expand their manufacturing facilities. The expansion plans require new machinery at a cost of £60,000 and a working capital injection of £10,000.

There are 3 different options for funding the expansion:

Option 1

- A bank loan of £60,000 secured on the new machinery. Capital repayments are to be made of equal amounts over 3 years. The interest rate is fixed at 4% per annum calculated on the capital balance outstanding at the beginning of each year.
- An arrangement fee equal to 0.5% of the bank loan is payable at the beginning of the loan term.
- The bank is also offering an overdraft facility of £15,000 which attracts an annual interest rate of 13%. Steinburgs believe that they will have an average overdraft of £8,000 for the first 7 months of the first year.

Option 2

- A bank loan of £80,000 secured on the assets of the partnership. Capital repayments are to be made over 3 years, with a 3 month payment holiday at the beginning of the loan term.
- The interest rate is fixed at 8% per annum for the first 2 years and will then revert to a variable interest rate 3% above the base rate.
- An arrangement fee equal to 0.9% of the bank loan is payable at the beginning of the loan term.
- No overdraft facility will be required.

Option 3

- Steinburgs' two owners each take out a personal secured loan for £35,000 repayable over 4 years at an interest rate of 4%. These monies will then be loaned to the partnership as increased capital. Interest of 7% per annum is payable by the business to the two owners.
- No overdraft facility will be required.

Required:

Calculate the cost of each of the above options for the first year. Which of the 3 methods would you recommend?

	Loan interest £	*Arrangement fee* £	*Overdraft interest* £	*Total cost* £
Option 1	2400	300	607	3307
Option 2	6400	720		7120
Option 3	4900	–	–	4900

Recommendation: Option 1

Activity 6

A company has two options available to raise finance to buy a new machine.

Option 1

A bank loan of £100,000 with capital repayments made over 5 years. The interest rate is fixed at 7% per annum for the first year and will then revert to a variable interest rate of 3% above the base rate for rest of the loan term.

Option 2

A bank loan of £100,000 with capital repayments made over 8 years. The interest rate is fixed at 5% for the first year and will then revert to a variable interest rate of 4% above the base rate for the rest of the loan term.

Required:

Calculate the total cost of both these options for the first 2 years. The base rate is predicted to be 1% in year 2.

	Option 1			*Option 2*		
Year	*Loan interest*	*Capital repayments*	*Total*	*Loan interest*	*Capital repayments*	*Total*
1						
2						
Total						

Which option should be chosen?

The company wishes to consider the whole life of the loans. Interest rates are as above but from year 3 to the term end the base rate will be 1.5%.

Which option should be chosen?

Activity 7

A business has paid £3,000 in interest on a £30,000 loan in one year. Calculate the flat rate applied to the loan.

Activity 8

A bank has offered to lend a company £90,000 to be repaid in 12 monthly instalments of £7,815. Calculate the flat rate of interest being applied to the loan.

8 Security

8.1 Security

In some cases the bank may only be prepared to advance the money on the basis of some security given by the business. Security can be in the form of a personal guarantee, a fixed charge or a floating charge.

Definition

A **fixed charge** is where the security is a specific and identifiable asset or group of assets.

The bank would have the right to sell this specific asset if the business defaults on the loan repayments.

Definition

A **floating charge** is where the security is supplied by a group of assets of a relevant value, such as receivables or inventory. The value of the security is constant but make up of the security will be changing.

If the business defaults on the loan then the bank will seize assets to the value of the outstanding repayment.

Activity 9

A fixed charge is security offered by a changing group of assets and a floating charge is security offered by a static asset.

True or false?

9 Gearing

9.1 Gearing ratio

Gearing is a measure of the company's capital structure – is the business being funded by equity (repayable to shareholders) or by debt (repayable to banks)?

If there is a lot of debt compared to the equity it is thought that a business is riskier as debt must be paid back to the banks when requested whereas equity does not have to be paid back to the shareholders on demand.

The gearing ratio in the CSHM assessment is calculated as:

$$\text{Gearing ratio} = \frac{\text{Total debt (short term and long term)}}{\text{Total debt + equity}} \times 100$$

It is usually long term debt, such as loans and debentures, that are included in this calculation but it is possible for overdrafts to be included if a business relies on them as a source of finance over the longer term.

The impact on the gearing ratio will need to be considered when deciding the type of finance to raise as a highly geared business may find sourcing funds in the future harder than a company with less debt compared to equity.

10 Relationship between the bank and the customer

10.1 Introduction

Whether an overdraft or a loan or a combination of the two is chosen to finance a deficit, a relationship is formed between the bank providing the finance and the company using the finance.

10.2 Facility letters

A **facility letter** will state all the terms that the overdraft is based on and will be signed by both parties and acts as a binding contract. It defines the legal rights of both bank and borrower and aims to protect both parties.

10.3 Fiduciary relationship

The bank and the customer also have a fiduciary relationship which means that the **bank is expected to act with the utmost good faith** in its relationship with the customer.

10.4 The duties of the bank

The bank has the following duties to its customers:

- It must honour customer's cheques as long as they are correctly made out, there is no legal reason for not honouring it and their customer has enough funds or overdraft limit to cover the amount of the cheque.
- The bank must credit cash/cheques paid in to the customer's account.
- If the customer makes a written request for repayment of funds in its account, for example by writing a cheque, the bank must repay the amounts on demand.
- The bank must comply with the customer's instructions by a direct debit mandate or standing order.
- The bank must provide a statement showing the transactions on the account and be prepared to provide details of the balance on the customer's account.
- The bank must respect the confidentiality of the customer's affairs unless the bank is required by law or public duty to disclose, or the interest of the bank requires disclosure or where the customer gives his consent for disclosure.
- The bank must tell the customer if there has been an attempt to forge the customer's signature on a cheque.
- The bank should use care and skill in its actions.
- The bank must provide reasonable notice if it is to close a customer's account.

10.5 The duties of the customer

The customer has two main duties:

- to exercise care in drawing cheques such that fraud is not facilitated
- to tell the bank of any forgeries known of.

10.6 The rights of the bank

The rights of the bank are:

- to charge reasonable charges and commissions over and above interest
- to use the customer's money in any way provided that it is legal and morally acceptable
- to be repaid overdrawn balances on demand
- to be indemnified against possible losses when acting on a customer's behalf.

11 Summary

There are many choices facing a business that needs to raise finance but it is important that the right choice of the form of finance is made. This will start with an initial consideration of the reason for the additional finance. If it is due to the need for increased working capital then a form of short-term or possibly loan finance would be most appropriate. If the finance is required for the purchase of non-current assets then long-term finance to match with the life of the asset is probably the best option.

Answers to chapter activities

Activity 1

Answer D

Activity 2

Answer A

Activity 3

- negotiate an increased overdraft
- delay payment to payables
- issue commercial paper
- take out a short term bank loan
- debt factoring
- invoice discounting

Activity 4

- negotiate an increased overdraft
- delay payment to payables
- take out a medium term bank loan
- purchase the vans on a finance lease

Activity 5

	Loan interest £	*Arrangement fee* £	*Overdraft interest* £	*Total cost* £
Option 1	2,400	300	607	3,307
Option 2	6,400	720	0	7,120
Option 3	4,900	0	0	4,900

Recommendation: Option 1 as it is the cheapest.

Activity 6

	Option 1			*Option 2*		
Year	*Loan interest*	*Capital repayments*	*Total*	*Loan interest*	*Capital repayments*	*Total*
1	7,000	20,000	27,000	5,000	12,500	17,500
2	3,200	20,000	23,200	4,375	12,500	16,875
Total	10,200	40,000	50,200	9,375	25,000	34,375

Recommendation: Option 2 as it is the cheapest over the first 2 years.

When the whole life of the loan is considered the capital repayments will be same – £100,000. The total interest paid will be the relevant cost.

Option 1		*Option 2*	
Year	*Interest*	*Year*	*Interest*
1	100,000 × 7% = 7,000	1	100,000 × 5% = 5,000
2	80,000 × 4% = 3,200	2	87,500 × 5% = 4,375
3	60,000 × 4.5% = 2,700	3	75,000 × 5.5% = 4,125
4	40,000 × 4.5% = 1,800	4	62,500 × 5.5% = 3,438
5	20,000 × 4.5% = 900	5	50,000 × 5.5% = 2,750
Total	**15,600**	6	37,500 × 5.5% 2,063
		7	25,000 × 5.5% = 1,375
		8	12,500 × 5.5% = 688
		Total	**23,814**

If total interest cost is considered then Option 1 is the cheapest but taking longer to pay back a loan may be more beneficial to the company.

Activity 7

3,000 ÷ 30,000 × 100 = 10%

Activity 8

£7,815 × 12 = £93,780

3,780 ÷ 90,000 × 100 = 4.2%

Activity 9

False

A fixed charge is security offered by a specific asset

A floating charge is security offered by a group of assets

12 Test your knowledge

Workbook Activity 10

Finalite are planning to expand their production facilities. The expansion plans require new machinery at a cost of £55,000 and a working capital injection of £20,000.

There are 3 different options for funding the expansion:

Option 1

- A bank loan of £55,000 secured on the new machinery. Capital repayments are to be made of equal amounts over 5 years. The interest rate is fixed at 5% per annum calculated on the capital balance outstanding at the beginning of each year.
- An arrangement fee equal to 0.7% of the bank loan is payable at the beginning of the loan term.
- The bank is also offering an overdraft facility of £22,000 which attracts an annual interest rate of 11%. Finalite believes that they will have an average overdraft of £11,000 for the first 6 months of the first year.

Option 2

- A bank loan of £75,000 secured on the assets of the partnership. Capital repayments are to be made over 5 years, with a 5 month payment holiday at the beginning of the loan term.
- The interest rate is fixed at 7% per annum for the first 2 years and will then revert to a variable interest rate 2% above the base rate.
- An arrangement fee equal to 0.8% of the bank loan is payable at the beginning of the loan term.
- No overdraft facility will be required.

Option 3

- Finalite's two owners each take out a personal secured loan for £37,500 repayable over 3 years at an interest rate of 5%. These monies will then be loaned to the partnership as increased capital. Interest of 8% per annum is payable by the business to the two owners.
- No overdraft facility will be required.

Required:

Calculate the cost of each of the above options for the first year. Which of the 3 methods would you recommend?

	Loan interest £	*Arrangement fee* £	*Overdraft interest* £	*Total cost* £
Option 1	2750	385	605	3740
Option 2	5250	600		5850
Option 3	6000			6000

Recommendation: option 1

Workbook Activity 11

Which of the following best describes the main features of an overdraft?

A Interest rates are low; it is available for as long as required; it is useful for capital purchases.

B Interest rates are low; it is payable on demand; it is useful for capital purchases.

C Interest rates are low; repayments can be negotiated; it is useful for capital purchases.

D Interest rates are high; repayments can be negotiated; it is a short-term form of finance.

E Interest rates are high; it is repayable on demand; it is a short-term form of finance.

F Interest rates are high; it is available for as long as required; it is a long-term form of finance.

Which of the following best describes the main features of a bank loan?

A Interest rates are low; it is available for as long as required; it is useful for capital purchases.

B Interest rates are low; it is payable on demand; it is useful for capital purchases.

C Interest rates are low; repayments can be negotiated; it is useful for capital purchases.

D Interest rates are high; repayments can be negotiated; it is a short-term form of finance.

E Interest rates are high; it is repayable on demand; it is a short-term form of finance.

F Interest rates are high; it is available for as long as required; it is a long-term form of finance.

Workbook Activity 12

The Board of Sleepy Ltd has approved an investment of £1 million for new cutting machinery which is planned to be made in July. Explain in a memo to the Board:

- the advantages and disadvantages of funding the purchase with either a bank overdraft or a bank loan
- which would be the preferred method of financing?

bank overdraft is payable on demand - high interest not recommended for long term short term source of finance

bank loan can be used with known exact length of payments, interest rate could be fixed set amount of monthly payments can be offset against profit loss.

preferred method of financing

bank loan

Which of the following best describes the main features of a bank loan?

A. Interest rates are low, it is available to be for a set period, it is useful for capital purchases.

B. Interest rates are low, it is repayable on demand, it is useful for capital purchases.

C. Interest rates are low, repayment can be renegotiated, it is useful for capital purchases.

D. Interest rates are high, repayment can be renegotiated, it is a short term form of finance.

E. Interest rates are high, it is repayable on demand, it is a short term form of finance.

F. Interest rates are high, it is available for as long as it's needed, it is a long term form of finance.

[illegible]

The Board of Sleepwell has approved an investment of [illegible] in new [illegible] machinery which is planned to be [illegible]. Prepare a report to the Board:

- the advantages and disadvantages of funding the purchase with either a bank loan or a [illegible]
- which would be the preferred method of financing.

Managing surplus funds

8

Introduction

In this chapter we will consider the ways in which any cash surplus can be invested and the factors that should be considered to determine the best type of investment.

KNOWLEDGE
Take account of trends in the economic and financial environment in managing cash balances (4.5S)
Assess different types of investment and the risks, terms and conditions associated with them (6.1S)
Analyse ways to manage risk when investing, to minimise potential losses to the organisation (6.2S)
Invest surplus funds according to organisational policy and within defined authorisation limits (6.3S)

CONTENTS

1 Business requirements for investing

1.1 Introduction

Cash budgets reveal, among other things, the **amount** of any surplus funds available to the company for short-term investment. Opportunities like this should always be taken; money **invested just overnight will be worth more than money left idle**. Surplus cash will therefore require an investment decision.

Many companies will have regulations and procedures to ensure that the liquidity of the business is safeguarded, for example:

- a certain amount of cash must be available immediately at any point in time
- investments in certain types of instrument may be limited to a financial amount
- investment of surplus funds might only be allowed in certain specified types of investment
- all investments must be convertible into cash within a certain number of days.

These procedures, regulations and limits must be followed at all times.

Public organisations have strict funding (cash) controls. They are required by Government to balance their budgets. Should they not spend all their granted cash and end up with a surplus, they do not have the freedom to choose an external investment.

Private organisations are allowed to invest their own funds as they wish but they still have regulations to adhere to through the Companies Act.

1.2 Investment strategy

Most organisations avoid the high risk investments. What to invest in depends on the following:

- **Size** of funds available for investment
- Length of **time** for which the funds are available
- **Certainty** of funds and **accuracy** of cash budget
- **Return** on invested funds – is it adequate? Does it compensate for the risk involved?
- **Risk** and variability of return from the investment if held for the full intended duration

- **Liquidity** of the investment. Whether there is any possibility that the cash may be required prematurely to make unexpected payments and whether there would be any costs in the event of an early termination.
- Risks associated with **early redemption**. A security which provides a fixed, risk-free return if held for the full term may prove costly if terminated early.
- **Realisation/Maturity**. In some circumstances it may be important that the investment can be realised easily. It provides a company with a reserve, or safety margin, in its cash planning.

The overall aim should be to secure the maximum interest possible, consistent with a satisfactory level of risk and the required degree of liquidity. The investing company has to balance the expected interest with the risks involved.

1.3 Main factors to consider

The main factors that should be considered when determining how to deal with surplus funds are:

- Maturity
- Return
- Risk
- Liquidity
- Diversification

1.4 Maturity

A cash surplus is usually temporary and may only available for some weeks or months. If an investment is cashed in or sold before it reached maturity there is as risk that there will be some loss in value or interest received, there may also be penalty charges.

1.5 Return

Return on an investment is the interest received over the period of time the investment. A business that has surplus funds to invest will wish those funds to earn a good profit or return but what is also paramount is the safety of the asset.

1.6 Risk

Risk refers to the probability that the investment might rise or fall in value. As a general rule risk and return should be related. The **higher the risk** of an investment the **higher the potential return should be.**

When cash is invested there are two potential risks. Firstly the risk that the **value of the investment will fall**, known as the capital risk, and secondly the risk that **the return from the investment will be lower than expected** due to changes in market rates, known as the return risk.

Example

A business has £10,000 of surplus cash to invest for a period of one month until it is needed to pay the quarterly VAT bill. The money could be paid into a bank deposit account earning 0.4% interest per month or it could be invested in shares purchased through a broker.

Consider the risks of these two options.

Solution

If the money is paid into the bank deposit account there is virtually no risk at all. The withdrawal in one month's time will total:

$$£10,000 + (0.4\% \times £10,000) = £10,040$$

The investment has earned £40 of income for the business.

If the £10,000 were to be invested in shares then in one month's time the share value may have increased to say £13,000, in which case the shares could be sold for that amount earning £3,000 of profit. However it is also possible that the share values have fallen and the shares can only be sold for £7,500 in one month's time meaning not only that a loss has been made but also that there is no longer enough cash available to pay the VAT bill.

1.7 Liquidity

Liquidity refers to the ease with which an investment can be cashed in or realised without significant loss of value or interest. When any surplus cash is invested it is important to ensure that it can be **realised when needed**. The ease of realisation will be reflected in the return that the investment gives.

For example the interest earned on a bank deposit account which requires a month's notice for any withdrawal will be higher than the interest on a deposit account where the funds can be withdrawn at any time.

1.8 Diversification

There is a general rule that a business should not put all its surplus funds into one investment. It is much better to diversify by investing in a number of different investments. This would lead to the business spreading the risk.

1.9 Treasury activities and risk

Whoever is in charge of the treasury function must ensure that, although surplus cash is invested profitably, excessive risks are not taken. There are many highly speculative and highly risky financial instruments on the market, which although they may yield very high returns, can also have huge losses.

The aim of the treasury activities in a trading company is to earn a reasonable return on any surplus cash but not to speculate.

1.10 Organisational rules and procedures

Many companies will have regulations and procedures to ensure that the liquidity of the business is safeguarded. For example that a certain amount of cash must be available immediately at any point in time, that investments in certain types of instrument may be limited to a financial amount, that surplus funds might only be allowed to be invested in certain specified types of investment or that all investments must be convertible into cash within a certain number of days. These procedures, regulations and limits must be followed at all times.

Activity 1

In the management of cash balances, surpluses may sometimes be forecast. These surpluses should be managed, taking liquidity, safety and rate of return into account.

(a) Describe **each** of these three factors:

(i) liquidity

(ii) safety

(iii) rate of return

(b) Briefly explain which of these three factors you consider to be the most important, giving reasons for your choice.

Activity 2

The benefits of good cash management to a company are:

(a) better control of financial risk

(b) opportunity for profit

(c) strengthened statement of financial position

(d) increased confidence of customers, suppliers, banks and shareholders.

Explain how good cash management may realise any **two** of these benefits.

2 Types of investment

2.1 Bank and building society deposit accounts

One of the safest and simplest forms of investment for surplus cash is to pay it into a high street bank or building society deposit account. There is a wide variety of such accounts available. For example:

- **Instant access deposit accounts** – money can be withdrawn when required without having to give any notice. There is no loss of interest but the **interest rate** is generally **quite low**.
- **Notice deposit accounts** – money can be withdrawn after a certain period of notice, for example 7 days or 30 days. These tend to have higher interest rates than instant access accounts but, if cash is withdrawn without notice, some loss of interest will be incurred.
- **High interest deposit accounts** – these will tend to be for larger amounts, for example at least £5,000, and for a fixed term with no withdrawal of funds permitted.

For cash that is definitely not going to be required in the near future there are deposits that can be made for a fixed term of up to three months at a variable rate of interest which is linked to money market rates. This will normally yield a higher rate of return due to the lower liquidity.

2.2 Bonds

There are lots of types of bonds, examples include:

- Local authority bonds – are certificates issued by local authorities backed by the government. They are also called local authority short-term loans, which are marketable. A lump sum can be invested for a fixed term at a fixed interest rate. They are considered low risk as they are backed by the government.
- Corporate bonds – are bonds issued by a company. These are long term bonds and can be high risk as the price will fluctuate with the movements in the general level of interest rates and can also be affected by the perceived credit risk of the company issuing the bonds.
- Government bonds or gilts – see below.

A bond will normally have a nominal (par) value (e.g. £1,000), a coupon rate (e.g. 5%) and redemption terms (e.g. redeem at par in 2015). The annual interest is the product of the nominal value and the coupon rate (e.g. £1,000 × 5% = £50 per annum).

Characteristics of a bond:

- Return – typically bonds have low returns because they are a lower risk investment.
- Risk – bonds are usually lower risk than equity. For example the bonds may be secured and the interest rate fixed.
- Timescales – the maturity is defined on the bond and varies from very short term (e.g. Treasury Bills) to long term (e.g. 25 year corporate bonds). Some bonds are redeemable but others irredeemable.
- Liquidity – if the bonds are unquoted then the investor has no choice except to wait for redemption. However, if quoted they will be easier to liquidate by selling on the bond markets. For example government bonds are usually very liquid. Note: high risk bonds will be sold at a large discount on face value.

There are a number of different ways of calculating the yield on bonds:

- **Coupon yield.** The coupon yield is the fixed rate of interest, expressed as a percentage of nominal value. So 7% Treasury Stock 2021 would have a coupon yield of 7%, regardless of its market price.
- **Interest yield.** The interest yield is the annual interest receivable, expressed as a percentage of the market price. For example, if 7% Treasury Stock 2001 has a market price of 103.80, the interest yield is 6.7% (100% × 7/103.80).

- **Redemption yield.** The interest yield measures the interest return on gilts, but ignores any capital gain or loss on investment when the gilts are eventually redeemed. Redemption yield is the interest yield plus or minus an amount to reflect the difference between the market price of the gilt and its eventual redemption value.

These calculations will be covered within the next section on Government securities.

2.3 Government securities

Government securities are also known as gilt-edged securities, gilts or Treasury stock. They are a type of bond.

Definition

Government securities or gilt-edged securities are **fixed interest** securities **issued by HM Treasury** which pays the holder a fixed cash payment (or coupon) every six months until maturity, at which point the holder receives his final coupon payment and the return of the principal.

The term 'gilt' or 'gilt-edged security' is a reference to the primary characteristic of gilts as an investment – the security. This is a reflection of the fact that the British Government has never failed to make interest or principal payments on gilts as they fall due.

Example

An issue of 9% Treasury stock has a par value of £100, a market value of £105.80, and it is redeemable at par in two years' time.

The **coupon rate** usually reflects the **market interest rate** at the time of the first issue of the gilt. The coupon indicates the cash payment per £100 nominal that the holder will receive per year.

This payment is made in two equal semi-annual payments on fixed dates.

For example, an investor who holds £100 nominal of 9% Treasury Gilt 2016 will receive two coupon payments of £4.50 each (9% × £100 = £9 split over two payments).

Gilts also have a specific maturity date.

The term can vary from less than one year up to 20 or more years. As this is a fixed rate interest, a change in base rates can affect the market price, and the attractiveness of the investment.

Interest yield

Definition

The interest yield or flat rate yield is the coupon rate of interest as a percentage of the current price of the gilt.

Example

An issue of 9% Treasury stock has a par value of £100, a market value of £105.80, and it is redeemable at par in two years' time. The interest yield on the stock is:

9%x£100

$$\frac{9\%\times£100}{£105.80}\times 100 = 8.5\%$$

This shows the return on the gilt if it were bought today and held for a year whereas the redemption yield is the return throughout the whole life of the security.

Redemption yield

Definition

The redemption yield is the **internal rate of return** (IRR) earned by an investor who buys the gilt today at the market price, assuming that the bond will be held until maturity, and that all coupon and principal payments will be made on schedule. Redemption yield is the discount rate at which the sum of all future cash flows from the gilt (coupons and principal) is equal to the price of the bond.

The redemption yield can be calculated for any fixed interest security. It is a way of comparing different securities and also comparing the return with the return from other forms of investment.

Example

An issue of 9% Treasury stock has a market value of £105.80, and it is redeemable at par (£100) in two years' time.

- £105.80 is the initial investment.
- Each year that the gilt is held the investor will receive 9% interest on the par value of the gilt = £9.
- At redemption the investor will receive £100.

An investor buying a quantity of the stock now at £105.80 and holding it until maturity will only receive £100 for every £105.80 of investment.

Although the investor will receive an interest yield of 8.5% per annum (see above), there will be a capital loss of £5.80 for each £105.80 invested.

Since the stock has two years remaining to maturity this represents an average loss of £2.90 each year, which is 2.7% of the investment value.

As a rough approximation, the redemption yield on the stock is 5.8% (8.5%–2.7%).

This can also be calculated as follows:

Calculate the NPV at two different discount rates and then calculate the IRR.

Note annuity factors have been used to calculate the present value of the interest received. This could equally been done by discounting the interest received each year.

	4%	£		8%	£
T_0 £105.80	× 1.000	(105.80)	T_0 £105.80	× 1.000	(105.80)
$T_1 - T_2$ £9	× 1.886	16.974	$T_1 - T_2$ £9	× 1.783	16.047
T_4 £100	× 0.925	92.5	T_4 £100	× 0.857	85.7
Present value		3.674	Present value		–4.053

The redemption yield:

$$IRR = L + \frac{N_L}{N_L - N_H} \times (H - L)$$

$$IRR = 4 + \frac{3.674}{3.674 - -4.053} \times (8–4)$$

L = Low interest rate

H = High interest rate

N_L = NPV at the low interest rate

N_H = NPV at the high interest rate

This means that over the term of the investment there will be a return of 5.90%.

Government securities can either be held to maturity or sold in a secondary market if the cash is needed. If they are sold before maturity a broker may be used which will incur costs (**brokerage fees**). In the UK Gilts are **almost risk free** and **very marketable** ensuring that they are a popular form of investment for companies. Beware that gilts in different countries may be a higher risk due to instability of governments.

Activity 3

An issue of 4% Treasury stock has a par value of £100, a current market price of £94.00. The stock has exactly three years to redemption, when it will be redeemed at par.

Required:

(a) Calculate the current interest yield on the stock. 4.26

(b) Calculate an approximate redemption yield. 6.25

(a) 4% × £100 / 94.00 × 100

b) 100 − 94.00 = £6

need more practise on this

2.4 Treasury bills

A business with a short-term cash surplus can arrange through its bank to invest in the discount market, by purchasing Treasury bills.

Definition

Treasury bills are short term government securities which pay no interest so are issued at a discount. They are issued by tender and have a minimum purchase value of £500,000.

Since Treasury bills are an undertaking to pay by the Government, the risk to an investor is very low. Treasury bills are commonly described as 'risk-free investments'. Treasury bills are negotiable instruments so they can be sold before maturity.

Bills are sold at a **discount** and **repaid at face value** at the end of the issue period, usually three or six months. The difference between the purchase price and the amount repaid represents the yield on the Bill.

Example

What is the yield (expressed in annual terms) on a three-month Treasury Bill initially sold at a price of 98% of face value?

Solution

For an investment return of say £500,000, the buyer only has to pay £490,000. The profit on holding to maturity is £10,000, or as a percentage:

$$\frac{£10,000}{£490,000} \times 100 = 2.04\%$$

This represents an annual yield of:

$(1.0204)^4 - 1 = 8.41\%$

An investor in bills needs to consider the risks and returns involved. There are two risks for an investor in bills.

- **Credit risk.** This is the risk that the bill will not be paid at maturity. As explained above, this risk is non-existent with Treasury bills.
- **The risk of a change in interest rates**. This risk does not exist for any investor who buys a bill and then holds it to maturity. Interest rate risk only exists for investors who buy bills with the intention of re-selling them before maturity. The risk arises because if market rates of interest go up, the market value of bills will fall. (Equally, if market rates of interest fall, the market value of bills will rise.)

Example

An investor buys a 91-day treasury bill with a face value of £1 million in the discount market for £987,500. Although the calculations are not shown, the bill will give the investor a return of 5% per annum if he holds the bill to maturity and takes the £1 million payment.

However, suppose that the investor sells the bill seven days later, when interest rates in the discount market have risen to 6%. The sale value of the bill would be about £986,000 (workings not shown) and the investor would have made a loss on his investment.

The market value of a bill goes down when interest rates rise, because when interest rates go up, investors want a higher return. To get a higher return, they must buy bills at a bigger discount to face value, in other words, bill prices will fall.

Activity 4

A Treasury bill with a face value of £1,000 is issued at a 5% discount for 91 days. Calculate the yield in annual terms.

2.5 Money market accounts

Money market deposits are amounts of money deposited through a bank in the money markets. These are the financial markets for short term borrowing and lending. The money markets are used largely by banks and other financial institutions, for depositing and lending funds.

Banks can deposit short term funds with other banks, or borrow short term from other banks in the interbank market.

Interest yields in the interbank market are often reasonably attractive, and it is now quite common for companies with large temporary cash surpluses to arrange with their bank to have the money deposited in the money markets (interbank market) or at money market interest rates.

Money invested in a money market deposit cannot be withdrawn until the deposit matures. It is therefore important that money should not be invested for a period longer than the investor's expected cash surplus.

Money market deposits can be for very short periods of time, as little as one day, or for as long as several months (and even up to one year). However, very short term deposits should be large amounts of money, so that the interest earned justifies the effort involved in making the deposits.

2.6 Certificates of deposit

Definition

A certificate of deposit (CD) is issued by a bank or building society which certifies that a certain sum, usually a minimum of £50,000, has been deposited with it to be repaid on a specific date.

The term can range from seven days to five years but is usually for three months (90 days). CDs are negotiable instruments; they can be bought and sold, therefore if the holder does not want to wait until the maturity date the CD can be sold in the money market.

The market in CDs is large and active therefore they are an ideal method for investing large cash surpluses. The sale value of a CD will depend on how much a buyer is willing to pay to obtain the right to the deposit plus interest at maturity.

Since CDs are negotiable, the holder can sell them at any time. This makes them far more liquid than a money-market time deposit, with the same bank.

CDs usually offer an attractive rate of interest when compared to deposit accounts and a low credit risk (as long as a reputable bank is used). They are useful for investing funds in the short term since they can be sold at any time on the secondary market.

An investor could ask the bank to make an early repayment, but there are normally penalty charges for doing this.

2.7 Shares

Shares in companies can be bought as an investment. Shares are bought and sold through a **broker for a fee**. Whilst being a share holder the company/person may have the right to vote in decisions and also receive **dividends** from the company they have invested in, depending on the class of shares held.

There are two main types of shares:

	Preference shares	**Ordinary shares (equity)**
Voting rights	None, or restricted	Full
Dividend rights	Fixed dividend paid in priority to other dividends	Paid after the preference dividend and the value can vary

Share prices can fluctuate depending on either, or both, the company and general market performance. If a company is achieving good profits and has a good reputation then the return possible from shares is higher than that of the other options discussed. Conversely if confidence in the company or in the general market drops then the loss can also be significant. Due to this shares are considered to be the **most risky** of investment opportunities.

Dividend yield is a financial ratio that shows how much a company pays out in dividends each year relative to its share price. In the absence of any capital gains, the dividend yield is the return on investment for a stock. Dividend yield is calculated as follows:

$$= \frac{\text{Annual dividend per share}}{\text{Market price per share}}$$

It is a way to measure how much cash flow you get for each pound invested in shares. Investors who require a minimum stream of cash flow from their investment portfolio can secure this cash flow by investing in stocks paying relatively high, stable dividend yields.

Example

If a company pays annual dividends of £1 per share and the shares are trading at £20 the company has a dividend yield of 5%.

$$= \frac{1}{20} \times 100 = 5\%$$

Activity 5

A company pays annual dividends of £1 per share and the shares are trading at £40 each. Calculate the dividend yield.

Activity 6

What type of investment do the following describe:

Interest rates are fixed and these types of securities are considered to be low risk because they are backed by the government.

A Certificates of deposit

B Government securities

C Bonds

D Bank deposit account

Certificates issued by banks that certify that an amount of money has been deposited and will be repaid at a specific date in the future. They can be traded on a market. They are considered to be a low risk investment.

A Certificates of deposit

B Government securities

C Bonds

D Bank deposit account

2.8 Land and property

Historically land and property were deemed to be a fairly safe investment as there is a finite supply. However in the last decade land and house values have been volatile sometimes resulting in a capital loss for investors. Therefore any initial investment may not be fully realised if the market value has dropped at the date of sale.

Land and property are usually seen as a long term investment and may take a long time to make a suitable return for the company. The investment can only be realised once the land or property is sold and the speed of this will depend upon the economic environment at the time of sale.

The liquidity of the company may be adversely affected if they are unable to realise the full investment at the point of sale. It is unlikely that the return could be forecast with any certainty at the time of purchase.

2.9 Gold

There are different forms of 'gold' that can be invested in, for example bullion, coins, and certificates of ownership.

Investment in gold can be thought of has high risk as the price can fluctuate. In the past gold prices have increased but recently the price of gold has dropped considerably ($1,800 per ounce to $1,228 per ounce between 2011 and 2013).

There is a limited supply of gold, which means it is becoming scarcer and more expensive to extract; this may lead to gold prices increasing. Some experts believe that long term gold prices could hit $2,000 an ounce but just as many believe gold prices will fall in the long run.

The return from investment in gold cannot be stated with any certainty at the time of investment because market fluctuations in price. There may be additional costs associated with storage and also an increase in insurance premiums if gold is to be kept on a company premises. There may also be broker charges for acquisition and sale.

Gold is tradable so liquidity is high. A company could realise its cash very quickly so long as it is happy to take the price offered at that point in time. Liquidity is good but return may be uncertain due to the volatility of the gold market.

2.10 Other ways to use surplus funds

Other than the investment opportunities mentioned above a business could choose to repay any loans early or to take advantage of a settlement discount a supplier offers. By doing this a business may be able to reduce finance charges or reduce the amount paid to payable. Overall this could provide a greater saving in monetary terms than the monetary return the various investment opportunities provide.

3 Making the right decision

3.1 Organisational policies and regulation

As noted earlier in the chapter each business will have certain criteria it will consider when deciding what to invest surplus funds in:

- Maturity
- Return
- Risk
- Liquidity
- Diversification

3.2 Attitudes to risk

There are two main types of risk with investments – capital risk and return risk. When investing in short-term investments it will be necessary to consider these risks and to take into account any expected changes in the economic and financial environment.

The decision makers' attitude to risk will have a bearing on the final investments chosen:

- **Risk neutral** decision makers consider all possible options and will try to select the one that maximises the expected return
- **Risk seekers** are likely to choose the option that will give the best return regardless of the risk involved
- **Risk averse** decision makers will consider the options and make a decision based on minimising the risk involved

All investments should be considered by a number of people as they may each have a different view point on the 'considered' level of risk. Company policy should also be robust enough to manage the risk levels.

3.3 Costs

There are a number of costs associated with making investments. Some of which are:

- **Brokerage fees** – some investments can be bought and sold through a broker, for example shares. There will be fees charged by the broker for making the sale or purchase.
- **Early termination costs** – if money is removed from some investments before it reaches maturity or realisation there may be a fee to apply. This also applies if the decision is to use surplus cash by repaying a loan early.
- **Interest rate changes** – increases or decreases in interest rates can have an impact on the value of the investment. See the next section for more detail.

3.4 Interest rate changes

Some short-term investments will have variable rates of interest. For example, many **bank deposit accounts** have **variable** rates of interest which means that if the bank base rate goes up or down the interest earned on the deposit will also increase or decrease. This is an **advantage** if interest rates go **up** but a **disadvantage** if they go **down**.

Other types of investment, such as **fixed rate deposit accounts and gilt edged securities**, are **fixed** rate investments. This means that if the general rate of interest changes there is no change in the interest paid on these investments. This is an **advantage** if interest rates go **down** but a **disadvantage** if interest rates go **up**.

Example

If an investment is made in a **fixed rate deposit account** and interest rates were expected to change then this would have **no effect on the amount deposited**. The principal amount invested will always remain the same and this is the amount that will be repaid at the end of the term of the investment no matter what happens to interest rates. What will be affected is the level of return in comparison to variable rate deposit accounts:

- If interest rates rise above the fixed rate then the investment will be returning less than a variable rate deposit account
- If interest rates drop below the fixed rate then the investment will be returning more than a variable rate deposit account

Example

An investment in **fixed rate gilts** is rather different. These are marketable securities, i.e. they can be sold on to another investor. As such, their **market value will fluctuate** with changes in underlying interest rates or the base rate.

- If a business has invested in gilts and the **interest rate increases** then the **value of the gilt will fall** in order to ensure that the return is in line with general interest rates.
- If the base rate of interest is decreased then the market value of the gilts will increase.

Therefore, the person responsible for such investments should take account of expected changes in economic and financial conditions before making an investment.

Activity 7

Task 1

Wilson Limited's long-term cash flow forecast to year ended 20X9 suggests a cash surplus of £1 million will be generated in 20X8 and £1.75 million in 20X9.

The company is considering its future cash management strategy and is considering four business strategies. For each of the following four scenarios, suggest what action you would take to manage the cash surplus and explain the reasons for your suggestion.

(a) Plans for an acquisition of a cycle parts manufacturer (value up to £5 million) when a suitable opportunity arises.

(b) Development in 20X8 and 20X9 of several new product lines requiring capital investment of £2.5 million.

(c) Phased development of two new product lines requiring capital investment of £1.25 million and the intention to acquire another cycle parts manufacturer (value up to £3 million) when a suitable opportunity arises.

Task 2

What are the main factors to consider when investing a cash surplus? Identify three factors and briefly explain their importance

4 Security of cash and investments

4.1 Introduction

At the start of this chapter it was argued that cash is an idle asset and ideally should be invested immediately to earn interest even if this is for a very short term, such as overnight. However, there are many businesses in the retail sector, or even manufacturing businesses with a retail outlet, which will necessarily have to deal with potentially large amounts of cash on a daily basis before it can be banked or otherwise invested.

4.2 Security of cash

Obviously cash is a highly risky asset to be holding on the business premises as it can so easily be misappropriated or stolen. Therefore, for any cash based business or part of a business, there must be strict procedures and policies to be followed to ensure that the cash and cheques taken from customers are secure and are **banked as quickly as possible.**

4.3 Security procedures for cash

Any business dealing with cash must have basic security procedures in place. The main ones that must be followed are:

- **Physical safeguards.** The cash taken must at all times be kept safe and only accessible to authorised individuals. This means that cash should be kept under lock and key either in a cash box or in a lockable till. Only authorised individuals should have access to the keys.
- **Valid payment.** If cheques are accepted as payment then they must be supported by a valid cheque guarantee card. If credit cards are accepted, authorisation must be sought for payments which exceed the limit.
- **Reconciliation.** A list of all cash, cheques and credit card payments taken during the day must be kept and this must be reconciled at the end of the day to the amount of cash in the till or cash box. The reconciliation should be carried out by someone other than the person responsible for making the sales. Any discrepancies between the amount of cash taken during the day and the amount left at the end of the day must be investigated.
- **Banking.** The receipts should be banked promptly each day. This not only ensures the physical safety of the cash in the bank and that it cannot be used by employees for unauthorised purposes, but also that it is earning the business the maximum amount of interest in the bank account. All cash should be banked as soon as possible but, if it is not to be banked until the following day, then either the cash must be left in a locked safe overnight or in the bank's night safe.
- **Recording.** The paying-in slip for the bank should be made out by someone other than the person paying the money into the bank and should be reconciled to the till records for the day.

4.4 Security procedures for investments

Any business that has made investments will need to keep the associated paperwork safe and secure. It is therefore recommended that businesses:

- Keep certificates in a safe
- Only allow few named employees bank authorisation for transfers
- Keep a list of all investments
- Keep records of authorised signatories

5 Summary

If a business has a short-term surplus of funds then these should be invested, rather than remaining as idle cash which is not earning any income for the business.

The main factors to consider when determining the type of investment are the risk, return and liquidity of the investment.

If a business deals with cash sales then management should ensure that basic security measures for the cash are in place.

Answers to chapter activities

Activity 1

(a) (i) **Liquidity**

The ability of a company to meet its debts as they fall due. The ability to change the liquidity profile (i.e. by selling investments) to meet unforeseen circumstances.

(ii) **Safety**

Investment of surplus cash must not be vulnerable to any unacceptable risk of loss through credit, market or exchange risk.

(iii) **Rate of return**

The return on the cash investment after taking into account transaction costs, management overheads and possible gains or losses on principal.

(b) Safety is the most important factor. Most short-term cash investments can be easily liquidated, even if at a discount. The difference between rates of return on high quality cash investments will be insignificant compared with the scale of loss encountered if there is loss of principal.

Activity 2

(a) **Better control of financial risk**

By determining and maintaining the proper level of cash within a company in accordance with the organisation's financial procedures and within defined authorisation limits.

(b) **Opportunity for profit**

By reducing to a minimum the opportunity cost associated with maintaining cash balances in excess of a company's operating needs. Earnings (or surpluses) are improved by freeing up surplus cash for investment purposes while reducing interest charged through minimising borrowing.

(c) **Strengthened statement of financial position**

By reducing or eliminating cash balances in excess of target balances and putting surplus cash to work by investing (e.g. in the overnight money market); by reducing or eliminating cash borrowing and keeping interest costs as low as possible.

(d) **Increased confidence of customers, suppliers, banks and shareholders**

By having access to funds to disburse to suppliers (payables), banks (interest, fees and principal payments) and shareholders (dividends) when due. By providing good instructions to customers (receivables) to enable the organisation to convert receipts into usable bank deposits.

Activity 3

(a) **Interest yield**

$$\frac{4\% \times £100}{£94} \times 100 = 4.26\%$$

(b) **Approximate redemption yield**

If an investor buys the stock now at £94.00 and holds it for three years until maturity, he will make a capital gain of 100 – 94 = £6 at redemption. In other words, there will be a capital gain of £6 for every £100 of stock, or for every £94 invested. This gives an average annual gain on redemption of £2 for each £94 invested, which is about 2% per annum.

The approximate redemption yield is therefore the interest yield of 4.25% plus 2%, which is 6.25%

£100 - £94 = £6.

∴ £6 per £100 or £94 invested.

Activity 4

$$\frac{500}{9{,}500} \times 100 = 5.26\% \text{ over 91 days}$$

Annual yield = 5.26 ÷ 91× 365 = 21.1%

Activity 5

$$\frac{1}{40} \times 100 = 2.5\%$$

Activity 6

What type of investment do the following describe:

Interest rates are fixed and these types of securities are considered to be low risk because they are backed by the government.

B Government securities

Certificates issued by banks that certify that an amount of money has been deposited and will be repaid at a specific date in the future. They can be traded on a market. They are considered to be a low risk investment.

A Certificates of deposit

Activity 7

Task 1

(a) Action – Invest cash in bank deposits or marketable securities (e.g. CDs, commercial paper).

Reason: To leave Wilson Limited with sufficient liquidity to help it make the acquisition, whilst receiving a market return on its cash investments.

(b) Action – Use cash to make the necessary capital investment in the new product lines.

Reason: Unless the cash is likely to be needed for a specific reason (such as an acquisition when cash will be needed immediately) it is unlikely that Wilson Limited will receive a return on its cash investments equivalent to the cost of raising debt finance.

(c) Action – Hold the cash to make the acquisition; either borrow or raise additional equity finance.

Reason: The cash will be required for the eventual acquisition at short notice. The new product lines should be easily financed using external funds.

Task 2

Risk	To ensure the investment is of acceptable credit standing.
Liquidity	To ensure the investment has sufficient marketability to allow the maximum availability of funds.
Return	To ensure the investment offers a good yield without unduly increasing risk or credit quality.

6 Test your knowledge

Workbook Activity 8

Four possible investment options are available:

Option 1

Investment of £60,000 required, there is a 90 day notice period, risk has been assessed as medium due to the inclusion of some shares in the portfolio and the interest rate is 5% per annum.

Option 2

Investment should be between £40,000 and £80,000, there is a 30 day notice period, interest is 3%, risk has been assessed as low as there is no inclusion of shares.

Option 3

Investment portfolio consists of stocks and shares so is high risk but with a projected interest rate of 8%. There is a minimum investment of £35,000 required and a 45 day notice period exists.

Option 4

A low risk investment opportunity with a guaranteed return of 2.5%, the minimum investment required is £40,000 and 10 working days notice must be given for withdrawals.

The treasury department has the following policy for investing surplus funds:

It must be possible to access the cash invested within 45 days.

The maximum investment amount is £45,000.

The interest rate must be 2.5% above base rate, which is currently 0.5%.

The investment must be low risk.

Complete the table below and decide which policy can be invested in, if any.

	Convertible within 45 days?	*Investment £45,000 or below?*	*Interest rate 2.5% above base rate?*	*Low risk?*	*Invest?*
Option 1					
Option 2					
Option 3					
Option 4					

Workbook Activity 9

Use the pick lists to complete the following sentences:

Certificates of deposit are certificates issued by [banks/local authorities/government]. They [can/cannot] be traded on a market. They are considered to be a [low risk/high risk] investment.

Local authority short term loans are certificates issued by [banks/local authorities/government]. They [can/cannot] be traded on a market. They are considered to be a [low risk/high risk] investment.

Government securities are also known as [gold-edged/gilt-edged/gilted] securities. They [can/cannot] be traded on a market. They are considered to be a [low risk/high risk] investment.

Workbook Activity 10

A company is looking to invest £50,000 for 6 months. Four possible investment options are available:

Option 1 – Bank notice deposit account

Fixed interest is 5% per annum, there is a 60 day notice period with an early redemption cost of £1,000

Option 2 – Bank deposit account

Fixed interest is 0.5% per month, there is a 30 day notice period, early redemption is not available

Option 3 – Gilts

Purchase of gilts, which reach maturity in 1 year, with a fixed interest rate of 6% per annum, payable quarterly.

Option 4 – Shares

An investment opportunity in shares with a possible return of 8% in 6 months.

The treasury department has the following policy for investing surplus funds:

It must be possible to access the cash invested within 30 days.

The investment must be low risk.

It has also been noted that the base rate is likely to rise over the next 6 months.

Which of the four options available is the most suitable for the company?

Workbook Activity 11

8% Treasury Stock 2012 has a par value of £100 and a market price of £126.9784 at 31 March 2006. Calculate the interest yield.

Assumed knowledge

1 Depreciation

1.1 Introduction

Non-current assets are capitalised in the statement of financial position at the point when they are purchased. However this is not the end of the story.

1.2 The accruals concept

The accruals concept states 'costs incurred in a period should be matched with the income produced in the same period'. Non-current assets are purchased to help generate income over a long period of time. In accordance with the accruals concept the cost of the asset should be matched to the period over which income is earned.

1.3 What is depreciation?

It is the measurement of the cost of the non-current asset consumed in a period. It reflects the wear and tear of a non-current asset in a period.

1.4 Calculating depreciation

There are three key factors to consider:

- Cost of the asset
- Useful economic life (period over which economic benefits are expected to be derived from asset)
- Residual value (amount that the asset is expected to be sold for at the end of its useful economic life)

There are two main ways of calculating depreciation:

1.5 Straight line method

This method assumes that the asset is used consistently throughout its life. Accordingly the depreciation charge is the same each year and the carrying value of the asset is reduced by the same amount each accounting period.

There are two different ways that you may be asked to calculate straight-line depreciation.

Example

$$\frac{\text{Cost – residual value}}{\text{Useful economic life}}$$

A new oven has been purchased by Ian for his cafe. Calculate the depreciation charge per year for the oven

Cost £100,000

Residual value £25,000

Useful economic life 5 years

$$\frac{£100{,}000 - £25{,}000}{5}$$

= £15,000 per year

Example

Cost – residual value × %

Roxanne's business policy for her hairdressing business is to depreciate non-current assets at 25% on cost each year

What is the depreciation charge each year if one of the assets costs £15,000?

£15,000 × 25% = £3,750

1.6 Diminishing (reducing) balance method

This method assumes that an asset is used less and less the older it gets. For this reason the depreciation charge falls each year.

It is calculated by multiplying the asset's carrying amount (the cost of the asset that has not been charged to the Statement of Profit or Loss) and multiplying it by a set percentage.

Example

Fixtures and fittings in Dev's corner shop cost £40,000. His business policy is to depreciate these assets at 10% per annum on a diminishing (reducing) balance basis.

Calculate the depreciation for the first three years of ownership.

Year 1 – £40,000 × 10% = £4,000

Year 2 – (£40,000 – £4,000) × 10% = £3,600

Year 3 – (£40,000 – £4,000 – £3,600) × 10% = £3,240

2 Accruals and prepayments

2.1 Introduction

An organisation's Statement of Profit or Loss and Statement of Financial Position are prepared on the basis of the accruals concept. Income is included on the basis of when it is earned, irrespective of whether it has been received in cash, and expenditure is included on the basis of when it is incurred, irrespective of whether it has actually been paid.

This principle applies not only to sales and purchases but also to other income and expenses.

2.2 Accruals

Definition

An accrual is an expense incurred in a period but not yet paid for.

Accounting for an accrual – Journal entry

Dr Expense account*	X	
Cr Accruals	X	(current liability in SoFP)

*Will depend on the expense to which the accrual relates.

Example

A business has a year end of 31 December 20X6. The last phone bill received and paid during the year covered the period to 31 October 20X6.

Post year-end an invoice that covered November, December 20X6 and January 20X7 was received. The phone charge for that period was £600.

Required

Calculate the year-end accrual for the phone expense.

Solution

£600 ÷ 3 × 2 = £400

Example

A business has a year-end of 31 December 20X5. The last gas bill received and paid covered the period from 1 January 20X5 to 31 July 20X5. The bill was for £1,400. Gas is expected to accrue evenly over the year.

Required

Based on the information provided, estimate the gas accrual for the year to 31 December 20X5.

Solution

£1,400 ÷ 7 × 5 = £1,000

2.3 Prepayments

Definition

A prepayment is a payment made in advance – the expense relates to a period following the current accounting period.

Accounting for a prepayment – Journal entry

Dr Prepayments X (current asset in SoFP)

Cr Expense account* X

*Will depend on the expense to which the prepayment relates.

Example

Andrews's year-end is 31 December 20X6.

The bank summary for premises insurance shows that Andrew paid £1,500.

This was to cover the period 1 January 20X6 to 31 March 20X7.

Required

Calculate the prepayment as at 31 December 20X6.

Solution

£1,500 ÷ 15 × 3 = £300

Example

Jason's year end is 31 December 20X8

Jason paid road tax of £120. This was for the period 1 July 20X8 to 30 June 20X9.

Required

Calculate the prepayment as at 31 December 20X8.

Solution

£120 ÷ 12 × 6 = £60

2.4 Opening accruals and prepayments

If there is a closing accrual or prepayment it will need to be brought down to be an opening accrual or prepayment for the next period.

Example

The electricity account for the year ended 30 June 20X3 included an accrual for £650. The bank payments for the next 3 months were £12,100. There was an accrual at the end of September of £650.

Write up the electricity expense account clearly showing the accrual balance brought forward and the balance carried forward for the three months ended 30 September 20X3.

Electricity account

Date	Detail	£	Date	Detail	£
30/06/X3	Closing Accrual	650			
30/09/X3	Bank	12,100	1/07/X3	Opening Accrual	650
30/09/X3	Closing Accrual	550	30/09/X3	Expense for the period	12,000
		12,650			12,650

Example

The insurance account for the year ended 30 June 20X3 included a prepayment for £300. The bank payments for the next 3 months were £4,300. There was a prepayment at the end of September of £600.

Write up the insurance expense account clearly showing the prepayment balance brought forward and the balance carried forward for the three months ended 30 September 20X3.

Insurance account

Date	Detail	£	Date	Detail	£
			30/06/X3	Closing Prepayment	300
1/07/X3	Opening Prepayment	300	30/09/X3	Expense for the period	4,000
30/09/X3	Bank	4,300	30/09/X3	Closing Prepayment	600
		4,600			4,600

3 Disposals

3.1 Introduction

When a non-current asset is disposed of (i.e. sold or scrapped), it is unlikely that the proceeds from sale will be equal to the carrying value of the asset in the statement of financial position.

The difference between the carrying value and the sale proceeds will be either a profit or a loss on the disposal of a non-current asset.

- Profit – this will occur where the sales proceeds exceed the carrying value.
- Loss – this will occur where the sales proceeds are lower than the carrying value.

3.2 Steps to disposing of a non-current asset

Firstly open a disposal T Account, then:

- Step 1 – Remove the original cost of the disposed asset from the asset account

  Dr Disposals

  Cr Non-current asset cost

- Step 2 – Remove the accumulated depreciation of the disposed asset from the accumulated depreciation account

  Dr Non-current asset accumulated depreciation

  Cr Disposals

- Step 3 – Enter the sale proceeds received/receivable for the disposed asset

  Dr Bank/Receivable

  Cr Disposals

- Step 4 – Balance off the ledger accounts and calculate whether a profit or loss has been made on disposal

Example

Veronica has a motor vehicle with a carrying value of £2,800. The motor vehicle had originally cost £7,000. Veronica sells the asset for £3,000 cash.

Required

Show the journal entries to dispose of the non-current asset above and calculate the profit or loss on the disposal of the non-current asset.

Solution

	£	£
Dr Disposal account	7,000	
Cr Motor vehicles cost account		7,000
Dr Accumulated depreciation – MV	4,200	
Cr Disposal account		4,200
Dr Cash	3,000	
Cr Disposal account		3,000

Disposal

Motor vehicles	7,000	Accumulated depreciation	4,200
Profit on disposal	200	Cash	3,000
	7,200		7,200

3.3 Part exchange of assets

You may come across a situation where instead of selling a non-current asset for cash, an old asset is taken by the supplier in part exchange for a new asset. A cheque/cash is paid for the net cost of the new asset, after offsetting the part exchange value of the old asset.

It is important that the new asset is recorded at its full cost, not the net amount for which a cheque/cash is paid. So in this situation you have got to deal with both the sale of one asset and the purchase of another.

Journals for part exchange		£	£
1	Dr Disposal account	X	
	Cr Non-current asset cost account		X
2	Dr Accumulated depreciation	X	
	Cr Disposal account		X
3	Dr Non-current asset cost account (part exchange value)	X	
	Cr Disposal account		X
4	Dr Non-current asset cost account	X	(net cost)
	Cr Bank/trade payables		X

Example

During the year Sarah part exchanged a machine that had originally cost £20,000 and had accumulated depreciation of £17,000.

The new machine cost £15,000 and a cheque for £14,000 was written for the remaining balance.

Required

Prepare the journal entries to account for the disposal and purchase of the assets and write up the disposal account to calculate the profit or loss on disposal.

Solution	£	£
Dr Disposal account	20,000	
Cr Machine cost account		20,000
Dr Accum dep'n – machines	17,000	
Cr Disposal account		17,000
Dr Machine cost account (part exchange)	1,000	
Cr Disposal account		1,000
Dr Machine cost account (net cost)	14,000	
Cr Cash		14,000

Disposal account

Machine	20,000	Accumulated depreciation	17,000
		Part exchange	1,000
		Loss on disposal	2,000
	20,000		20,000

4 Irrecoverable debts

4.1 Introduction

Trade receivables should only be included as assets in a statement of financial position if they are expected to settle the amounts due from them. The prudence concept requires an organisation to recognise future losses as soon as it becomes aware of their existence. This means that as soon as an organisation is aware that a debt may not be settled, then the asset value should be reduced by an adjustment being put through the accounts.

4.2 Irrecoverable debts

This is a debt that the business believes will NOT be recovered. It should be completely removed from the ledger accounts and therefore from the statement of financial position.

Double entry to account for an irrecoverable debt:

Dr Irrecoverable debt	X (SoPL)	
Cr SLCA		X (SoFP)

4.3 Doubtful debts

This is a debt about which there is some question as to whether or not the amount will be settled. We must recognise this doubt in the accounts but we should not write off the debt completely, because the cash may be received. In any event we need to keeping pressing for it to be settled. Therefore we still need to show the debt as outstanding.

Example

Shauna has trade receivables at her year-end of £25,000.

There is concern about whether £5,000 of this will be settled.

Dr Irrecoverable debt expense	5,000 (SoPL)	
Cr Allowance for doubtful debts		5,000 (SoFP)

The allowance for doubtful debts is offset against the trade receivables balance in the statement of financial position.

Statement of financial position extract

Trade receivables	25,000
Less allowance for doubtful debts	(5,000)
	20,000

This treatment clearly shows that there is doubt as to whether the debt will be received but does not write it off and we can continue chasing it.

4.4 Types of allowance for doubtful debts

There are two main types:

- **Specific allowance** – calculated by reference to a particular invoice or trade receivables balance.
- **General allowance** – this is an allowance against trade receivables as a whole, normally expressed as a percentage of the trade receivables balance.

5 The statement of financial position

	£	£
Non-current assets		
Property, plant and equipment		X
Goodwill		X
Investments in associates		X
		X
Current assets		
Inventories	X	
Trade and other receivables	X	
Cash and cash equivalents	X	
		X
Total assets		**X**
Equity		
Share capital		X
Share premium account		X
Retained earnings		X
Revaluation reserve		X
Total equity		X
Non-current liabilities		
Loans or debentures		X
Current liabilities		
Trade and other payables	X	
Bank overdrafts	X	
Tax payable	X	
		X
Total liabilities		X
Total equity and liabilities		**X**

6 The statement of profit or loss

	£
Revenue	X
Cost of sales	(X)
Gross profit	X
Distribution costs	(X)
Administrative expenses	(X)
Operating profit	X
Finance costs	(X)
Profit before tax	X
Tax	(X)
Profit for the period	**X**
Other comprehensive income	
Gain on revaluation of land	X
Total comprehensive income for year	X

7 Net assets

7.1 The accounting equation

The basic accounting equation is that:

Net assets = Capital

Remember that net assets = business assets – business liabilities

This can be expanded to:

Increase in net assets = Capital introduced + profit – drawings

This is important: any increase in the net assets of the business must be due to the introduction of new capital and/or the making of profit less drawings.

7.2 Using the accounting equation

If the opening net assets of the business can be determined and also the closing net assets then the increase in net assets is the difference.

Therefore if any capital introduced is known together with any drawings made by the owner, then the profit for the period can be deduced.

Alternatively if the profit and capital introduced are known then the drawings can be found as the balancing figure.

Example

Archibald started a business on 1 January 20X1 with £2,000. On 31 December 20X1 the position of the business was as follows:

	£
It owned	
Freehold lock–up shop, at cost	4,000
Shop fixtures and equipment, at cost	500
Inventory of goods bought for resale, at cost	10,300
Debts owing by customers	500
Cash in till	10
Cash at bank	150
It owed	
Mortgage on shop premises	3,000
Payables for goods	7,000
Accrued mortgage interest	100

Archibald had drawn £500 for personal living expenses.

The shop fixtures are to be depreciated by £50 and certain goods in inventory which had cost £300 can be sold for only £50.

No records had been maintained throughout the year.

You are required to calculate the profit earned by Archibald's business in the year ended 31 December 20X1.

Solution

This sort of question is answered by calculating the net assets at the year-end as follows:

Net assets at 31 December 20X1

	Cost	Depreciation	CV
	£	£	£
Non-current assets			
Freehold shop	4,000	–	4,000
Fixtures and fittings	500	50	450
	4,500	50	4,450
Current assets			
Inventory at lower of cost and net realisable value (10,300 – 300 + 50)		10,050	
Trade receivables		500	
Cash and bank balances (150 + 10)		160	
		10,710	
Current liabilities			
Trade payables	7,000		
Mortgage interest	100		
		(7,100)	
			3,610
			8,060
Mortgage			(3,000)
Net assets			5,060

The profit is now calculated from the accounting equation.

Note that the opening net assets will be the cash paid into the bank when the business was started on 1 January 20X1.

Change in net assets =		Profit + capital introduced – drawings
£5,060 – 2,000	=	Profit + Nil – 500
£3,060	=	Profit – 500
Profit	=	£3,560

Example

Jones and Sons is a firm of builders who have been trading for just over a year. The tax authorities have just raised a tax assessment on the firm based on profits of £42,000. The owner David Jones does not believe that the firm has done that well because they have an overdraft at the year end. He needs a profit figure with which to counter the claim by the tax authorities. Unfortunately proper accounting records have not been kept. However the following facts have been established in respect of the year end.

- Depreciation needs to be charged at 25% on a straight line basis against the van. The van cost £12,000.
- Sundry building tools purchased in the year cost £4,000 of which £1,000 is to be written off.
- Inventory of cement and sand at cost £1,000.
- Owed by clients – £26,000. A debt of £1,000 is to be written off for work in dispute and a receivables allowance of 2% is required.
- There is an overdraft of £2,000.
- Trade payables amount to £7,000.
- There are accrued expenses of £150.
- The Jones family introduced £10,000 at the start of the year and have drawn out an average of £2,000 per month.

Calculate the profit of Jones and Sons for the year, based upon the above information.

Solution

Year end Statement of Financial Position

	£
Van (12,000 – (12,000 × 25%))	9,000
Tools (4,000 – 1,000)	3,000
Cement and sand	1,000
Receivables (26,000 – 1,000)	25,000
Less allowance ((26,000 – 1,000) × 2%)	(500)
Overdraft (remember this is negative)	(2,000)
Trade payables	(7,000)
Accrued expenses	(150)
Net assets at year end	28,350

Profit calculation

	£
Net assets at end of year	28,350
Less net assets at beginning of year	(nil)
Increase in net assets	28,350
Less capital introduced in the year	(10,000)
Add drawings for the year (12 months × £2,000)	24,000
Profit for the year	42,350

8 Internal rate of return

8.1 Definition

Definition

The **IRR** calculates the **rate of return** (or discount rate) that one project is expected to achieve if it **breaks even** i.e. no profit or loss is made. The IRR is therefore the point where the **NPV of an investment is zero**.

For one investment, a graph of NPV against discount rate looks like the following:

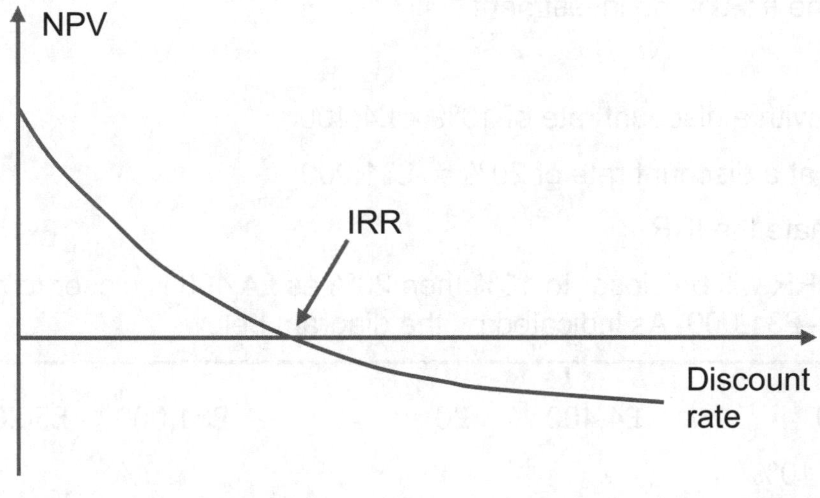

As the discount rate gets higher, the NPV gets smaller and then becomes negative. The cash flows are being discounted by a higher percentage therefore the present value of the cash flows becomes less.

The internal rate of return (IRR) is the discount rate that will cause the cash flow of a project to have a net present value equal to zero.

To decide on whether to invest using the IRR you need to compare the IRR with the discount rate that the company would like to use. If the chosen discount rate was somewhere between 10% and 15%, and the IRR of a project was 22% then we can still accept the project as our rate is less than the IRR, giving a positive NPV.

8.2 Calculation of the IRR

The approximate IRR of a project can be estimated by considering how close the NPVs are to zero.

The method used to estimate the IRR is as follows:

- Calculate two NPVs for the investment at different discount rates.
- Estimate the IRR with reference to the NPV values.

Example

A machine costs £150,000 now. We expect the following cash flows:

	Year 1 (t = 1) £000	*Year 2 (t = 2)* £000	*Year 3 (t = 3)* £000	*Year 4 (t = 4)* £000	*Year 5 (t = 5)* £000
Scrap value					30
Sales revenues	40	50	60	50	40
Variable costs	(10)	(12)	(15)	(13)	(11)

Estimate the IRR of the investment.

Solution

1 NPV with a discount rate of 10% = £4,400

2 NPV at a discount rate of 20% = -£31,000

3 Estimate the IRR

The IRR will be closer to 10% then 20% as £4,400 is closer to zero than –£31,000. As indicated by the diagram below:

£50,000 £4,400 £0 £31,000 –£50,000

10% 20%

From this we could estimate the IRR as approximately 11% or 12%

The IRR of an investment can also be calculated using linear interpolation i.e. it uses two known points on a graph and joins them with a straight line. The point where the line crosses the x-axis will be calculated to provide the IRR.

The method used to calculate the IRR is as follows:

- Calculate two NPVs for the investment at different discount rates
- Use the following formula to find the IRR:

$$\text{IRR}(\%) = L + \frac{N_L}{N_L - N_H} \times (H - L)$$

Where:

L = Lower rate of interest

H = Higher rate of interest

N_L = NPV at lower rate of interest

N_H = NPV at higher rate of interest

Example

A machine costs £150,000 now. We expect the following cash flows:

	Year 1 *(t = 1)* £000	*Year 2* *(t = 2)* £000	*Year 3* *(t = 3)* £000	*Year 4* *(t = 4)* £000	*Year 5* *(t = 5)* £000
Scrap value					30
Sales revenues	40	50	60	50	40
Variable costs	(10)	(12)	(15)	(13)	(11)

Calculate the IRR of the investment.

Solution

1 NPV with a discount rate of 10% = £4,400 positive

2 NPV at a discount rate of 20% = £31,000 negative

3 Using the formula – you need to remember the rules of maths. Remove the brackets first, then deal with and division or multiplication and finally addition and subtraction (BODMAS)

$$IRR = L + \frac{N_L}{N_L - N_H} \times (H - L)$$

$$IRR = 10 + \frac{4{,}400}{4{,}400 - -31{,}000} \times (20 - 10)$$

$$IRR = 10 + \frac{4{,}400}{35{,}400} \times 10$$

$$IRR = 10 + 0.1243 \times 10$$

$$IRR = 10 + 1.243 = 11.24\%$$

WORKBOOK ACTIVITIES ANSWERS

Workbook Activities Answers

1 Cash and profit

Workbook Activity 7

	Working	£
Sales receipts	1,520 + 3,000 – 1,400	3,120
Purchases payments	400 + 1,400 – 520	1,280
Wages paid	As per SoPL	300
Advertising expenses paid	As per SoPL	100
Travel expenses	50 + 400 – 80	370
Competition fees paid	150 + 110 – 80	180

2 Forecasting cash flows

Workbook Activity 12

Month	*Sales volume*	*3 Month trend*	*Seasonal variation*
Jan	49		
Feb	37	48	(11)
Mar	58	48	10
Apr	50	49	1
May	38	49	(11)
Jun	60	50	10
Jul	51	50	1
Aug	40	51	(11)
Sept	61	51	10
Oct	53	52	1
Nov	41	52	(11)
Dec	61		

Month	*Forecast sales trend*	*Variation*	*Forecast sales volume*
Jan	53	1	54
Feb	54	(11)	43
Mar	54	10	64

Workbook Activity 13

(a)

	Sales volume (units)	*Trend*	*Monthly variation*
May	11,000		
June	11,850	11,800	50
July	12,550	12,100	450
August	11,900	12,400	–500
September	12,750		

(b)

	Forecast trend	*Variation*	*Forecast sales volume*	*Forecast sales £*	*Forecast purchases £*
October	13,000	450	13,450	282,450	169,470

Workbook Activity 14

Answer D

45/132 × 154 = £52.50

Workbook Activity 15

Answer C

Production	2,000 shirts
Usage per shirt	× 1 m^2
Material usage	2,000 m^2
Opening inventory	(100 m^2)
Closing inventory 100 × 1.10	110 m^2
Purchases of material	2,010 m^2

3 Patterns of cash flow

Workbook Activity 10

Cash budgets, June – August

	June	*July*	*August*
	£	£	£
Receipts of cash			
Cash sales	4,500	5,000	6,000
Credit sales 30%	9,990	12,150	13,500
Credit sales 70%	18,900	23,310	28,350
	33,390	40,460	47,850

Workbook Activity 11

(a)

	Actual		*Forecast*			
	Oct	*Nov*	*Dec*	*Jan*	*Feb*	*Mar*
Total sales	11,000	14,000	16,000	18,500	19,900	22,100
Cash sales	2,200	2,800	3,200	3,700	3,980	4,420
Credit sales	8,800	11,200	12,800	14,800	15,920	17,680

(b)

		Cash received				
	Credit sales £	*Nov* £	*Dec* £	*Jan* £	*Feb* £	*Mar* £
October	8,800	2,200	6,600			
November	11,200		2,800	8,400		
December	12,800			3,200	9,600	
January	14,800				3,700	11,100
February	15,920					3,980
Monthly credit sales receipts			9,400	11,600	13,300	15,080

Workbook Activity 12

	Nov	*Dec*	*Jan*	*Feb*
Receipts:	£	£	£	£
Cash sales (W1)	18,000	17,600	16,800	20,000
Credit sales (W2)	24,000	27,000	26,400	25,200
	42,000	44,600	43,200	45,200
Payments:				
Purchases (W3)	16,000	18,000	17,600	16,800
Wages	2,000	2,000	2,000	2,000
Fixed costs (W4)	6,000	6,000	6,000	6,000
	24,000	26,000	25,600	24,800

Workings

(W1) Since 60% of sales are credit sales, 40% are cash sales, e.g.

November cash sales = £45,000 × 40% = £18,000

(W2) October credit sales are paid in November, and so on.

Credit sales = 60% so the October receipt = 60% × £40,000 = £24,000.

(W3) 40% of the next months sales paid 2 months later i.e. the purchases in November will ordered and received in September and will be 40% of October sales

e.g. November: (40% × £40,000) = £16,000

(W4) Fixed costs: £6,000 (£7,500 – £1,500)

4 Preparing cash budgets

Workbook Activity 9

Cash flow forecast for the first three months of next year

	January £	*February* £	*March* £
Cash received			
Sales: cash	18,000	18,500	20,000
Sales: credit	7,000	6,000	7,000
Grant	20,000	0	0
Total	45,000	24,500	27,000
Cash paid			
Equipment: deposit	–50,000	0	0
Equipment: instalment	0	–50,000	0
Rent	–5,000	0	0
Wages	–6,000	–6,000	–6,000
Purchases	–10,000	–10,000	–10,000
Selling/administration	–2,400	–2,500	–2,600
Overdraft interest	0	0	–324
Total	–73,400	–68,500	–18,924
Net cash flow	–28,400	–44,000	8,076
Opening cash balance	40,000	11,600	–32,400
Closing cash balance	11,600	–32,400	–24,324

Workbook Activity 10

Cash flow forecast for the first three months of next year, new division

	January £	*February* £	*March* £
CASH RECEIVED			
Sales: cash	12,000	12,500	13,000
Sales: credit	–	12,000	12,500
Grant	20,000		
Total	32,000	24,500	25,500
CASH PAID			
Equipment: deposit	–50,000		
Equipment: instalment		–50,000	
Rent	–5,000		
Wages	–6,000	–6,000	–6,000
Purchases			–10,000
Selling/administration	–2,400	–2,500	–2,600
Total	–63,400	–58,500	–18,600
Net cash flow	–31,400	–34,000	6,900
Opening cash balance	0	–31,400	–65,400
Closing cash balance	–31,400	–65,400	–58,500

Workbook Activity 11

	January £	*February* £	*March* £	*April* £
Original value of sales	30,000	45,000	51,000	57,000
Original timing of receipts (W1)	12,000	36,000	47,400	53,400
Revised value of sales	28,800	43,200	48,960	54,720
Revised timing of receipts (W2)	5,760	17,280	37,152	47,232
Increase/(decrease) in receipts	–6,240	–18,720	–10,248	–6,168

	January £	*February* £	*March* £	*April* £
Original timing of payments	4,000	4,200	4,400	4,600
Revised timing of payments (W3)	0	1,600	4,080	4,280
(Increase)/decrease in payment	4,000	2,600	320	320

	February £	*March* £	*April* £
Original net cash flow	20,000	20,300	20,800
Changes in receipts	–18,720	–10,248	–6,168
Changes in payments	2,600	320	320
Revised net cash flow	3,880	10,372	14,952
Opening bank balance	7,500	11,380	21,752
Closing bank balance	11,380	21,752	36,704

Workings

(W1)

	January	*February*	*March*	*April*
In month	12,000	18,000	20,400	22,800
In following month	0	18,000	27,000	30,600
Total	12,000	36,000	47,400	53,400

(W2)

	January	*February*	*March*	*April*
In month	5,760	8,640	9,792	10,944
One month following	0	8,640	12,960	14,688
Two months following	0	0	14,400	21,600
Total	5,760	17,280	37,152	47,232

(W3)

	January	*February*	*March*	*April*
One month following	0	1,600	1,680	1,760
Two months following	0	0	2,400	2,520
Total	0	1,600	4,080	4,280

Workbook Activity 12

Impact on bank balance if receivables pay one month later

	January	*February*	*March*
	£	£	£
Cash received			
Sales: cash	18,000	18,500	20,000
Sales: credit	10,000	7,000	6,000
Grant	20,000	0	0
Total	48,000	25,500	26,000
Cash paid	–73,400	–68,500	–18,924
Net cash flow	–25,400	–43,000	7,076
Opening cash balance	40,000	14,600	–28,400
Closing cash balance	14,600	–28,400	–21,324

Workbook Activity 13

(a) Cash flow forecast for the three months ended 31 December 20X3

	October £	*November* £	*December* £
Receipts			
Trade sales (W)	240,000	240,000	246,000
Shop sales (4,000 × £3.50)	14,000	14,000	14,000
Total receipts	254,000	254,000	260,000
Payments			
Trade suppliers (W)	93,600	98,100	107,100
Production wages (£1 per unit)	109,000	119,000	129,000
Production overheads	16,000	16,000	16,000
Sales department costs	9,500	9,500	9,500
Retail shop costs	7,000	7,000	7,000
Administration costs	20,000	20,000	20,000
Overdraft interest (at 0.75%)	1,425	1,444	1,572
Total payments	256,525	271,044	290,172
Net cash flow	(2,525)	(17,044)	(30,172)
Opening cash balance	(190,000)	(192,525)	(209,569)
Closing cash balance	(192,525)	(209,569)	(239,741)

Working

	October (units)	November (units)	December (units)
Sales			
Credit	100,000	110,000	120,000
Shop	4,000	4,000	4,000
	104,000	114,000	124,000
Closing inventory	45,000	50,000	55,000
Opening inventory	(40,000)	(45,000)	(50,000)
Production required	109,000	119,000	129,000
	£	£	£
Purchases (at 90p per unit)	98,100	107,100	116,100

	October £	November £	December £
Receipts			
B/fwd	240,000	180,000	12,000
October sales	0	60,000	168,000
November sales	0	0	66,000
December sales	0	0	0
	240,000	240,000	246,000

(b) **Effect of 10% reduction in price**

If price reduced from £2.40 to £2.16 on 1 October 20X3, the effect on sales will be:

	Volume	*Reduction*		*Received*	
			October	*November*	*December*
		£	£	£	£
October	100,000	24,000	0	6,000	16,800
November	110,000	26,400	0	0	6,600
December	120,000	28,800	0	0	0
			0	6,000	23,400
Original overdraft			(192,525)	(209,569)	(239,741)
New overdraft			(192,525)	(215,569)	(269,141)
Interest charge			0	0	(45)
Final overdraft				(215,569)	(269,186)

Therefore, the final overdraft will increase by £29,445.

Action that could be taken:

(i) Receivables could be collected more quickly.

(ii) Additional credit could be taken from suppliers.

Workbook Activity 14

	Jan	*Feb*	*March*	*April*	*May*	*June*
	£	£	£	£	£	£
Cash receipts						
Sale of shares	5,000	0	0	0	0	0
Receivables (W1)	200	1,500	4,000	6,750	9,300	12,500
Government grant	0	0	0	0	0	10,000
	5,200	1,500	4,000	6,750	9,300	22,500

Overdraft facility would need to be £15,000 to cover the cash shortfall in May.

Workings

(W1) **Receipts from receivables**

	Jan	*Feb*	*March*	*April*	*May*	*June*
	£	£	£	£	£	£
Sales	2,000	5,000	8,000	10,000	15,000	15,000
Receipts						
Jan	200	1,000	700			
Feb		500	2,500	1,750		
March			800	4,000	2,800	
April				1,000	5,000	3,500
May					1,500	7,500
June						1,500
	200	1,500	4,000	6,750	9,300	12,500

(W2) **Payments for purchases**

		Jan	*Feb*	*March*	*April*	*May*	*June*
		£	£	£	£	£	£
Sales		2,000	5,000	8,000	10,000	15,000	15,000
	Dec	*Jan*	*Feb*	*Mar*	*Apr*	*May*	*June*
	£	£	£	£	£	£	£
Purchases	1,000	2,500	4,000	5,000	7,500	7,500	
Paid							
Dec			1,000				
Jan			2,500				
Feb				4,000			
March					5,000		
April						7,500	
May							7,500
			3,500	4,000	5,000	7,500	7,500

5 Monitoring cash flows

Workbook Activity 6

(a) **Reconciliation of budgeted cash balance to actual cash balance**

	£
Budgeted cash balance	46,300
Shortfall in receipts from receivables	(26,400)
Additional payments to suppliers	(9,000)
Additional production wages	(500)
Additional production expenses	(500)
Shortfall in selling expenses	600
Unbudgeted dividend	(20,000)
Actual overdraft	(9,500)

(b) **Answer C**

A Chased customers to pay sooner – would cover overdraft but the company does not have complete control on when the receivables pay

B Delayed payments to suppliers – would not remove the overdraft

C Avoided dividend payment – covers overdraft and company has more control over the payment of dividends

D Reduced selling expenses – not required

Workbook Activity 7

Customers are buying lower value products	Actively market more expensive product lines
Customers are taking more days to settle their debts	Offer a settlement discount
Electricity cost increases	Install energy saving lights
Customers are delaying payments due to invoice queries	Improve credit control by agreeing invoices before they are posted

6 Liquidity management

Workbook Activity 8

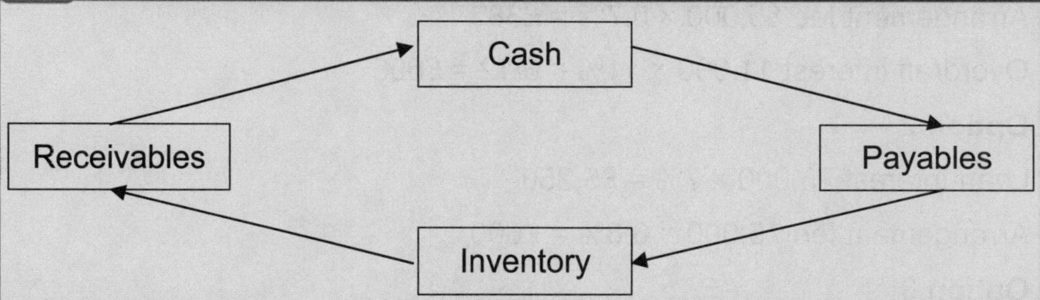

Workbook Activity 9

Overtrading can occur when working capital levels are too low.

True

Over-capitalisation can occur when working capital levels are too high.

True

7 Raising finance

Workbook Activity 10

	Loan interest £	*Arrangement fee* £	*Overdraft interest* £	*Total cost* £
Option 1	2,750	385	605	3,740
Option 2	5,250	600	0	5,850
Option 3	6,000	0	0	6,000

Recommendation: Option 1

Workings

Option 1

Loan interest 55,000 × 5% = £2,750

Arrangement fee 55,000 × 0.7% = £385

Overdraft interest 11,000 × 11% × 6/12 = £605

Option 2

Loan Interest 75,000 × 7% = £5,250

Arrangement fee 75,000 × 0.8% = £600

Option 3

Loan interest (37,500 × 8%) × 2 = £6,000

Workbook Activity 11

Which of the following best describes the main features of an overdraft?

E Interest rates are high; it is repayable on demand; it is a short-term form of finance.

Which of the following best describes the main features of a bank loan?

C Interest rates are low; repayments can be negotiated; it is useful for capital purchases.

Workbook Activity 12

MEMO

To: The Board of Directors

From: Pat King, Accounting Technician

Re: Loan and overdraft finance

Date: January 20X5

A bank overdraft is effectively a short term source of finance. An overdraft facility is made available by the bank in order to fund short term shortfalls of income compared to outgoings. A bank overdraft attracts a relatively high rate of interest and therefore would be a very costly form of finance for a £1,000,000 investment.

Companies should aim to match their sources of finance to the purposes for which they were raised. A bank overdraft is a short term source of finance suitable for funding short term working capital changes. However the purchase of machinery is a medium to long term investment and as such would be more appropriately funded by a medium to long term source of finance such as a bank loan.

The bank loan could be negotiated to be paid off over the approximate life of the machinery with repayments covering both interest and capital. Alternatively the interest could be paid off periodically but the repayment of the capital would all happen at the end of the loan term. Bank loan finance will tend to be at a lower interest rate than a bank overdraft.

For the purchase of non-current assets a bank loan will generally be the preferred method of financing rather than a bank overdraft.

8 Managing surplus funds

Workbook Activity 8

	Convertible within 45 days?	*Investment £45,000 or below?*	*Interest rate 2.5% above base rate?*	*Low risk?*	*Invest?*
Option 1	N	N	Y	N	N
Option 2	Y	Y	Y	Y	Y
Option 3	Y	Y	Y	N	N
Option 4	Y	Y	N	Y	N

Workbook Activity 9

Certificates of deposit are certificates issued by banks. They can be traded on a market. They are considered to be a low risk investment.

Local authority short term loans are certificates issued by local authorities. They can be traded on a market. They are considered to be a low risk investment.

Government securities are also known as gilt-edged securities. They can be traded on a market. They are considered to be a low risk investment.

Activity 10

	Meets policy guidelines?	*Risk*	*Return*	*Cost*	*Invest?*
Option 1	Yes	Low	1,250	1,000	No
Comments: Can access cash in 30 days but there is a charge of £1,000, the risk is low and the return = (£50,000 × 5%) × 6/12 = £1,250. Giving a net return of £250.					
Option 2	Yes	Low	1,500	0	Yes
Comments: Cash can be accessed within 30 days with no fee, the risk is low and the return = (£50,000 × 0.5%) × 6 = £1,500.					
Option 3	Yes	Low	1,500	Unknown but fees may be charged for sale	No
Comments: Cash can be accessed by selling the gilts but there may be a brokerage charge for doing so. The risk is low and the return = (£50,000 × 6%) × 6/12 = £1,500. Interest rates are likely to rise so the market value of the gilt will drop.					
Option 4	No	High	4,000	Brokerage fees to buy and sell shares	No
Comments: A high risk investment, with a high return = (£50,000 × 8%) = £4,000.					

Option 2 is the most suitable for the company.

Option 1 has the lowest net return, Option 3 may drop in market value and has unknown fees associated with the sale, Option 4 is high risk.

Workbook Activity 11

$$\text{Interest yield} = \frac{\text{Coupon rate}}{\text{Market price}} \times 100 = \frac{8}{126.9784} \times 100 = 6.3\%$$

MOCK ASSESSMENT

1 Mock Assessment Questions

Task 1

(a) Cash receipts and payments take many different forms, but they can be broadly categorised into regular, capital, exceptional and drawings.

Complete the table by selecting the correct description from the list of options below to match the type of cash receipt or cash payment.

Type of receipt or payment	*Description*
Capital payments	
Regular revenue receipts	
Drawings	
Exceptional payments	

Options:

Payments that relate to the acquisition of non-current assets.

Payments made to the owners of the business.

Income received from the operating activities of the business that are expected to occur frequently.

Payments that do not arise from the operating activities of the business and that are not expected to occur frequently.

(b) B Clarke owns a gardening business and prepares quarterly statements of profit or loss and financial position. These are prepared on an accruals basis.

The forecast Statement of profit or loss for B Clarke's business for the quarter ended 31 March is as follows:

	£	£
Revenue		128,400
Less: Purchases		(25,510)
Gross profit		102,890
Less: Expenses		
Wages	35,100	
Rent of tools	10,550	
General expenses	15,540	
Van expenses	10,120	
Van depreciation	3,190	
		74,500
Operating profit		28,390

Additional information

1 Gardening materials are purchased when required and therefore very little inventory is maintained.

2 All purchases are to be made on credit terms. The balance of trade payables at 1 January is forecast to be £1,050. Total payments for purchases during the quarter have been forecast as £25,202.

3 The balance of trade receivables at 1 January is forecast to be £18,720 and the company expects the trade receivables at 31 March to be equivalent of 20% of credit sales for the quarter. B Clarke believes that 90% of total sales will be on credit terms.

4 The Statement of Financial Position shows an accrual for general expenses of £541 at 1 January. B Clarke predicts that at 31 March there will be an accrual of £541 for general expenses.

5 There are also two prepayments at 1 January:

- Van expenses £388
- Rent of tools £1,200

B Clarke predicts that the closing prepayments for the quarter ended 31 March will be:

- Van expenses £395
- Rent of tools £1,450.

6 The forecast cash position at 1 January is £10,000 in hand.

Forecast the closing cash position at the end of March.

Use brackets or minus signs where appropriate.

	£
Operating profit	28390
Change in trade receivables	-4392
Change in trade payables	308
Rent adjustment	-250
General expenses adjustment	0
Van expenses adjustment	-7
Adjustments for other non-cash items	3190
Net change in cash position	27239
Forecast cash position 1 January	10000
Forecast cash position 31 March	37239

Task 2

A company is preparing its forecast sales and purchase information for April.

The sales volume trend is to be identified using a 3-point moving average based on the actual monthly sales volumes for the current year.

(a) **Complete the table below to calculate the monthly sales volume trend and identify any monthly variations.**

	Sales volume (units)	*Trend*	*Monthly variation*
November	425		
December	570		
January	625		
February	545		
March	690		

Additional information

The production cost per unit has been set at £13.

Assume that the increase in the trend is constant and the seasonal variations are cyclical.

(b) **Using the trend and the monthly variations identified in part a. calculate the forecast production cost for April**

The forecast production cost for April is £__________

(c) **Calculate the forecast sales value if the company requires a mark up of 25% or a margin of 10%**

The forecast sales value if the company requires a mark up of 25% is: £______(to the nearest £)

The forecast sales value if the company requires a margin of 10% is: £________(to the nearest £)

Additional information

The company uses an index to forecast future monthly wage costs. The January monthly wage cost of £11,700 was calculated when the wage index was 100.

(d) **Create an index (to one decimal place) for the wage cost for February, March and April with January as the base period.**

Month	*January*	*February*	*March*	*April*
Price	£11,700	£12,004	£11,928	£11,320
Index				

Task 3

Canvas Canopies has been trading for a number of years. The business has supplied information regarding its forecast sales, purchases and expenses.

Sales

Sales values have been forecast for January to May.

Canvas Canopies estimates that cash sales account for 15% of the total sales. The remaining 85% of sales are made on a credit basis.

	January	*February*	*March*	*April*	*May*
Total sales £	8,000	10,000	15,000	18,000	23,000

Canvas Canopies estimates that 70% of credit sales are received in the month after sale with the balance being received two months after sale.

(a) **Complete the table below to calculate the total sales receipts forecast for April and May.**

Identify the forecast trade receivables balance at the end of May.

	April £	*May* £
Total sales receipts		

The trade receivables balance at the end of May is forecast to be:

£____________

Purchases

Canvas Canopies pays their suppliers on the basis of 40% one month after date of purchase, 20% two months after purchase and the remainder three months after the date of purchase.

At the end May the balance on the trade payables is forecast to be:

	£
January	5,280
February	8,640
March	16,800
Trade payables at the end of March	30,720

(b) **Complete the table below to identify the value of trade payables at the end of March that will be paid in April and May.**

	April £	*May* £
Settlement of trade payables		

Expenses

A new machine is to be purchased in January at a total cost of £60,000. Payment for the machine is to be made in three equal monthly instalments, beginning in January.

The machine is to be depreciated monthly on a straight-line basis at 20% per annum. This has been included in the expenses of the business.

Expenses are paid in the month they are incurred.

(c) **Complete the table below to show the expenses to be included in the cash budget.**

	January £	*February* £	*March* £	*April* £	*May* £
Expenses	4,512	4,951	5,541	5,745	6,785
Expenses to be included in cash budget					

Task 4

The cash budget for Walldoor for the three months ended June has been partially completed. The following information is to be incorporated and the cash budget completed:

- A bank loan of £60,000 has been negotiated and this will be paid into the business bank account in April. The loan term is 48 months beginning in May.
- The loan attracts 5% interest per annum calculated on the amount of the loan principal advanced in April. The annual interest charge is to be paid in equal monthly instalments beginning in May.
- The company has contracted to purchase plant and machinery for £80,000. The supplier has agreed hire purchase terms. The hire purchase interest is 3% of the purchase price. The interest and instalments will be paid in 10 equal monthly amounts starting in April.
- The company plans to issue 115,000 ordinary share of £1 each in May at an issue price of £1.25 per share.
- Overdraft interest is payable monthly and is estimated at 1% of the previous months overdraft balance. The interest is to be rounded to the nearest £.
- At 1 April the balance of the bank account was £5,214.

Using the additional information above, complete the cash budget for Walldoor for the three months ending June.

Cash inflows should be entered as positive figures and cash outflows as negative figures. Round to the nearest whole £ throughout. Zeroes must be entered where appropriate to achieve full marks.

	April £	*May* £	*June* £
RECEIPTS			
Cash sales	2,700	3,450	3,900
Credit sales	15,300	19,550	22,100
Proceeds from share issue			
Bank loan			
Total receipts			
PAYMENTS			
Purchases	–13,200	–14,400	–16,800
Wages	–10,541	–10,685	–10,852
Expenses	–5,541	–5,745	–6,785
Hire purchase of plant and machinery			
Bank loan capital repayment			
Bank loan interest			
Overdraft interest			
Total payments			
Net cash flow			
Opening bank balance			
Closing bank balance			

Task 5

A cash budget has been prepared for Boxlid Ltd for a new product the next four periods.

The budget was prepared based on the following sales volumes and a selling price of £180 per item.

	Period 1	*Period 2*	*Period 3*	*Period 4*
Sales volume (items)	800	850	875	925

The pattern of cash receipts used in the budget assumed 50% of sales were received in the month of sale and the remaining 50% in the month following sale.

	Period 1 (£)	*Period 2* (£)	*Period 3* (£)	*Period 4* (£)
Original value of forecast sales	144,000	153,000	157,500	166,500

Boxlid needs to make adjustments to its cash budget to take account of the following:

- The selling price will be reduced by 15% per item.
- The pattern of sales receipts changes to 30% of sales received in the month of sale, 50% in the month following sale and the remaining 20% two months after sale.

(a) **Complete the table below to calculate the sales receipts expected in periods 1 to 4 if the selling price and receipts pattern changes (round down to the nearest £).**

	Adjusted forecast sales value £	*Sales receipts*				
		Period 1 (£)	*Period 2 (£)*	*Period 3 (£)*	*Period 4 (£)*	*Total*
Period 1 sales						
Period 2 sales						
Period 3 sales						
Period 4 sales						
Revised forecast sales receipts						

(b) **Complete the sentences below.**

If the selling price and receipt patterns change total receipts from sales in periods 1 to 4 will increase/fall by _____% (2 decimal places)

(c) **Which one of the following identifies the impact on cash flow of offering an early settlement discount to credit customers?**

A Total cash receipts remain the same but customers take less time to pay

B Total cash receipts reduce but customers take less time to pay

C Total cash receipts increase but customers take less time to pay

D Total cash receipts remain the same but customers take longer to pay

E Total cash receipts reduce but customers take longer to pay

F Total cash receipts increase but customers take longer to pay

Task 6

The quarterly budgeted and actual figures for an organisation are provided below:

	Budgeted	*Actual*
	£	£
Receipts from receivables	89,142	90,654
Cash sales	22,541	19,874
Payments to payables	(54,214)	(52,965)
Cash purchases	(6,951)	(7,841)
Capital expenditure	–	(24,850)
Wages and salaries	(20,100)	(19,540)
General expenses	(18,654)	(19,876)
Net cash flow	11,764	(14,544)
Opening bank balance	15,541	15,541
Closing bank balance	27,305	997

(a) **Prepare a reconciliation of budgeted cash flow with actual cash flow for the quarter. Select the appropriate description for each entry.**

	£
Budgeted closing bank balance	
Surplus/Shortfall in receipts from receivables	
Surplus/Shortfall in cash sales	
Increase/Decrease in payments to payables	
Increase/Decrease in cash purchases	
Increase/Decrease in capital expenditure	
Increase/Decrease in wages and salaries	
Increase/Decrease in general expenses	
Actual closing bank balance	

(b) **Discuss the variances that have arisen from this investigation.**

Task 7

(a) **Complete the diagram of the working capital cycle below, by identifying the missing phase.**

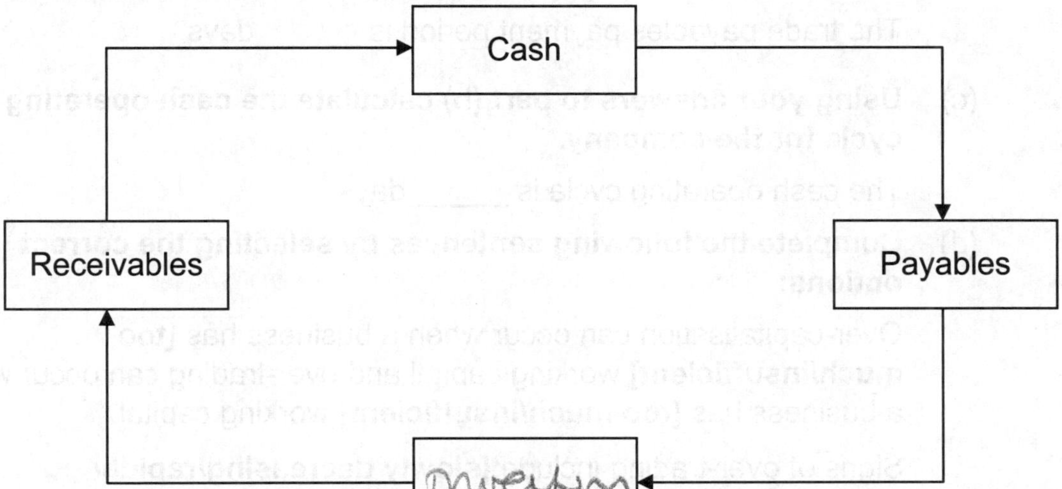

Options:

A Cash at bank

B Inventory

C Profit

D Assets

The following figures have been extracted from the financial statements of a company for the year ended December 20X3.

Statement of Financial Position (Extract)	£000	*Statement of Profit or Loss (Extract)*	£000
Inventories	150	Revenue	2,700
Receivables	300	Cost of sales	1,300
Cash	25	Gross profit	1,400
Payables	230	Admin costs	500
Overdraft	90	Distribution costs	350
		Profit from operations	550
		Finance cost	75

(b) **Calculate the following (to the nearest day):**

The inventory holding period is________days

The trade receivables collection period is ______days

The trade payables payment period is ______days

(c) **Using your answers to part (b) calculate the cash operating cycle for the company.**

The cash operating cycle is ______days

(d) **Complete the following sentences by selecting the correct options:**

Over-capitalisation can occur when a business has **[too much/insufficient]** working capital and over-trading can occur when a business has **[too much/insufficient]** working capital.

Signs of over-trading include **[slowly decreasing/rapidly decreasing/slowly increasing/rapidly increasing]** sales volumes, **[reducing/increasing]** profit margins, **[shorter/longer]** receivables collection periods, **[shorter/longer]** payables payment periods.

Task 8

(a) **Which one of the following best describes the main features of an overdraft?**

A Interest rates are low; it is available for as long as required; it is useful for capital purchases

B Interest rates are low; it is repayable on demand; it is useful for capital purchases

C Interest rates are low; repayments can be negotiated; it is useful for capital purchases

D Interest rates are high; repayments can be negotiated; it is a short-term form of finance

E Interest rates are high; it is repayable on demand; it is a short-term form of finance

F Interest rates are high; it is available for as long as required; it is a long-term form of finance

(b) **Which one of the following best describes the main features of a bank loan?**

A Interest rates are low; it is available for as long as required; it is useful for capital purchases

B Interest rates are low; it is repayable on demand; it is useful for capital purchases

C Interest rates are low; repayments can be negotiated; it is useful for capital purchases

D Interest rates are high; repayments can be negotiated; it is a short-term form of finance

E Interest rates are high; it is repayable on demand; it is a short-term form of finance

F Interest rates are high; it is available for as long as required; it is a long-term form of finance

(c) **How much will an investor need to invest for one year to earn £4,000 interest, assuming a fixed annual rate of interest of 8%?**

£____________will need to be invested

(d) **A bank has offered to lend a company £96,000 to be repaid in 12 monthly instalments of £8,400 per month.**

The flat rate of interest being charged is _____%

(e) Calculate the approximate yield to redemption of a 5% Treasury Stock with a current market price of £110, redeemable in 4 years.

The approximate redemption yield is _____%

Task 9

Evans & Sons is planning to expand its production facilities. The expansion plans will require the purchase of new machinery at a cost of £65,000.

The company has been seeking possible means of funding the expansion and has been offered three options:

1 A bank loan

2 An operating lease

3 Issue of equity shares to cover the cost of the purchase.

Prepare notes for the company which identify:

- **the main features of each of the options**
- **the implications on the gearing of the company.**

1 Bank loan fixed amount, agreed period pre arranged terms

low risk borrowing
know exactly how much interest payable
terms of loan.
affects gearing ratio as debt to the company ∴ less profit available for shareholders
security may be required
term of loan should not exceed assets life

∴ gearing will increase

2 Operating lease

Do not have risks/rewards
off balance sheet, to
expenses in profit & loss like rental payment
doesn't affect gearing ratio as
do not own
just has to be mentioned in the footnotes
useful for short period
finance lease more appropriate for longer term
lessee simply has use of the asset lessor responsible for maintenance when lease expires lessor can lease same asset to another lessee.

3 Share issue

shares are high risk
volatile market
cost implication of selling & acquisition of shares
value can go up or down
~~could~~ return could be less than investment depending on market.
can easily buy & sell quickly but have to accept price at the time
companies issues shares to raise capital
redeemable preference shares can be brought back at the time agreed.
dividends are only paid if the company has available profits
Raising cash through shares reduces the gearing of the firm

Task 10

(a) **Select the correct options to complete the following sentences:**

Government securities are also known as **[gold-edged/gilt-edged/gilted]** securities and **[can/cannot]** be traded. Interest rates are **[fixed/variable]** and these types of securities are considered to be **[low risk/high risk]** because they **[are/are not]** backed by the government.

A company has £750,000 surplus cash and the treasurer estimates that the cash is free for to be invested for up to two years.

(b) **Write a report to the finance director of the company which considers the risk, return and liquidity of the following investment options:**

- Treasury bills
- Certificate of deposit

Treasury bills – short term government securities pay no interest but are issued at a discount

difference between purchase price & amount repaid represents the yield on the bill

Low rate compared to other investment options

maturity period usually 91 days

risk free investment – as undertaking to pay by the government. They can be sold before maturity so they are a liquid investment

Interest risk only for those who buy with intention to sell before maturity. If interest rates go up their value falls

CD low risk issued by bank/building society

2 Mock Assessment Answers

Task 1

(a)

Type of receipt or payment	*Description*
Capital payments	Payments that relate to the acquisition of non-current assets.
Regular revenue receipts	Income received from the operating activities of the business that are expected to occur frequently.
Drawings	Payments made to the owners of the business.
Exceptional payments	Payments that do not arise from the operating activities of the business and that are not expected to occur frequently.

(b)

	£	**Working**
Operating profit	28,390	
Change in trade receivables	–4,392	Opening = £18,720 Closing = £128,400 × 90% × 20% = £23,112
Change in trade payables	308	Opening = £1,050 Closing = £1,358
Rent adjustment	–250	SOPL = £10,550 Cash paid = £10,800
General expenses adjustment	0	SOPL = £15,540 Cash paid = £15,540
Van expenses adjustment	–7	SOPL = £10,120 Cash paid = £10,127
Adjustments for other non-cash items	3,190	Depreciation
Net change in cash position	27,239	
Forecast cash position 1 January	10,000	
Forecast cash position 31 March	37,239	

Task 2

(a)

	Sales volume (units)	*Trend*	*Monthly variation*
November	425		
December	570	540	30
January	625	580	45
February	545	620	–75
March	690		

(b) The forecast production cost for April is £9,685

Trend = 620 + 40 + 40 = 700 units

Variation = 700 + 45 = 745

Cost = 745 × £13 = £9,685

(c) The forecast sales value if the company requires a mark up of 25% is: £12,106 (to the nearest £)

Working: £9,685 ÷ 100 × 125

The forecast sales value if the company requires a margin of 10% is: £10,761 (to the nearest £)

Working: £9,685 ÷ 90 × 100

(d)

Month	*January*	*February*	*March*	*April*
Price	£11,700	£12,004	£11,928	£11,320
Index		102.6	101.9	96.8

Task 3

(a)

	April £	*May* £
Total sales receipts	14,175	17,985

The trade receivables balance at the end of May is forecast to be:

£24,140

(b)

	April £	*May* £
Settlement of trade payables	14,800	9,120

Workings

		£
April:	All of January's outstanding balance	5,280
	February £8,640 ÷ 60 × 20	2,880
	March £16,800 × 40%	6,720
		Total 14,800
May:	February £8,640 ÷ 60 × 40	5,760
	March £16,800 × 20%	3,360
		Total 9,120

(c)

	January £	*February* £	*March* £	*April* £	*May* £
Expenses	4,512	4,951	5,541	5,745	6,785
Expenses to be included in cash budget	23,512	23,951	24,541	4,745	5,785

Monthly depreciation = £60,000 × 20% = £12,000 ÷ 12 = £1,000

Purchase of machine = £60,000 ÷ 3 = £20,000

Task 4

	April £	*May* £	*June* £
Receipts			
Cash sales	2,700	3,450	3,900
Credit sales	15,300	19,550	22,100
Proceeds from share issue	0	143,750	0
Bank loan	60,000	0	0
Total receipts	78,000	166,750	26,000
Payments			
Purchases	–13,200	–14,400	–16,800
Wages	–10,541	–10,685	–10,852
Expenses	–5,541	–5,745	–6,785
Hire purchase of plant and machinery	–8,240	–8,240	–8,240
Bank loan capital repayment	0	–1,250	–1,250
Bank loan interest	0	–250	–250
Overdraft interest	0	0	0
Total payments	–37,522	–40,570	–44,177
Net cash flow	40,478	126,180	–18,177
Opening bank balance	5,214	45,692	171,872
Closing bank balance	45,692	171,872	153,695

Task 5

(a)

	Adjusted forecast sales value £	*Sales receipts*				
		Period 1 (£)	*Period 2 (£)*	*Period 3 (£)*	*Period 4 (£)*	*Total*
Period 1 sales	122,400	36,720	61,200	24,480		
Period 2 sales	130,050		39,015	65,025	26,010	
Period 3 sales	133,875			40,162	66,937	
Period 4 sales	141,525				42,457	
Revised forecast sales receipts		36,720	100,215	129,667	135,404	402,006

(b) Total receipts from sales in periods 1 to 4 will fall by 25.24%

Working

	Period 1 (£)	*Period 2 (£)*	*Period 3 (£)*	*Period 4 (£)*	*Total*
Original value of forecast sales	144,000	153,000	157,500	166,500	
Original sales receipts	72,000	148,500	155,250	162,000	537,750

(537,750 – 402,006) ÷ 537,750 × 100 = 25.24%

(c) B

Task 6

(a)

	£
Budgeted closing bank balance	27,305
Surplus in receipts from receivables	1,512
Shortfall in cash sales	–2,667
Decrease in payments to payables	1,249
Increase in cash purchases	–890
Increase in capital expenditure	–24,850
Decrease in wages and salaries	560
Increase in general expenses	–1,222
Actual closing bank balance	997

(b)

Receipts from receivables were better than budget but cash receipts fell. We need to investigate if this is because more customers are taking credit terms. The net effect is an overall reduction in cash inflows in the period.

Payable payments decreased but cash purchases increased. This could be due to improved credit terms (i.e. taking longer to pay) or worse credit terms (i.e. payables insisting on cash payments). The net effect is that purchase payments have decreased.

There has been an unplanned amount spent on non-current assets. Investigation is needed to see if this was an oversight at the time the budget was put together or whether there was, for example, an unforeseen breakdown of machinery.

Wages and salaries have decreased. This could be due to less overtime being worked or due to staff leaving.

General expenses have increased. This needs to be looked into to find out the cause as it is unclear what is included in general expenses.

Overview

From the variances identified it may be that production has been lower than expected (net purchases have decreased and wages have decreased), leading to a reduction in sales volume/value (net sales have decreased) as the products have not been available to sell. The cause of the reduction in production could be due to a machine breaking down and having to be replaced (capital expenditure increased).

Task 7

(a) B

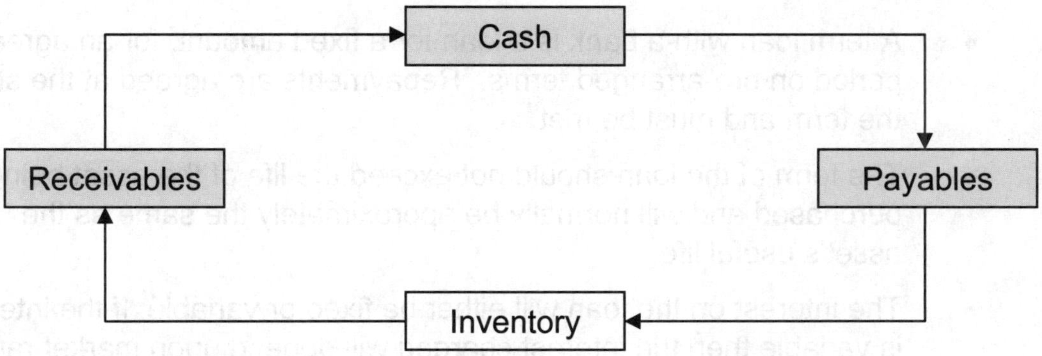

(b) The inventory holding period is 150 ÷ 1,300 × 365 = 42 days

The trade receivables collection period is 300 ÷ 2,700 × 365 = 41 days

The trade payable payment period is 230 ÷ 1,300 × 365 = 65 days

(c) The cash operating cycle is 42 + 41 – 65 = 18 days

(d) Over-capitalisation can occur when a business has **too much** working capital and over-trading can occur when a business has **insufficient** working capital.

Signs of over-trading include **rapidly increasing** sales volumes, **reducing** profit margins, **longer** receivable collection periods, **longer** payable payment periods.

Task 8

(a) E

(b) C

(c) £4,000 ÷ 8 × 100 = £50,000 will need to be invested

(d) The flat rate of interest being charged is (8,400 × 12 – 96,000) ÷ 96,000 × 100 = 5%

(e) The approximate redemption yield is 2.28%

Interest yield = 5 ÷ 110 × 100 = 4.55%

Capital loss = £10 ÷ 4 = £2.50 per year

Represents 2.5 ÷ 110 × 100 = 2.27% of investment value

Approximate redemption yield = 4.55% – 2.27% = 2.28%

Task 9

Bank loan

- A term loan with a bank is a loan for a fixed amount, for an agreed period on pre-arranged terms. Repayments are agreed at the start of the term and must be met.
- The term of the loan should not exceed the life of the asset being purchased and will normally be approximately the same as the asset's useful life.
- The interest on the loan will either be fixed or variable. If the interest is variable then the interest charged will depend upon market rates of interest and will normally be a certain percentage above the bank's base rate or the London Inter-Bank Offered Rate (LIBOR).
- Security of some form may be required; in this case the loan may be secured on the new machinery.
- The gearing of the firm will increase as this type of finance is debt finance.
- In most cases a bank loan is most appropriate for the purchase of major assets which will hopefully provide income over the loan period out of which the loan interest and repayments can be made.

Operating lease

- An operating lease is where the lessor hires out the asset to the lessee for a short period which is normally substantially less than the asset's total life.
- The asset is not treated as if it is owned, and lease payments are an expense in the Statement of Profit or Loss, rather like rental payments. This means there is no effect on gearing.
- Once the lease period is over then the lessor will lease the same asset to another lessee. The lessor is responsible for servicing and maintaining the asset and the lessee simply gets the use of the asset for the lease period in return for the lease payments.
- This type of lease might be useful if the machinery is only required for a fairly short time period. However if it is required for substantially the entire useful life of the asset then a finance lease would be a more appropriate form of leasing.

Equity shares

- Companies issue shares to raise capital, usually in the form of cash although shares may be issued in exchange for assets.
- A shareholder is a member of the company and therefore, depending on the class of shares held, has voting rights. They are also entitled to dividends depending on the availability of profits.
- There are costs involved in issuing shares.
- Redeemable preference shares could be used as an alternative to borrowing as they can be bought back by the company at the time agreed.
- In times of high interest rates redeemable preference shares may be particularly attractive to companies. This is because if a company borrows money, interest at the agreed rate must be paid whether or not the company is making a profit.
- Dividends to the preference (and ordinary) shareholders are only paid if the company has available profits.
- Raising cash through the issue of shares reduces the gearing of the firm as shares increase the equity in the business rather than the debt.

Task 10

(a) Government securities are also known as **gilt-edged** securities and **can** be traded. Interest rates are **fixed** and these types of securities are considered to be **low risk** because they **are** backed by the government.

(b) **Treasury bills**

- Treasury bills are short term government securities which pay no interest but are issued at a discount.
- The difference between the purchase price and the amount repaid represents the yield on the bill. The yield is often low compared to other investment options.
- They usually have a maturity of 91 days.
- Treasury bills are an undertaking to pay by the Government, the risk to an investor is very low. Treasury bills are commonly described as 'risk-free investments'.

- Treasury bills are negotiable instruments so they can be sold before maturity; therefore they are a liquid investment.
- Interest rate risk only exists for investors who buy bills with the intention of re-selling them before maturity. The risk arises because if market rates of interest go up, the market value of bills will fall.

Certificates of deposit

- A certificate of deposit (CD) is issued by a bank or building society which certifies that a certain sum, usually a minimum of £50,000, has been deposited with it to be repaid on a specific date.
- The term can range from seven days to five years but is usually for three months (90 days). CDs are negotiable instruments; they can be bought and sold, therefore if the holder does not want to wait until the maturity date the CD can be sold in the money market.
- The market in CDs is large and active therefore they are an ideal method for investing large cash surpluses. The sale value of a CD will depend on how much a buyer is willing to pay to obtain the right to the deposit plus interest at maturity.
- Since CDs are negotiable, the holder can sell them at any time but there are normally penalty charges for doing this. This makes them more liquid than a money-market time deposit, with the same bank.
- CDs usually offer an attractive rate of interest when compared to deposit accounts and a low credit risk (as long as a reputable bank is used). They are useful for investing funds in the short term since they can be sold at any time on the secondary market.

Glossary

Term	Description
Accrual	An expense that has been incurred during the period but has not been paid for by the end of the period.
Annual percentage rates (APR)	The APR is annual rate that is charged for borrowing (or made by investing), expressed as a single percentage number. It represents the actual yearly cost of funds over the term of a loan. This includes any fees or additional costs associated with the transaction.
Broker	A broker is an individual or party that arranges transactions between a buyer and a seller, and gets a commission when a deal is executed.
Capital receipts/payments	Receipts/payments that relate to the disposal/acquisition of non-current assets.
Capped interest rates	A capped interest rate means that there is an upper limit on the level the interest charge can go to.
Depreciation	An annual internal charge to the income statement that spreads the net cost of a non-current asset over the number of years of its useful life.
Exceptional receipts/payments	Receipts/payments that are not expected to occur on a regular basis.
Fiduciary duty of banks	The bank is expected to act with the utmost good faith in relationship with the customer.
Fixed charge	A fixed charge is where the security is a specific and identifiable asset or group of assets.
Fixed interest rate	A fixed interest rate provides an unchanging percentage charge over the length of the borrowing period.
Flat rate interest	Interest rate is calculated based on the loan principle. It is applied to the whole of the loan every year and does not take into account any repayments.

Term	Description
Floating charge	A floating charge is where the security is supplied by a group of assets of the relevant value which can change in make-up i.e. inventory or receivables.
Loan principal	The amount that is borrowed.
Maturity date	The final payment date of a loan.
Money markets	A market for the buying and selling of short term, highly liquid investments.
Personal guarantee	A form of security offered by an individual.
Prepayment	A payment made during the period that relates to an expense in a future period.
Regular receipts/payments	Receipts/payments that are expected to occur frequently.
Simple interest rate	This can be calculated by taking the total interest as a percentage of the original principal.
Term loans	A term loan is a loan from a bank for a specific amount that has a specified repayment schedule and a variable interest rate. Term loans almost always mature between one and 10 years.
Variable interest	A variable interest rate changes over the period of the borrowing, usually in line with base rate.
Yield	The return from an investment.

INDEX